CONTENTS

W9-CDG-896

The Backstreet Philosophy

Don't panic.

Douglas Adams, *The Hitchhiker's Guide to the Galaxy*

Moving is always a traumatic and unsettling experience, but it can be even more insane if you're moving to a new city. Not only do you have to uproot your life from one place, but you need to plant it again in another—all while finding a new place to live, a new job, new friends, new places to hang out, and new places to have fun.

But like the man said, *don't panic*. Because these are not your average guides.

Most guidebooks to the major cities are written for tourists—visitors to the city in question. But Backstreet Guides were created specifically for people who are going to live in the major cities.

These books were created to be your inside perspective on a new city. The information they provide is the kind of information you could only get from a friend who has lived in the city for years. In fact, you can think of these books as your "all-knowing friends," something to refer to, with inside tips about what it's really like in the city, where you might want to live, how to settle in quickly and comfortably, and what to do when you get there and want to start exploring.

These guides don't have everything—they aren't directories or phone books. They're opinionated guides with this point of view:

Cities are a lot of fun once you get to know them.

The problem is that it usually takes several years to really *get to know* a city. And that's where we come in. Our writers grew up in these cities, lived in them, and have loved them for years. The listings in this book come from the "insider's" perspective—from the native's body of knowledge about the city—not from what other guides, magazines, newspapers, and ratings sources say.

Within, you'll find information that no other books have. You'll find sidebars throughout with essential and interesting info

The Practical Companion

to Your New City,

From Settling In

to Stepping Out

by Candace Walsh

alpha books

A Division of Macmillan Publishing
A Simon & Schuster Macmillan Company
1633 Broadway, New York, NY 10019-6785

MOVING TO NEW YORK CITY

International Standard Book Number: 0-02-861279-5
Library of Congress Catalog Card Number: 96-086490

98   97   96   8   7   6   5   4   3   2   1

Interpretation of the printing code: the rightmost double-digit number
is the year of the book's first printing; the rightmost single-digit number
is the number of the book's printing. For example, a printing code of
96-1 shows that this copy of the book was printed during the first printing
of the book in 1996.

Printed in the United States of America

Publisher: Theresa Murtha
Development Editor: Nancy Mikhail
Cover Designer: Michael Freeland
Designer: Francine Fishpaw
Indexer: Tom Simons
Contributing Writers: Rachel Aydt, Nilofar Motamed, Tim Harper
Creators: James Grace and David Borgenicht

You'll find easy-to-use maps that will help you navigate the city streets. You'll find great sites to see, restaurants to try, things to do, and places to go—some of which are the essential "tourist" attractions and establishments, but most of which are places where *actual people* (without cameras) go. And the establishments listed in these guides are here because they deserve to be—not because they paid to be. What you'll find here is the best the city has to offer.

But like we said, Backstreet Guides aren't meant to have it all. Instead, they have what you need for your first year in the new city. Backstreet Guides will help you to:

- Select a neighborhood
- Find a place to live
- Move in
- Set up your utilities and your new home
- Decide what to do when you want to explore
- Help you locate good restaurants and bars
- Help you find exciting and fun things to do
- Provide a comprehensive listing of essential numbers and addresses

And much more. We hope you'll find your own favorites in this book, but we know you'll find others on your own. When you do, don't hesitate to drop us a line. Send your comments via e-mail to Book Soup at BookSoop@aol.com.

Have fun in your new city.

THE BACKSTREET GUIDES EDITORS

Chapter One
MEET THE CITY

NO MATTER WHAT YOU'RE INTO, Manhattan probably is the place where it's being done best. Whether it's jazz, fashion, cuisine, clubbing, decorating, or just enjoying life, it's happening here. Every American city strives, at some point, to emulate the groove of Manhattan, and for good reason—but there's only one New York City.

Manhattan would not be the mecca it is if it weren't for the fresh crop of the world's most ambitious and talented people that arrive every day. It takes a strange creature to want to look past the grit, overpopulation, and expensiveness to appreciate the glittering, constantly changing, and oddly beautiful face of this city. Then again, perhaps we don't choose New York at all—perhaps it chooses us, and divides the lifers from the ones who scurry off to the suburbs at the first provocation.

In any event, welcome to New York, the greatest city in the world.

N.Y. STORY

Before it became the lush concrete jungle it is today, Manhattan was originally a lush forest. It was bought by the Dutch in 1624, from Native Americans for $24 in trinkets (New York's first raw deal).

Since then, many Brooklyn Bridges have been sold to many poor trusting souls, but they emerged wiser from the experience, as do we all.

Christened "New Amsterdam" by the Dutch, the area quickly became a booming business center which attracted traders, entrepreneurs, and others from all over the world. In 1664, Britain swooped down on New Amsterdam in characteristic colonial fashion. Surprisingly enough, the British war fleet cruised into the New York Harbor and intimidated the Dutch so much that they surrendered without firing a single gun. King Charles II gave the colony to his brother, the Duke of York. He, of course, gave Dutch Governor Peter Stuyvesant the boot. And that's how New York got its name, which it managed to keep, even after the Revolutionary War.

The city developed from North to South, and its oldest neighborhoods are what is now known as the Wall Street area. New York became the epicenter of resistance to royal authority, with George Washington leading the way. Washington read the Declaration of Independence on the site where City Hall now stands, which initiated the Revolutionary War. After the American Revolution, from 1785 to 1790, New York served as the capital of the United States, and it was here that Washington was inaugurated as President, in 1789.

Development progressed northwards, into a rolling wilderness. Reminders of New York City's original topography can be found in the northern reaches of Central Park—its rocky outcroppings and lush forest have not yet been conquered. The thriving economy drew people steadily, and by 1790, the population had grown to 33,000. By 1830, it had grown to 200,000.

"New York. Women look like flowerpots, hats of lilies, poppies, cherries. Windows full of orange and shocking pink dresses. An explosion of color. Dogs running away from their masters in the park. The Village is full of Bowery bums, beggars, staring tourists."

ANAIS NIN, THE JOURNALS OF ANAIS NIN, VOLUME SIX

"No one should come to New York to live unless he is willing to be lucky."

E.B. WHITE, HERE IS NEW YORK

During the 19th Century, New York became the place to go if you were a European immigrant in search of a better life. Many a crestfallen face was seen when the noisy, dirty city was exposed to the hopeful eyes of newcomers expecting a paradise. Numerous pioneers stayed on in the city, trading their labor for what they hoped would become the American Dream.

New York City (including the boroughs) is home to a whopping 7,322,564 people—give or take a few.

Immigrants continue their pilgrimage here to this day, cementing the New York tradition of multicultural enrichment that has made New York City so full of life, diversity, and ethnicity.

"New York is the meeting place of the peoples, the only city where you can hardly find a typical American."

DJUNA BARNES, NEW YORK

"There are roughly three New Yorks. There is, first, the New York of the man or woman who was born here, who takes the city for granted and accepts its size and its turbulence as natural and inevitable. Second, there is the New York of the commuter— the city that is devoured by locusts each day and spat out each night. Third, there is the New York of the person who was born somewhere else and came to New York in quest of something. Of these three trembling cities the greatest is the last—the city of final destination, the city that is a goal."

E.B. WHITE, HERE IS NEW YORK

WHO NEW YORKERS ARE

Manhattan's population was close to 1.5 million in 1990—pretty crazy when you think that we're all living on a mere 22 miles. And New York's ethnic composition is extraordinarily rich. New York City is home to the largest African-American population in the United

States. Many live in Harlem, and in the Bedford-Stuyvesant and Brownsville sections of Brooklyn. The world's largest Jewish population lives in the metropolitan New York area (which includes Long Island, parts of southern New York State, northeastern New Jersey, and southwestern Connecticut). Puerto Ricans and other Hispanics from the Caribbean and Latin America make up the most recent large-scale immigrant to settle here. Both Little Italy and Chinatown are located in Manhattan. Other significant foreign-born groups living in the city that never sleeps include Russians, English, Irish, and Poles. Unlike most other American cities, non-Hispanic whites are not a majority of the population in New York City, although they are the largest population group.

The majority of us are in our twenties and thirties, and half of us have never been married. A third of us are married, and are sticking it out here as we strive to make the city a good place to bring up children.

HOW WE PAY FOR IT ALL

New York is a global business, entertainment, and publishing epicenter. The radio and television broadcasting industry is based here, and the New York and American stock exchanges and the commodity exchanges are found in the Wall Street area, whose siren song calls everyone from blue-blood WASP bankers to outer-borough secretaries who've seen *Working Girl* and want a piece of the same fairy tale.

New York City is also the biggest headquarters of the wholesale and retail trade. Naturally, all these businesses need advertising, which explains the huge presence of advertising agencies in New York, especially on Madison Avenue.

On the manufacturing end, the garment and publishing industries are the two largest and most well-known industries in New York. This explains the presence of all those fashionistas and serious-looking, bespectacled people in black. New York also endures about 17 million tourists annually, who make a large, positive impact on the city's income.

WEATHER AND CLIMATE

New York City's climate is officially billed as temperate (cool winters, warm, humid summers). However, a more realistic description would be this: **In the summer, it's Africa-hot, and in the winter, it varies from plain old cold to freezing.** What keeps us going are the in-between seasons—autumn stretches into late November, and spring into mid-June. Most people favor these in-between seasons, as they provide perfect weather for walking around.

Summer is beastly here, but proximity to beaches and beach communities make this bearable, as does a good air conditioner or fan. Due to the heat given off by the buildings, and the lack of breezes, summer temperature in the city is often higher than in surrounding areas like Long Island and Westchester County. Little wonder that sweltering kids jimmy the fire hydrants to get some relief. Everyone who can afford to leaves on the weekends.

AVERAGE TEMPERATURES PER MONTH

Month	High	Low
JAN	H, 38.0	L, 25.6
FEB	H, 40.1	L, 26.6
MAR	H, 48.6	L, 34.1
APR	H, 61.1	L, 43.8
MAY	H, 71.5	L, 53.3
JUN	H, 80.1	L, 62.7
JUL	H, 85.3	L, 68.2
AUG	H, 83.7	L, 67.1
SEPT	H, 76.4	L, 60.1
OCT	H, 65.6	L, 49.9
NOV	H, 53.6	L, 40.8
DEC	H, 42.1	L, 30.3

WHY WE DO IT

So why live here? Everyone seems to have an opinion about New York City. It's simultaneously touted as Shangri-la and Sodom and Gomorrah, but the truth lies somewhere in between.

Efforts by the local government and law-enforcement agencies to increase the quality of life have yielded positive results—subway cars are almost 100% graffiti-free, belligerent beggars have become near-Southern in their polite requests for assistance, murders and muggings have dropped significantly, and neighborhood groups have turned many eyesore vacant lots into lovely community gardens.

Yes, it smells. Yes, it's often dirty. (Try the word "sooty"—it sounds more romantic.) But at this point, you can almost choose to avoid the grimier areas simply by gravitating toward the more manicured ones—the Upper East and West Sides, parts of Midtown East, parts of the West Village, and Soho.

Another popular gripe is that Manhattan is overpriced. You bet your bippie. But where else will a person with fleet typing and word-processing skills command a whopping $20-25 an hour? And that's just word-processing. Wages are high here as well, which makes paying for that $2 muffin seem less egregious.

People also say that Manhattanites are rude and nasty. Let's put it this way. If you're lollygagging down 34th street at 5:15p.m., you will probably get shoved, cursed at, and feel many satanic stares boring into the back of your head. But that's because the 300 business women and men behind you have a train to catch, so that they can go home, kiss their spouses, and indulge in a little familial bliss before jumping back into the rat race the next morning. Good Samaritans are everywhere—It's all a matter of a city's pace. Manhattan is so fast paced that it seems rude, but it's really just very focused. Don't take it personally. Toughen up, will ya?

"I began to like New York, the racy, adventurous feel of it at night and the satisfaction that the constant flicker of men and women and machines gives to the restless eye. I liked to walk up Fifth Ave. and pick out romantic women from the crowd and imagine that in a few minutes I was going to enter into their lives, and no one would ever know or disapprove . . . At the enchanted metropolitan twilight I felt a haunting loneliness sometimes, and felt it in others—poor young clerks who loitered in front of windows waiting until it was time for a solitary dinner—young clerks in the dusk, wasting the most poignant moments of night and life."

F. SCOTT FITZGERALD, THE GREAT GATSBY

The Grid

E. 67th St
E. 66th St
E. 65th St
E. 64th St
E. 63rd St
E. 62nd St
E. 61st St
E. 60th St
E. 59th St
E. 58th St
E. 57th St
E. 56th St
E. 55th St
E. 54th St
E. 53rd St
E. 52nd St
E. 51st St
E. 50th St
E. 49th St
E. 48th St
E. 47th St
E. 46th St
E. 45th St
E. 44th St
E. 43rd St
E. 42nd St
E. 41st St
E. 40th St
E. 39th St
E. 38th St
E. 37th St
E. 36th St
E. 35th St
E. 34th St
E. 33rd St
E. 32nd St
E. 31st St
E. 30th St
E. 29th St
E. 28th St
E. 27th St
E. 26th St
E. 25th St
E. 24th St
E. 23rd St
E. 22nd St
E. 21st St
E. 20th St
E. 19th St
E. 18th St
E. 17th St
E. 16th St
E. 15th St
E. 14th St
E. 13th St

0   440 y
     400 m

Central Park S
The Pond
East River

York Av
Roosevelt Island Tram
Queensboro Bridge
Queens

From Lower Level
To Upper Level

Sutton Pl
Sutton Pl South
Beekman Place
Mitchell Place
FDR Drive

MIDTOWN EAST

Sixth Av
Fifth Av
Madison Av
Park Av
Lexington Av
Third Av
Second Av
First Av

Rockefeller Center

Bryant Park
New York Public Library

Vanderbilt Av
Depew Pl
Grand Central Terminal

United Nations
Queens-Midtown Tunnel

MURRAY HILL

Tunnel Exit
Tunnel Entrance

Empire State Bldg.
Broadway
Park Av. S.

Madison Square Park

FLATIRON DISTRICT

Gramercy Park
GRAMERCY PARK

Union Sq W
Union Square
Union Sq E
Irving Pl
Perlman Pl

Asser Levy Pl
Av. C
Peter Cooper Village
Stuyvesant Town

East River

Subway stop

Chapter Two

GETTING AROUND

THE LAY OF THE LAND

One of the hardest things for nouveau New Yorkers can be orienting themselves when going somewhere. The worst part is that when you finally drum up enough nerve to ask someone for directions, they tell you to walk west for three blocks and south for two. West? South? What does that mean? "Okay, thanks," you say, even more confused than before.

The good news is that although Manhattan may seem really confusing, there is a grid system in place that has logical constants. The bad news is, you're going to have to devote some time to familiarizing yourself with this grid and the compass points before you feel totally confident about your sense of direction. But once you do, you'll feel so much more at home.

THE GRID

Manhattan's avenues run north and south. They are numbered west of Avenue A, and lettered east of Avenue A. From West to East, they run: **Twelfth, Eleventh, Tenth, Ninth, Eighth, Seventh, Sixth (Avenue of the Americas), Fifth, Madison, Park, Lexington, Third, Second, First, A, B, C, D.**

Manhattan's streets run east to west. **Fifth Avenue** divides the city like a y-axis, and all streets to the east and west of it become **East or West** depending on what side of Fifth Avenue they're on.

Street address numbers ascend as they travel away from Fifth

Avenue. The higher the street address number, the farther east or west the address is. (for example, 700 E. 5th Street is far east between Avenues C and D). In general, each city block is equal to 50 address numbers.

Street numbering begins north of **Houston Street,** which is downtown between Soho/the Lower East Side and the Villages. It begins with 1st Street and ends in Harlem in the 200's.

Broadway bisects the entire isle of Manhattan, starting in the Financial District and extending north up through Harlem. It veers off to the west after Union Square, ending up in the Upper West Side.

ORIENTATION ABCs

Seems pretty simple, right? Wrong. There are a ton of streets that are not numbered, and instead have names like Astor Place, Rector Street, and Sutton Place. It would take about fifty pages to describe it all to you, and I don't think either of us want to go there.

You'll need to get a good detailed map of the city to puzzle out the rest.

Most things take place in the grid, anyway, and people are more than happy to give you orienting directions if you ask. They're used to people who've lived here for years not knowing where streets are, too.

Nowhere else in America are the compass points so important. For twentysomethings who grew up in the digital watch age, telling analog time is a feat in itself, let alone figuring out directions. So here are a few tricks:

1) Look at a street sign, and determine whether you are on an avenue or a street. This you can figure out from looking at signs on the corner. Streets run east and west, and avenues run north and south.

2) **If you're on an avenue,** look at the avenue's building numbers as you walk. Are they ascending or descending? If they're ascending, you're walking north. If they're descending, you're walking south. **If you're on a street** on the westside (the street sign would have a little W next to the number) and the numbers are ascending, you're walking west. If you're on the westside and the numbers are descending, you're walking east. Similarly, if

you're on the eastside (the street sign will have a little E next to the number) and the numbers are ascending, you're walking east. If the numbers are descending, you're walking west.

3) In the West Village, Soho, Tribeca, and all of Downtown, this whole system ceases to apply. Oops.

4) Other random tips:

- Walk in well-lit areas whenever possible.

- Avoid Central Park after dark.

- If you like to take long walks (or must out of necessity), make sure you go to the bathroom before you leave. There's no guarantee that you'll be able to find a public restroom without buying a cup of coffee. If you're near City Hall, however, you can use our city's one public self-cleaning toilet. It's located behind City Hall, and it costs 25 cents.

- Be on the lookout for swift bicyclists. They can come out of nowhere and ruin your day.

BASIC SAFETY TIPS

1. If you're lost, try not to look lost. Walk authoritatively, and scout out a safe place to ask for directions, i.e. a deli, restaurant, or other enclosed area. Also, if you see one of New York's finest, don't hesitate to ask him or her either. If it's late at night, and you're packing some cash, hail down a cab and let him worry about where you are and where you're going.

2. Don't necessarily assume bicyclists and in-line skaters will stop for you—even if you have the right of way.

3. Don't stand on the edge of subway platforms.

4. Always carry at least a little money on you. It's important to be able to a) use a pay phone; b) hop into a passing cab if you feel unsafe; c) buy a beverage on a hot summer day to avoid dehydration; d) take advantage of the odd sidewalk vendor deal.

5. Carry a map of Manhattan with you if you don't know the city well.

6. Learn which main streets are on the East Side and which ones cover the West Side.

7. Don't jog alone.

8. With the exception of lifetime friends or lovers, don't let anyone know your ATM code.

"A CLEAN WELL-LIGHTED PLACE"

Although the acronym ATM actually stands for Automated Teller Machine, in New York, it might as well stand for All-Night Trouble Magnet, or more simply, the most likely place to run into one of the city's many homeless trying to make a quick buck. This, however, should not make you run for the hills. Just use your common sense and before you know it you will have your own trusted ATM and you won't need to worry.

Stay away if the ATM door is not magnetically locked, the ATM is not well-lit, there are no windows facing the street, a homeless person is holding the door open or sleeping inside, or anyone is loitering outside or inside.

NILOUFAR MOTAMED

GETTING AROUND IN MANHATTAN

Manhattan is a walker's delight. If you're not going too far, (say, 20 blocks), or if you have time to kill, walking is the best way to see the city, and to learn it. In most parts of the city, anything you might need is down the block or around the corner—dry cleaner, grocery store, pharmacy, restaurant—even art gallery or gift shop. And taking a walk in New York City usually yields some wonderfully weird or beautiful (or both) sight, whether it be the Flatiron building or a bevy of summer punk-rock squatters. It's also good for epiphanies and gaining perspective.

When you need to travel greater distances, though, buses, subways, and taxis are at your disposal most any time of the day and night.

INSIDER TIP: *The subway is almost always the fastest way around town, but buses are usually the best way to go east to west, particularly through Central Park. They're also good when you're not near a subway. (Duh.)*

SUBWAY SMARTS

For the newcomer to New York, traveling on the subways can be a real mystery. So let's start with some basics.

First of all, leave your preconceptions behind. As long as you follow certain precautions, you have a reasonable chance of survival. (That would be some New York humor, by the way.) But seriously, folks . . .

Subway maps are free for the asking at every subway station. Just ask the token clerk.

Learn your route before you descend. The subway token clerk doesn't have a lot of time and may not be inspired to give you directions, especially if there's a line of growling commuters behind you. When in doubt, call the number below for guidance on getting from point A to point B.

Subway, City Information, (718) 330-1234

If you have plans to go somewhere (a restaurant, for example) **call the destination** and ask which subways run near there. You can then figure out which stop to aim for.

If you don't have a subway map, **you can usually find an enlarged subway map on the wall of the subway station.**

Until you get comfortable with the vibe of your local subway station late at night, **don't take the subway after, say, 9:30 p.m.**—unless you're with a group.

In the subway station **make sure you're on the right platform.** Each train runs east and west, or north and south, so look at the signs before the turnstiles to make sure you're not going to the wrong train. It'll usually say something like "Uptown and Queens" or "Downtown and Brooklyn."

Subway Basics

Upper East Side:

The **4, 5, 6 line (green)** runs up and down the east side, and is the only north/south subway that provides access to the Upper East Side. It also heads down into the financial district via points in the East Village and Soho.

Upper West Side:

The **1, 2, 3, 9 line (red)** and the **A, C, E line (blue)** run up and down the west side.

However, the E turns east at 50th Street and runs east to Queens. They both run downtown via the West Village and Soho.

Crosstown Lines:

The **L line (black)** runs east and west along 14th Street. The **7 line (purple)** runs east and west along 42nd Street. The **S (Shuttle)** connects Grand Central and Times Square at 42nd Street.

These days, **it costs is $1.50** to ride the bus or subway. You'll need exact change or a token for the bus. It's best to buy a ten-pack or a metro card, which is gradually being accepted in more and more subway stations. For **Subway and Bus Info** call (718) 330-1234.

Everyone's got a different "safety barometer" when it comes to using public transportation, but until 9 p.m. is a safe bet, later if you're with a friend.

INSIDER TIP: *You can get free jumbo subway and bus maps from any subway station or bus, but for a handier solution, business-card sized ones are sold in stationery stores that will fit in your wallet. Additionally, if you carry a standard-sized daily planner, Filofax sells a mini-foldout laminated subway and bus map that snaps into the binder.*

BUS BASICS

Buses are both a bane and a blessing. First of all, you must have a token or change in the amount of $1.50. They don't take dollar bills or pennies. They offer an above-ground option to getting around the city, but they're not a good idea if you're in a rush. As a rule, crosstown buses are great for shooting across Houston, 14th, 23rd, 42nd, 57th and other main streets.

Manhattan Subways

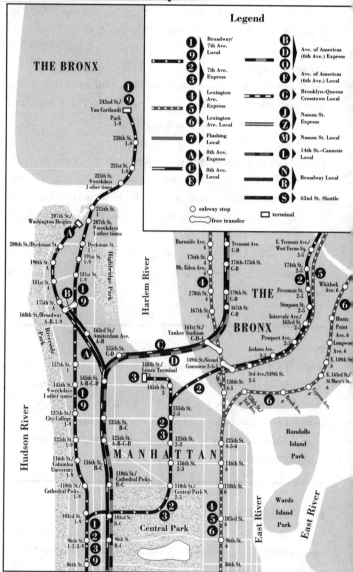

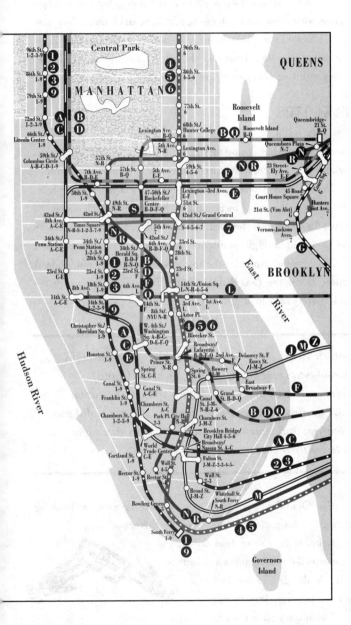

Buses are also a salvation to subway-deprived East Villagers—buses that run up and down Avenues A and B drop folks off at Union Square, where they can catch the N, R, 4, 5, 6, and L trains. New York City buses are clean, pleasant and reliable most of the time, but can get crowded at rush hour. Don't take the bus up or downtown in midtown during rush hour—you could walk there faster.

TAXI TIPS

New York might be the only city in which there's no such thing as phoning for a cab. Because they're so ubiquitous (11,787 and counting), it's just a matter of venturing streetside and hailing one down.

The entire city has recently had to adjust to a 20% taxi meter hike, which has sent many of us running to the subway (which also had a recent 25-cent hike). However, the Taxi and Limousine Commission has acquired a high profile of late, with TLC Commissioner Christopher Lynn espousing the apotheosis of a kinder, gentler ride. A yellow sticker, the **Taxi Rider's Bill of Rights,** is plastered on the back of every cab's front seat at eye level.

INSIDER TIP: *If you're venturing to the outer boroughs (Brooklyn, Queens, the Bronx, or State Island), plant your butt in the seat before you tell the cabbie your destination, or risk his flooring the gas pedal away from you and your remote address. They don't like to leave their turf.*

The Bill of Rights spells out your rights as a passenger: You have the right to designate the route, to ask the driver not to smoke, to turn down loud music, and what to do if the driver takes a circuitous route. It also directs the rider as to when to refrain from tipping.

Which leads us to the topic of taxi tipping. There are no hard and fast rules, although the rule of thumb is to tip at least a dollar, and more if the fare grows to more than $8.

GETTING TO AND FROM THE AIRPORTS

If you are traveling with one or more people, sharing a taxi is by far the fastest and most economical method of transport to JFK and La Guardia. If not, expect to spend around $30 for the ride. (You're expected to pay for all bridge and tunnel tolls.) However, you can take . . .

The Bus

The New York Bus Station is called the **Port Authority,** and this is probably the cheapest (if not the cleanest) way to get to the airport. For General Port Authority Information call 1-800-AIRRIDE.

The **Carey Bus** service goes to JFK and LaGuardia from the Port Authority and Grand Central Station. For information and exact times, call (718) 632-0500. Buses leave every 20-30 minutes, depending on the time of day.

Port Authority—La Guardia: Travel Time: 40-60 minutes, $10
Port Authority—JFK: Travel Time: 60-75 minutes, $13
Grand Central Station—LaGuardia. Bus leaves from Carey
    Ticket Office, 125 Park Ave. between 41st and 42nd Streets.
    30-45 minutes, $10
Grand Central Station—JFK. Bus leaves from Carey Ticket
    Office, 125 Park Ave. between 41st and 42nd Streets. Travel
    Time, 60-75 minutes, $13
Olympia Trails (Newark), 964-6233
Greyline, 1-800-451-0455
#300 bus to Newark Airport, 24 hours/day

TRAINS TO AND FROM NEW YORK

For service to Connecticut and upstate N.Y., you'll want to go to

Grand Central (located at 42nd St. and Lexington Ave.). Contract **Metro North** for ticket and schedule info at (212) 532-4900.

For trains to **Long Island, New Jersey,** and all **Amtrak services,** you'll want to go to **Penn Station** (located at 34th Street between Seventh and Eighth Avenues). Contact the following for information:

To Long Island: **Long Island Railroad:** (718) 217-5477
To New Jersey: **New Jersey Transit,** (201) 762-5100,
     or **PATH,** 1-800-234-7284.

PATH trains run about every 15 minutes during the day and once every half hour at night. Provides service to **Hoboken, Jersey City** and **Newark** 24 hours a day. Call **New Jersey Transit** for schedule information.

PATH Stations are at:
World Trade Center
Sixth Ave. &: 33rd St., 23rd St., 14th St., 9th St., and
     Christopher St.

To Other Cities via Amtrak: **1-800-USA-RAIL**

You can also get to other cities by taking a bus. You'll board at the **Port Authority Bus Terminal,** at 42nd St. and 8th Ave., 564-8484. Whether it's to Atlantic City, New Jersey, or Spokane, Washington, there are buses here to get you there. Just don't mind the underworld feel.

FERRY SERVICES

Plodding through Manhattan's gridlock, it can be easy to forget that you're on an island. But not for those who commute via ferry from Staten Island or Hoboken, New Jersey. And at fifty cents round trip, the Staten Island ferry can't be beat—even just for an excursion or quick escape from urban life.

Staten Island Ferry: 806-6940
New Jersey passenger ferries: 1-800-533-3779

HOW TO HAIL A CAB

The true sign of a seasoned New Yorker is the ease with which they step out into traffic and summon a taxi. Here are a few tips to help you fake it until it becomes second nature. And it will.

If lit, the white light on the roof of the taxi indicates that it is free. If it's not lit, set your sights on the next one. The unlit sign means it's occupied.

If the yellow "Off Duty" light is on, it means that the cab will not be picking up any fares.

It is especially difficult to find a taxi when it's raining and between four and six p.m. (when the drivers change shifts and everyone else is looking for a cab after work).

You'll have the best luck finding a cab at busy intersections, where you will have twice the opportunity to get an available taxi.

When hailing a taxi, don't scream "Taxi!", don't whistle, and don't flail your arms. Simply extend your arm upward, with your hand open. Like waving without the motion.

If you see someone disembarking a cab and you want to take the cab next, hold the door open for the passenger, which will claim the taxi as yours, (and win you brownie points) and then hop in. Being demure about it will only guarantee you another five minutes of waiting.

If there's already someone waiting for a taxi at your corner, ask if they're heading in the same direction, and if so, offer to split the fare.

If there's already someone waiting for a taxi at your corner and you don't want to share a fare, walk past them, against the direction of traffic, with your arm extended. That way, you'll get the taxi first (although you might feel like a jerk, you won't be late for work).

NILOUFAR MOTAMED

INSIDER TIP: *When in a position to pick between taxis dueling for your attentions, choose the shiny new one, not the old piece of crap. The best drivers get the best machines.*

Chapter Three

FIRST THINGS FIRST:

CHOOSING A NEIGHBORHOOD

MOVING TO NEW YORK is one of the most radical things a person can do. Whether you hail from a small town or a modest metropolis, nothing quite approaches being enveloped in the grasp of this unique and ever-evolving, grand and gritty sliver of land.

It's the actual moving in that can give one pause. When attempting to move into New York city, you may feel like you're waiting in front of the velvet ropes at a mobbed club. You know there are fabulous people inside having a fabulous time, but you're sort of stuck outside with the Bridge-and-Tunnel crowd. There seem to be arbitrary rules that govern who gets in and who gets stiffed, who pays the cover charge and who's greeted with open arms. You look down at your suave threads (at least you thought so before you left the house) and check your hair in a nearby car window, and hope to catch the suddenly omnipotent club vibe controller's eye and favor. (Funny, he kind of looks like a Bridge-and-Tunnel type with a flashlight). It's you against the rest of the crowd, and things seem a bit worrisome. Until the door guy points his beefy finger in your direction and you're in.

It's an insider's city, and this is an insider's guide to getting your foot (and the rest of your body) in the door of your very own Manhattan nest. Landing a swanky pad or even a bearable hole-in-the-wall may be one of the biggest challenges you ever face. The good news is, you get it out of the way rather primarily. The bad news is that it's kind of a drag. Manhattan is arguably the ultimate urban experience, and so lots of people flock here, which creates a bit of a housing crunch. Rents are high, space is at a premium, and often you may feel like you are doing the equivalent of a tapdance medley just to achieve your goal.

THE TRADEOFF

The biggest tradeoff for residing within this urban jewel is kissing goodbye the luxuries of two bathrooms, restaurant-sized kitchens, and re-adjusting your definition of a what a master bedroom is. Of course, there are sprawling apartments out there, with dimensions that defy their environment—if you can afford them. If you can, I'll try to forgive you.

But for those of you coming to New York to make your fortune, it's wise to put aside all notions of room dimensions based on the apartment layouts of la-la land sitcoms such as *Seinfeld*, *Friends*, *Caroline in the City*, and *Mad About You*. Instead, go hunting in your closet for shoeboxes. Set them up in an apartment formation. Meditate on these shoeboxes. Then, when you start looking at apartments, they won't seem so small in comparison.

Besides, after being in Manhattan for a few months, you'll start to think like a lot of us New Yorkers who have decided that the concept of space is overrated. Once you've discovered your own set of local haunts, you may come to think that your favorite little bistro is an alternate dining room, the corner cafe is your den, and so on. Nearby public parks certainly double as a back yard (with lots of guests that you don't know wandering around).

CHOOSING A NEIGHBORHOOD

Manhattan is all about having a ridiculous amount of choices—and that extends to housing as well. You may not be able to snag the apartment of your dreams, but you can choose the neighborhood and method of residence (renting, buying co-ops or condos)—depending on your means, of course. Money will certainly play a role in your options, but fear not. For every lady-who-lunches in New York, there is a starving artist whose muse and home is Manhattan as well. This is where people come to make their fortunes, as well as to spend them.

Although many folk are quite happy living in the outer boroughs, the focus of this book is on *Manhattan*, and we will tour its nine major neighborhoods, as well as give 25-cent tours of the meta-neighborhoods within them. Each neighborhood has its own distinct personality, idiosyncrasies, comforts, and detractions, and there is a dazzling array of possible environments. From the discreet charm of the Upper East Side to the unabashed sass of the East Village, the hipper-than-thou Euro vibe of Soho to the historic, diverse candor of the Upper West Side, and everything in between, this chapter will give you a sense of the habits, folkways, price range, and personality of Manhattan's many faces. Not to mention the inside scoop on the best way to catch a flick, walk your dog, strike a pose, sip a microbrew, and make your kid's day.

What to Think About When Choosing a Neighborhood

Be sure to choose your neighborhood well—it will have a marked effect on your New York experience. Things to consider:

- Do you want to be near work or near your post-work stomping grounds?
- Do you want to be in a neighborhood made up of mostly people your age, or do you not care?
- If you are raising a family, is it a neighborhood you want your child to be surrounded by?
- Young singles usually want to be near each other and near places where they can socialize together, such as Yorkville and the Villages, whereas families often prefer a quieter, more residential area, such as parts of the Upper East and West Sides, Gramercy and Battery Park City.
- Examine the block you are considering. Does it embody the best or worst the area has to offer? Be sure to check out the block at night to see how much the mood changes.

HOW TO FIND AN APARTMENT

There are many ways to go about finding an apartment, and the smartest way to go about your quest is to take advantage of all methods simultaneously.

Comb classified listings, in newspapers such as the *New York Times*, the *New York Post*, the *Daily News*, the *Village Voice*, and

CHEAP HOTELS TO STAY IN WHILE YOU'RE SEARCHING

CARLETON ARMS, 160 E. 25th St., 679-0680. In this Gramercy-ish spot, rates start at $49 and it's $69 for a double with a private bath. Students and tourists receive a $5 discount per night.

CHELSEA PINES INN, 317 West 14th St., 929-1023. "A cozy bed and breakfast in the heart of Gay New York." This 1850s row house was recently renovated with A/C and TVs, and offers single rooms with shared bath at $55—private bath at $85. Included: fresh fruit and homeade bread in the morning.

HOTEL 17, 225 E. 17th St., 475-2845. Not for the faint of heart—this is a clubby, modern-day Hotel Chelsea, sans any obvious resident geniuses. Their ad boasts "mod crowd, cool grunge, glamour decor, special events, rock stars..." and rates start at $65, $90 with bath, and give the deal of $210/week for a single and $315/week for a double.

OFFSOHO SUITES, 11 Rivington St., 353-0860. If you want to see if you can make it as a renter in the Lower East Side, this is a good litmus test. This below-Houston, off-Ludlow and sort-of off-Soho hotel has fabu rates: an air-conditioned suite for two (kitchen, bedroom and bath) is $79; a suite for four (bedroom, living room with pull-out bed, kitchen and bath) is $129. But it is a little intimidating, especially if you've watched too many episodes of NYPD Blue.

YMCA, 206 West 23rd St., 741-9226. They win the prize for inexpensiveness—$36 gets you a single room without a TV, along with free use of the pool and gym, clean sheets, and weekday maid service. $52 for a double.

smaller neighborhood newspapers. The best listings come out on Sundays, but you can pick up the Sunday Real Estate section on Saturdays after 9 p.m. (this varies, depending on your deli's alacrity).

Realtors and brokers are also more than happy to help you find a place—that's how they make their living, after all. And there are also services such as Roommate Finders and Apartment Source, where you pay a fee to be matched up with compatible roommates.

Word of mouth is very important, maybe even crucial. Manhattan is the city of connections and networking. If you have any, and I mean any, connections in Manhattan, use them. It doesn't have to be your best friend—it could be your friend's second cousin. Whoever they are, phone them up and ask them to put the word out that you're looking for a place to live. People are always much more comfortable rooming with or renting to those they have some sort of a personal connection with, as opposed to taking chances with a complete stranger. I think we all remember the movie "Single White Female." Need I say more?

Last but not least, check bulletin boards, whether they be in a funky cafe, a church, a bookstore, your college student union or local alumni chapter office. If you have been transferred here by your company, they may be able to give you some leads as well.

APARTMENT HUNTER TIPS

Get the Voice on Tuesday Night at Astor Place. The rest of the world gets it on Wednesday morning, so this gives you a jump-start.

Get the Sunday Times on Saturday evening, so you can spend the night cruising the ads and start phoning early Sunday morning.

Scour the Times on off-days midweek—most people just look at their classified on the weekends. ALSO: if your internet service provider is America Online, you can use their @Times connection to cruise their online classifieds.

Buy Gabriel's Apartment Rental Guide, available at NYC Barnes & Noble bookstores. You can also order it by calling 423-9000.

What to Think About When Choosing an Apartment

It's very important to have a certain set of personal guidelines in mind when beginning your search. Beyond which corner of the city you pick, it's also crucial to know which things you can't live without and which things are not so vital to your housing happiness. The key considerations:

- Do you want to live in a doorman building?
- If you're single, do you want your own place or do you mind a roommate? (For young people moving into the city, roommates are often a big plus. If friendly, they can hook you up with anything from a hot restaurant tip to a circle of acquaintances who may eventually grow into friends. New York can be a lonely place when you first get here, and living alone may prove to further enunciate this feeling of isolation. But make sure you really suss out the personalities of these potential bathroom-sharers. No matter what city you're in, bad roommates are a domestic pothole to avoid. Laying down ground rules, and respecting existing ones, really preserves domestic harmony, which is more fragile than it would be if everyone had more space.)
- Do you want a washer/dryer? If laundry is coin-operated, is there a change machine or quarters available at the front desk?
- How is the water pressure in the shower?
- How is the height of the shower head? (If you are tall and the shower head hits your back, you'll be stooping to get clean.)
- Are there hardwood floors, and if so, what condition are they in?
- Is there air conditioning? Manhattan summers are harsh, so if you don't have A/C, get a fan or two—before the summer price hike.
- Is a parking space included? If not, is one available for an additional charge?
- How high were the utility bills of the previous tenants?
- Is the apartment cable-ready?
- Why did the previous tenants leave?
- Does the bedroom face a busy street?
- How much light shines into the bedroom in the morning?
- Are there enough windows?
- Is there a garden or lawn, patio, a deck or a balcony? Are you allowed to go up on the roof?
- Is an elevator available?
- Does the super live on the premises?
- Can you take bicycles in the elevator?
- Is a secure storage space available for bicycles or furniture?
- Are there specific rules about parties, pets, or days you can or cannot move in?

- Are there any move-in fees?
- What kind of security does the place have?
- Do the windows have security bars on them? (In New York, landlords are required to install bars on all windows not opening onto a fire escape.)
- If you have a window opening onto a fire escape, is there a gate on this window? (Window gates usually run about $200-300.)
- What is the penalty for breaking the lease? (Don't ask this question until the lease is in your hand. The landlord will pass on you and go to the candidate who would never think of breaking his or her lease)
- Check the pilot light on the stove.
- Turn on and off all the lights.
- Test the dishwasher, the disposal, the microwave.
- Check the number, placement and condition of phone jacks and electrical outlets.
- If you are not familiar with the neighborhood, consider going back to the area at night.
- Would you be comfortable walking around after dark?
- Is parking a problem after 8 p.m.?
- Keep in mind that you can ask a landlord to exterminate, have the apartment cleaned, have carpets steam-cleaned and walls repainted before you move in.
- Ask landlord or other tenants in the building if they have had problems with bugs or safety (i.e. break-ins or burglaries).

TO RENT OR TO BUY

Those of us who are looking to rent and those of us who are looking to buy are almost certainly coming to New York with an entirely different, and equally valid, set of priorities and means. Buying property in Manhattan is smart for those who can afford to do so. But most lifers (those of us who are never leaving this burg) start out renting and eventually make arrangements to buy their apartment, or another one, after they have become established in their careers and have the money. Renting is the way to go (and perhaps the only option) for those of us who don't have the capital to buy, aren't planning on being in New York for the long haul, or simply don't want to make such a permanent arrangement.

THE RENTAL SITUATION

The process of renting an apartment in New York can be anything from easy as pie to labyrinthine. You could be lucky enough to land a share with some friends, or friends of friends, and not have to sign

APARTMENT STICKER SHOCK

For people who buy co-op apartments in New York, the maintenance fee is a shock. Besides paying off their own mortgages, they have to make a monthly payment that might be as much as they were paying in rent back in Omaha or Springfield. The maintenance fee covers the co-operative's expenses for the building: taxes, the mortgage on the building, maintenance fees, repairs, etc. Look at it this way: if you bought a house back in Omaha or Springfield, how much would you pay for property taxes, to have someone tend the lawn and garden, to have the place painted every three or four years, and to fix the cracks in the sidewalk or ceilings? Doesn't help much, does it?

a single piece of paper. Or, you could have to fill out a small file cabinet's worth of information, list a zillion references, and pay off everyone from the realtor, to the super, to the wino who camps out in front of the building. If you're renting an apartment on your own, make sure to have all your papers, references, intended roommates, and money at close hand.

What You Usually Need Is:

- References: a neat list of former landlords, and their numbers and addresses
- Driver's License or Passport (i.e., a photo ID that proves you are who you say you are)

How Much You'll Need

The standard cash you should expect to have to put down when renting an apartment is:

Choosing a Neighborhood p.33

REAL ESTATE ABBREVIATIONS

Get to know the abbreviations in the classified ads: WBFP, for example, is "wood-burning fireplace." FLR-THRU is "floor-through," which refers to an entire floor of a townhouse, with windows front and back. JR 2BR means one small bedroom and a closet that a single bed could fit in, maybe. Here are some others:

BAL—balcony	*LG—large*
BRNSTN—brownstone	*LNDRY—laundry*
CONV—converted	*LOC—location*
CUST—custom	*MOD—modern*
DRMN—doorman	*MW—microwave*
DW—dishwasher	*PARQ—parquet floors*
EIK—eat-in kitchen	*PH—penthouse*
ELEV—elevator	*PVT—private*
EXPO BRK—exposed brick	*REN, RENO—renovated*
FSB—full-service building	*RFTP SNDK—rooftop sundeck*
GAR, GDN—garden	*RIV VU—river view*
HRDWD—hardwood	*SEP—separate*
IMM OCC—immediate	*SF—square feet*
occupancy	*TERR—terrace*

- First and last month's rent
- A security deposit (equal to another month's rent)
- A finder's fee (equal to 15% of your first year's rent). Many apartments can't be seen without an agent, who usually charges you 15-20% of a year's rent.

The Rent Race

Those who snooze, lose in the mad dash for pads, and I wouldn't even recommend blinking. Don't be surprised if you show up at your appointment and find a queue of shifty-eyed hopefuls waiting ahead of you. It's a landlord's market. If at all possible, try to land a place through word of mouth. There is a tremendous amount of rental housing in New York, yet there always seems to be a shortage of good, affordable places.

Most apartments are **studios** or **one-bedrooms.** In most parts of Manhattan, anything under $1,000 is a good price for a studio, while a one-bedroom typically is $1,200 to $1,500, and a luxury one-bedroom can easily cost twice that.

Family-size apartments—two, three, and even four bedrooms—are available to rent in Manhattan, but they are also in demand, with prices to match. Figure on paying $1,000 per bedroom, conservatively.

RENTAL FACTOIDS: *The rent may be higher for apartments on high floors, or with doormen. A gym or a health club in the building can also add to the cost.*

An apartment on the fourth floor is going to cost more if there's an elevator in the building than if it's a walkup. (There are many fourth-floor and fifth-floor walkups, particularly in brownstone townhouses.)

Most apartments are rent-stabilized, which means landlords are limited in the amount they can raise your rent when you renew your lease.

THE BUYING SITUATION

There are usually a few family houses for sale at any one time in Manhattan, but they typically start at several hundred thousand dollars, not counting the work that most families will have to do for another hundred thousand, or more.

LOFTY IDEAS

The loft is a very New York-specific term which refers to old industrial spaces which have been revamped into living quarters, boasting high ceilings and big windows—both rarities in Manhattan. Lofts are the perfect solution for space-starved New Yorkers who don't mind paying for the extra breathing room.
Loft Specialist: Patrick Lilly, 112 Fourth Ave., 353-3003.

RECOMMENDED BROKERS

Very High End Buying/Rental:

BROWN, HARRIS, STEVENS, 655 Madison Ave.,
   906-9200 (Saul Howard)

SOTHEBY'S, 980 Madison Ave., 606-7660

ALICE MASON, 635 Madison Ave., 832-8870

EDWARD LEE CAVE INC., 33 E. 68th St., 772-8510

STRIBLING ASSOCIATES LTD., 924 Madison, 570-2440

GREENTHAL RESIDENTIAL, 4 Park Ave., 340-9300

Rental:

THE HALSTEAD PROPERTY CO., 451 West Broadway, 475-4200

CROMAN REALTY, 611 Broadway, 228-9300

CITY CONNECTIONS REALTY CO., 165 Ninth Ave., 242-5050
   All of Manhattan to 96th St.

CORCORAN GROUP INC., 25 E. 21st St., 979-7700
   Has a relocation department especially for
   non-native New Yorkers.

THE FEATHERED NEST, 310 Madison Ave., 867-8500
   Rentals only.

SOPHER REAL ESTATE, 2162 Broadway, 469-3000

J.I. SOPHER & CO., 250 Mercer, 475-8888

SWIFT & WATSON, 552 LaGuardia Place, 995-0001

Roommate Services:

ROOMMATES NYC, 543 E. 5th St. (A&B), 982-6265. This is a
   do-it-yourself, cheapie service, where a measly 20 beans gets
   you four months of access to on-site, city-wide, daily-updated
   apartment listings. If looking for a roommate, you can list
   your apartment for free. Rent range: $300-$1000.

RAINBOW ROOMMATES NY., 312 West 15th St., 627-8612,
   Rainbowroommate@nycnet.com, http://nycnet.com/rainbow-
   roommates. If you're gay, this a surefire way to avoid the
   headache of homophobic roommates. It's free to list your share,
   and costs $40 until you find one. To receive applications via
   fax, call: 1-800-529-0292. All major credit cards accepted.

ROOMMATE FINDERS, The Fisk Building, 250 West 57th St. (off

Broadway), Suite 1629, 489-6918. $200 flat fee. (50% money-back guarantee). This high-volume organization offers many listings. Used by big corporations' relocation departments, like American Express and the United Nations. Large range of rents.

APARTMENT SOURCE, 580 Broadway (Houston & Prince), 343-8155. (www.apartmentsource.com) For a $145 fee, you can call or come in to the office, and arrange to see apartments on your own. They will also fax you daily listings. Studios, 1-3 bedrooms, city-wide. Rent range: $800 and up.

THE APARTMENT FONE: 278-3663, http://www.aptfone.com. Free 24-hour service, updated daily.

CONDOS VS. CO-OPS— WHAT DOES IT ALL MEAN?

Condo:

• You are full owner of your apartment, and joint owner of common areas.

• You are responsible for paying your own monthly mortgage, and real estate taxes. Monthly maintenance is smaller than a co-op's.

• If an owner defaults on his mortgage payments and common charges, the other owners are only responsible for making up the difference of the common charges.

• A condo board of directors is elected, but they can't tell any unit owner to whom they can sell or rent their apartment.

Condos tend to be modern buildings.

Co-Op:

• You own shares of stock in a corporation worth the value of your apartment. You get a proprietary lease.

• Your monthly maintenance covers the entire building's mortgage payments and real estate taxes as part of common charges.

• If one owner defaults on his payments, or if any units are unsold, the other owners could be responsible for making up the difference.

• A co-op board has the right to accept or nix you as a future neighbor. If you decide to sell, they must approve your buyer.

If you're buying an apartment, there are two choices. **Cooperative apartments,** or co-ops, and **condominiums.**

When you buy a co-op, you're literally buying a share in a cooperative building. The co-op board decides whether you will get in. There have been a number of stories in recent years about celebrities being rejected because co-op boards fear they will cause some sort of uproar—but most rejections are because board members feel the applicant's financial position is not strong enough. The co-op board also sets rules for the members (no using the freight elevator before 9 a.m. on Sundays, no loud music after 11 p.m., and so forth), as well as the monthly maintenance fee. A typical monthly maintenance fee is several hundred dollars, and can easily be more than $1,000 for larger apartments in nicer buildings. A rule of thumb is that the maintenance fee will usually be $1 to $1.25 per square foot.

In some ways, condos are in more demand than co-ops, and therefore often carry higher asking prices, because you can actually buy the apartment instead of merely a share in the building. Without a co-op board, there are usually fewer restrictions on what you can and cannot do. You still pay monthly common charges—for repairs, janitors, doormen and such—that are usually significantly lower than the maintenance fees for co-ops.

CAR TALK

Although the parking situation varies by neighborhood, it's safe to say that overall, parking is a total headache and will cost you in one way or another. However, there are many ways to circumvent this headache, or at least ease its pain.

For starters, if you actually want to park on the streets, you must keep abreast of the myriad rules and regulations that change by the day. Each street has signs that designate the daily schedule. Additionally, every Sunday and during the week, the *New York Times* carries parking information.

Many people avoid the whole problem by picking a parking garage or lot. You can either choose one nearby, or a cheaper one in an out-of-the-way location like on the far east or west side of Manhattan, or in New Jersey or the outer boroughs. This way, if you only use your car for weekend getaways, you can cab, subway, or bus to it. In each neighborhood, there will be a sampling of area garages and prices, as well as a description of the general street-parking situation.

SCHOOL INFORMATION

The following organizations and publications will help parents, when selecting a school, negotiate the daunting maze of information out there.

Public Education Association, 39 W. 32nd St., 868-1640, is a non-profit civic organization whose focus is on obtaining quality public education for children.

National Training and Evaluation Center, Inc., 15 W. 84th St., 877-4480. Testing center administers tests for admission into public schools. Offers consultation to parents who want to find the right public school for their child.

The Fund for NYC Public Education, 96 Morton St., 645-5100. Talk to Beth Leif, Executive Director, about your district or any particular school.

Parents League of New York, 115 E. 82nd St., 737-7385, is a non-profit organization of parents and independent schools proving guidance on private schools.

Catholic Schools of the Archdiocese, 240 Bleecker St., 691-3381 (elementary) and 371-1000 (high school), will provide information on parochial education opportunities.

Center for Educational Innovation at the Manhattan Institute, 52 Vanderbilt Ave., 559-7000

NY's Neighborhoods

New York can be broken down into 10 primary neighborhoods, although each neighborhood can have several sub-neighborhoods within it. They are:

- The Upper East Side
- The Upper West Side
- Midtown East
- Midtown West
- Chelsea
- Gramercy Park
- The East Village
- Greenwich Village
- Soho and Tribeca
- Downtown

Here's your guide to what life is like there, along with the essential resources they offer.

THE UPPER EAST SIDE

For many people, the **Upper East Side** is where to live when you've "arrived," and I don't mean stepped off the plane, train, or bus, blinking and disoriented. Bordered on the south by E. 59th Street, 96th Street on the North, and cinched between the East River and Fifth Avenue, it boasts beautiful buildings, relatively immaculate streets, and a conservative, insular demographic. For people who don't want to be exposed to the grittier aspects of urban life, it's a refuge, offering many benefits of suburban life along with cosmopolitan advantages. Exclusive boutiques line the avenues and streets, Central Park's arboreal bliss beckons from the west, and four-star restaurants are within a stone's throw of each other. Culturally, it offers the **Museum Mile,** which consists of the august Whitney, Metropolitan Museum of Art (the Met), the Guggenheim, and the Frick Collection, to name a few.

The Upper East Side has always had a patrician reputation. Its proximity to Central Park earmarked the area, which was already *chi-chi,* as the ultimate in luxury living. Fifth Avenue soon became known as "Millionaire's Row," boasting society lions such as the Astors, Vanderbilts, and Whitneys. A strong neo-classical influence permeated the architecture, much to the bane of later, modernist architects such as Frank Lloyd Wright, who eschewed aping the old world traditions and sought instead to establish a new, organic American architecture (he got his revenge with the Guggenheim, no?).

The Upper East Side is an ideal place to raise children, if you can afford it—it's probably the safest (or feels safest, anyway) area to live in. Pre-war buildings predominate, with uniformed doormen holding court at the front door. Most of N.Y.'s exclusive private schools, such as Brearley, Chapin, Dalton, and Sacred Heart, are right in the neighborhood. Central Park offers children a close approximation of their US RDA of nature, with parental supervision required, of course. It's a neighborhood that has residential roots, and it shows. The further east you go, the more the mood relaxes.

Carnegie Hill, a sub-neighborhood of the Upper East Side, takes "residential" to a higher level. It extends from 86th to 96th Streets between Fifth and Third Aves. and up to 98th Street from Fifth to Madison Avenue. Its mood is decidedly family-oriented, upper-crust, and quiet. Landmarks include the Cooper-Hewitt Museum (formerly

Manhattan Neighborhoods

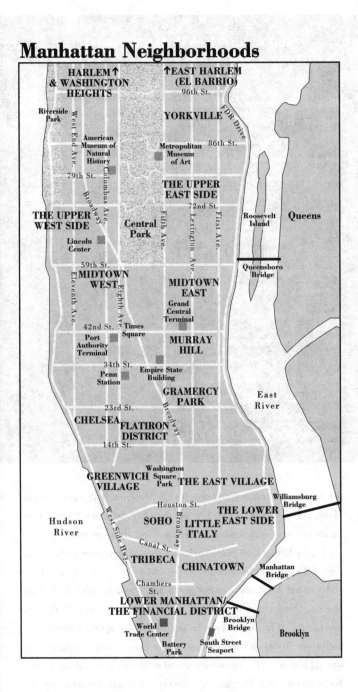

How to Find Out About Schools on the Upper East Side

Most of Manhattan is divided into two school districts. COMMUNITY SCHOOL DISTRICT ONE covers most of the Lower East Side. COMMUNITY SCHOOL DISTRICT TWO covers all of Manhattan below 96th St. on the East Side and below 59th St. on the West Side, exempting the part of the Lower East Side in District One. COMMUNITY SCHOOL DISTRICT THREE covers the West Side from 59th St. to 122nd St.

For public schools, the Upper East Side belongs to COMMUNITY SCHOOL DISTRICT 2, 330 West 18th St., 337-8700. Make an appointment with Ms. Marjorie Robbins, Director of Pupil Personnel, or Mr. Michael Dance.

Private Schools to look into:

THE BREARLEY SCHOOL, 610 E. 83rd, 744-8582.
THE BROWNING SCHOOL, 52 E. 62nd, 838-6280.
THE CHAPIN SCHOOL, 100 E. End Ave., 744-2335.
THE DALTON SCHOOL, 108 E. 89th St., 722-5160.
THE EPISCOPAL SCHOOL, 35 E. 69th St., 879-9764.
THE SPENCE SCHOOL, 22 E. 91st, 289-5940.

the Carnegie Mansion) and the Jewish Museum. The Park Avenue Malls, between 86th and 96th Street, beautify the area with their profusion of spring and summer flowers and fruit-bearing trees.

On the Upper East Side, **Yorkville** used to be known as the wrong side of the tracks. It is bounded on the east and west by the East River and Central Park, and on the north and south by 96th and 72nd Streets. Once home to German, Czechoslovakian, and Hungarian immigrants, it has since become gentrified, and sports many luxury high-rises. Today, it's the destination for many young single professionals who want the convenience and ready-made social scene that Yorkville provides. For many, the area emulates a fraternity scene and is populated by nostalgic recent graduates. Bars that line First,

Second, and Third Aves. play host to the locals, and the scene is often crowded with weekend warriors reveling in each other's company. However, many hipper types prefer to travel deep south (below 14th Street, that is) for their cruisy and boozy adventures.

Carl Schurz Park is a highlight of Yorkville, and contains, along with lovely landscaped grounds, a playground and a dog run, **Gracie Mansion,** which is home to the mayors of this city during their oft-beleaguered tenures.

Another sub-neighborhood on the Upper East Side is **Lenox Hill**—the slightly hilly area in the East 70's which was formerly owned by the Lenox family. It combines the aura of both its neighbors to the north and south, to provide a refined, residential feel. Lenox Hill Hospital is in this area, and has a very good reputation.

Advantages of the Upper East Side are numerous. Its proximity to the park is a real plus, and the environment lends itself to raising a family, unlike most other parts of the city. There's a real emphasis on keeping the streets clean and preserving historical buildings. Fans of the Upper East Side cite accessibility and convenience when it comes to services, and they enjoy the variety of choices available to them.

Drawbacks include the general expensiveness of everything (from rent to coffee), the homogeneity, and the lack of funk. Also, since there is only one subway line that runs up there (the 4, 5, 6), it's over-crowded and under-sufficient for the needs of the area. What the Upper East Side lacks in funk, it makes up for in posh.

INSIDER TIP: *If you want information about the crime rate in a particular neighborhood, call the local police station. You'll find their names and numbers in the "Essential Neighborhood Resources" sections of each neighborhood.*

If You're Looking to Rent:

It's possible, but not probable, to find a studio apartment for less than $1,000/month, especially in Yorkville. In general, however, a range of $1,000 to $1,400 is more realistic for a studio. A one-bedroom for under $1,400 is usually a good deal or has some serious flaw—such as an inconvenient location, a kitchen the size of a closet, or a bedroom that actually is a closet. A range of $1,500 to $2,000 is common for one-bedroom apartments. Most two-bedroom places are $2,000 a month and up. The one type of apartment that longtime New York residents say is a relative bargain nowadays is the three-bedroom family place that can still be found for $3,000 to $4,000—not much more than the going rate back in the mid-1980s.

If You're Looking to Buy:

Studios can be found for under $100,000, with monthly maintenance fees, or common charges, of $500 to $800. But think twice about buying a studio—let's hope at some point you'll require more living space, and when you try to unload your studio, people will be thinking twice because at some point, *they'll* require more living space. There's a wide range in prices for **one-bedroom** places, from $100,000 to $300,000, depending on the swank factor. The typical one-bedroom sells for around $120,000 to $150,000, with monthly maintenance fees from $600 to $1,000. Most two-bedroom apartments are between $200,000 and $300,000, with the majority falling between those two figures.

Essential Neighborhood Resources

Area Code: 212

Zip Codes: 10128, 10028, 10021

Police:
19th Precinct, 153 E. 67th St., 452-0600

Hospitals:
Mt. Sinai, 1 Gustav Levi Place, 241-6500
Lenox Hill, 100 E. 77th St., 439-2345
Metropolitan, 1901 First Ave., 230-6262

Post Offices:
Cherokee, 1483 York Ave., 288-3724
Gracie, 229 E. 85th St., 988-6681

Lenox Hill, 221 E. 70th St., 870-4401
Yorkville Finance Station, 1619 Third Ave., 369-2230

Libraries:
96th Street, 112 E. 96th St., 289-0908
Webster, 1465 York Ave., 288-5049
67th Street, 328 E. 67th St., 734-1717

Community Resources:
Community Board 8, 309 E. 94th St., 427-4840
Lenox Hill Neighborhood Association, 331 E. 71st St.,
 744-5022, runs a school, as well as a community center.
Carnegie Hill Neighbors Inc., 1234 Madison Ave., 966-5520
Central Park Conservancy, 315-0385

Churches:
Church of the Heavenly Rest, Fifth Ave. and 90th St.
St. Jean Baptiste Church, 184 E. 76th St., 288-5082
All Saints Episcopal Church, 230 E. 60th St., 758-0447
Zion Saint Mark's Evangelical Lutheran Church,
 339 E. 84th St., 650-1648

Synagogues:
Temple Emanu-El, 1 E. 65th St. (5th Ave. between
 65th and 66th St.), 744-1400
Lisker Congregation, 163 E. 69th St., 472-3968
Manhattan Sephardic Congregation, 325 E. 75th St., 988-6085
Park Avenue Synagogue, 50 E. 87th St., 369-2600
Temple Israel of the City of New York, 112 E. 75th St.,
 249-5000
Temple Shaaray Tefila, 250 E. 79th St., 535-7597

Landmarks:
The Metropolitan Museum of Art, Fifth Ave. at 82nd St., 570-
3753. This grand neoclassical behemoth has both an imposing
permanent collection as well as exciting temporary exhibits. Don't
miss the Egyptian collection.

The Frick Collection, 1 E. 70th St., 288-0700. Formerly Henry Clay Frick's domicile, this mansion is now merely home to a large, mostly European Renaissance art collection, featuring Fragonard. Note the period furnishings.

The Cooper-Hewitt Museum: The Smithsonian Institution's National Museum of Design, 2 E. 91st St., 860-6868. Formerly Andrew Carnegie's home, this museum now preserves over 30,000 drawings and prints, mostly depicting architecture, ornament, and design.

The Jewish Museum, 1109 Fifth Ave. at 92nd St., 860-1888. Formerly the home of Felix M. Warburg, this museum is devoted to Judaica, and offers changing collections.

The Solomon R. Guggenheim Museum, 1071 Fifth Ave. (at 89th St.), 360-3500. Frank Lloyd Wright's fab modern structure is home to over 4,000 pieces of art, from the Impressionist period to the present.

The Whitney Museum of American Art, 945 Madison Ave. (at 75th St.), 570-3600. Like the Guggenheim, this Marcel Breuer-designed building has a brave, new look to it. Patron and Trustafarian Gertrude Vanderbilt Whitney was responsible for this—her interest in things artsy and bohemian led to the funding of this institution. The Whitney's permanent collection is largely composed of 20th Century art.

Gracie Mansion, 88th St. and E. End Ave., 570-4751, Go on a tour at our local White House. It's surrounded by Carl Shurz Park (from 90th St. to Gracie Square at 84th St.), which has a promenade by the East River, a dog run, a playground, and other good things.

Main Drags:

First, Second and **Third Aves.** have lots of weekend nightlife, from 95th St. down to 72nd St. Irish bars, like **Pat O'Brien's** (628-7242) at 1497 Third Ave., between 84th and 85th streets, are plentiful, and are perfect for pounding an unpretentious beer with friends. **The Yorkville Brewery** (517-2739), 1359 First Ave. at 73rd St., offers mediocre home-grown brews, but a packed house.

The Great Outdoors:

Central Park, (see page 47) 840 acres, bounded on the north by 110th St., on the South by 59th St., on the West by Eighth Ave., and on the East by Fifth Ave.

Central Park Attractions

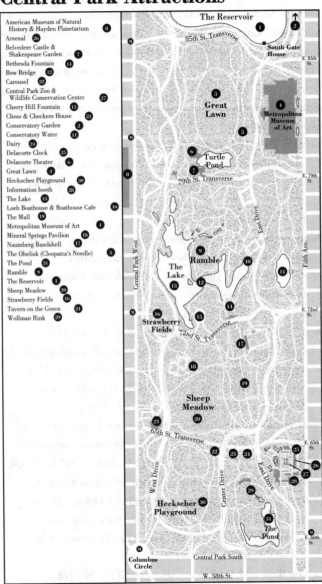

American Museum of Natural History & Hayden Planetarium **8**
Arsenal **26**
Belvedere Castle & Shakespeare Garden **7**
Bethesda Fountain **14**
Bow Bridge **12**
Carousel **22**
Central Park Zoo & Wildlife Conservation Center **27**
Cherry Hill Fountain **15**
Chess & Checkers House **23**
Conservatory Garden **2**
Conservatory Water **11**
Dairy **24**
Delacorte Clock **25**
Delacorte Theater **6**
Great Lawn **3**
Heckscher Playground **30**
Information booth **28**
The Lake **13**
Loeb Boathouse & Boathouse Cafe **10**
The Mall **19**
Metropolitan Museum of Art **4**
Mineral Springs Pavilion **18**
Naumberg Bandshell **17**
The Obelisk (Cleopatra's Needle) **5**
The Pond **31**
Ramble **9**
The Reservoir **1**
Sheep Meadow **20**
Strawberry Fields **16**
Tavern on the Green **21**
Wollman Rink **29**

What's an Upper East Sider to do for nature? Go to Central Park, of course. Naturally, every Manhattanite can claim a stake in this Frederick Law Olmsted-designed mega-oasis, but for Uptowners, it's their lush back yard, the rolling hills and vegetation a reminder of the wilderness Manhattan used to be. Now suitably colonized with benches, paved jogging, cycling, and rollerblading paths, as well as baseball diamonds, roller/ice rinks, tennis courts, and amphitheaters, Central Park offers a variety of activities for both the athlete and sedentary nature lover in you. Below are some Central Park highlights to get you started.

Central Park Visitor and Information Center, 794-6564.
> The quaintly-named Dairy (no milk here) serves as the eye of the storm for visitors and locals who want to be in the know. A small gift shop, calendars of events, family workshops and tours are among its offerings.

Summerstage, The Rumsey Playfield, at 72nd St. and East Dr.
> Host to a FREE array of dance, opera, alterna-rock, spoken word, and global music. Schedules are distributed in most weekly newspapers at the beginning of the season, or call 360-2777 if you miss it.

New York Road Runners Club, 9 E. 89th St., 860-4455,
> E-mail: http://www.membership@nyrrc.org. This august running organization has partnered with the park, and has a multitude of programs for all ages and skill levels. It also offers a safety pairing system, so that no runners have to go it alone.

Shakespeare in the Park, Every summer, the Joseph Papp
> Shakespeare Festival takes place at the Delacorte Shakespeare Theatre (mid-park, at 79th St.) It's free! Call 861-7277 for details.

Model Boat Pond, Conservatory Water, 74th St. and Fifth Ave.

Central Park Zoo/Wildlife Conservation Center, Fifth Ave.
> and 64th St., 439-6500. Bring the little ones to this global collection of animals. Behind bars, unlike the ones on you see on the subway.

Lasker Rink and Pool, Mid-park at 106th St., 996-1184.
> Depending on the season, you can swim or skate here.

Tennis, Obtain an annual tennis permit from the **Arsenal** at
> Central Park (near Fifth Ave. at 64th St.) or call 360-8133.

Fees: adults, $40; Seniors, $20; and under 18, $10. For a single-play ticket, (guest pass) you must pay $5.00. Sign up beforehand.

Parking:

Street parking on the Upper East Side is very hard to come by—between the residents and the visitors, parking is next to impossible. If you can get a spot, it's relatively safe, especially if you have a visual deterrent like a Club on your steering wheel. Regardless, you should seriously consider a building with a garage, or a separate parking garage.

GARAGES (Rates are monthly):

Kinney Systems, 222 E. 65th St., 355-9451, $350 w/tax; 1110 First Ave., 355-8082, $260 w/tax.

Garage Management Corp, 113 E. 84th St., 888-7400, $473 w/tax; 203 E. 71st St., 888-7400, $473 w/tax.

Square One Parking, 82nd St., First Ave., 650-1882, $305, w/tax.

Banks and ATMs:

The following banks and ATMs are safe and well-lit:

Apple Bank for Savings, 1555 First Ave. (81st), 472-4545

Chase Manhattan, 1-800-AT-CHASE, 1025 Madison Ave., at 77th; 201 E. 79th St. between Second and Third Aves.; 255 E. 86th St. between Second and Third Aves.

Chemical Bank, 770 Lexington Ave. (60th), 935-9935; 360 E. 72nd, at First Ave.; 1003 Lexington Ave., at 72nd; 501 E. 79th St. at York Ave.; 126 E. 86th, at Lexington Ave.

Citibank, 1078 Third Ave. (64th), 627-399; 757 Madison Ave. (65th).

Grocery Stores:

Food Emporium. This upscale supermarket has good produce, an excellent deli, and they deliver. They also have 8 locations on the Upper East Side, so call 650-1260 for the location nearest you.

D'Agostino's Supermarkets. We call it D'Ag's for short (rhymes with bags), 1031 First Ave., 486-0340; 1074 Lexington Ave., at 76th

St. 988-8813; 1507 York Ave., at 80th St. 734-6317; 1233 Lexington Ave., at 83rd, 570-6803.

There are also many **Sloan's** and **Gristede's** supermarkets, for a more basic supermarket experience. Call 956-5770 for the location nearest you.

Beer and Liquor:
K & D Wines & Spirits, 1366 Madison Ave. at 96th St., 289-1818. Renowned among wine-lovers around the world.

Pharmacies:
Cambridge Chemists, 215 65th St. (Madison and Fifth) 734-5678

Drug Loft, 1103 Lexington Ave. (77th St.), 879-0910

Zitomer Pharmacy, 969 Madison Ave., 737-5560. Veronica Webb's fave pharmacy. They're actually more of a department store, and they deliver.

Alexander Pharmacy, 1751 Second Ave. (91st), 410-0060. Free delivery.

Duane Reade, 1191 Second Ave., 355-5944; 1279 Third Ave., 744-2688. Discount prices and a good selection.

Eastside Pharmacy, 1394 York Ave., 249-1777. Free pickup of prescriptions and delivery.

Gas Stations:
Atlas Auto, 410 E. 60th , 838-9000

1855 First Avenue Service Station, 1855 First Ave., 534-9044

Mobil Oil Service Station, 1730 First Ave., 369-3365

96th and First Avenue Service Station, 534-5411

Dry Cleaners:
Madame Paulette Dry Cleaners, 1255 2nd Ave., 838-6827

Fashion Award Cleaners, 1462 Lexington Ave. (95th St.), 289-5623. A place to have valuable garments cleaned, such as wedding dresses.

Lady Dubonnet French Dry Cleaners, 1143 First Ave. (63rd), 371-0373. Also good for valuable or special garments.

Laundry King, 343 E. 66th St., 879-5141. Free pickup and delivery.

Perry Process Cleaners, 1315 Third Ave., 628-8300.

Good for leather and suede items. Pick up and delivery.

Ace Cleaners, 1701 First Ave., 427-7111.

Chang's Cleaners, 1031 Lexington Ave., 734-8360.

Laundromats:

Many Upper East Side buildings have their own laundry facilities on-site. But if you want to stray, or aren't that lucky, here are some viable possibilities. You can either have your laundry done for you, or do the dirty deed yourself (saving money in the process).

The Mat, 1717 First Ave. (89th St.), 426-9207. Where else but New York would you be able to shoot pool, watch TV and chill out while your laundry does its thing? And can you say singles bar of the nineties?

Five Star Laundry, 1396 Lexington Ave. (91st St.), 289-7245. 50 cents/pound, minimum 8 pounds. No pickup/delivery.

One Stop Do All Laundromat, 318 E. 70th St., 517-7861. 7 pound minimum at $5, 50 cents each additional pound. $2 for pickup and delivery.

Royal Sutton Laundromat, 318 E. 70th St., 838-0910. They pick up and deliver. Up to 8 lbs, $6. Each additional pound is 65 cents.

Waterworks II, 357 E. 68th St., 439-9467. 7 pounds for $5, each additional pound, 50 cents.

Hardware:

Gracious Homes, 1217 Third Ave., 988-8990

Feldman's House of Wares, 1071 Madison, 879-8090

AB Locksmith & Hardware, Inc., 1603 York Ave., 734-1112

K&G Hardware & Supply, 401 E. 90th St. 831-3140

Lemmon W. G., Ltd., 755 Madison Ave., 734-4400

Lexington Hardware and Electric Co., Inc., 797 Lexington Ave., 838-5586

Video Stores:

Video Room, 1487 Third Ave. (84th), 879-5333. Specializes in foreign and classic movies. Membership Policy: Walk-In plan simply entails getting your credit card imprint, and movies are $3.99 each.

Their Delivery plan is $89/year, for free pick-up and delivery, with 12 free rentals. New releases 1 day, all others, 2 days.

Couch Potato Video, 1302 Second Ave., 288-6620; 1456 Second Ave., 517-8666. They just need a major credit card to get you started. For $10, you get free delivery and they throw in two free rentals.

Blockbuster Video, 205 E. 95th St. 423-0332; 1251 Lexington Ave., 439-0960. To start a membership, you need a major credit card and photo ID. If you don't have a credit card, you need to bring in 2 utility bills, and there's a $5 fee. $4.35 per rental for 1-3 evenings.

THE COST CHART

Throughout this book you'll see dollar signs after establishments. Here's what it all means:

$: $10-$15 $$: $20-$30 $$$: $30 and up

Cafes, Delis, Coffeeshops, and Diners:

Eat Here Now, 839 Lexington Ave. (64th), 751-0724. $
   Kid-friendly.
Hunter Coffee Shop, 966 Lexington Ave. (70th St.), 432-6240.
   $ Kid-friendly.
Peppermint Park, 1225 First Ave. (66th St.), 288-5054.
   Maybe the best ice cream on the East Side. $ Kid-friendly.
Million Dollar Deli, 1264 Madison Ave., 348-7070.
Lorenzo & Maria's Kitchen, 1418 Third Ave. (80th & 81st),
   794-1080.

Best Pizza:

Sofia Fabulous Pizza, 1022 Madison Ave. (79th St.), 734-2676
Garlic Bob's Pizza Bar, 1325 Third Ave. (at 76th St.), 772-2627
Petaluma Restaurant, 1356 First Ave., 772-8800. A restaurant
   that also happens to deliver a tasty brick oven pizza.

Miscellaneous Neighborhood Fun:

Vico Restaurant, 1306 Madison Ave. (92nd & 93rd) 876-2222,

This boisterous Italian restaurant also manages to be somewhat highbrow, but the pasta and salads are, according to *Zagat's*, "perfection."

E.A.T., 1064 Madison (80th and 81st), 772-0022, Eli Zabar's upscale deli has elevated standards like soup and sandwiches to the sublime. Pricey but never dicey.

Corner Bookstore at 93rd Street, 1313 Madison Ave., 831-3554, Ray and Lenny Sherman have run this community-oriented bookstore for close to two decades, and have preserved its architectural integrity by maintaining the terrazzo floors, tin ceiling, and extant woodwork. They carry books to interest each member of the family, with an eye toward belles lettres.

Christie's East, 219 E. 67th St., 606-0400. This auction house offshoot tends to have more inexpensive items than its higher-end mom. Drop in to "just look," and perhaps an item will strike your fancy, without giving your bank account a drubbing.

Barnes & Noble, 120 Lexington Ave. (86th St.), B&N is synonymous with "huge," and this holds true here as well. When looking for a good deal on bestsellers, as well as randomly marked-down gems, stop in to this location for a nice browse.

Yorkville Brewery and Tavern, 1359 First Ave. (73rd St.), 517-BREW. This brewpub offers as-yet undistinguished brews, but a very distinguished bunch of post-Wall Streeters stopping off for a fancier pint than what's found at the local Irish pub.

DINNER THE FIRST NIGHT

SARABETH'S, Hotel Wales, 1295 Madison Ave. (between 92th and 93th), 410-7335; Whitney Museum, 945 Madison, (at 75th), 570-3670. A "girly" place to eat the homey baked goods and just-like-mom's entrees. Comforting, yet classy.

BARAONDA, 1439 Second Ave. (75th St.), 288-8555. Good Northern Italian fare, married with sophisticated environs.

JACKSON HOLE, 232 E. 64th St. (between Second and Third Aves.), 371-7187. Comforting, greasy spoon burgers and

Polo Grounds, E. 83rd St. and Third Ave., 570-5590.

This sports bar features 14 screens, high-end pub fare, and post-jock businessman types.

Hi-Life Bar & Grill, 1340 First Ave. (72nd St.), 249-3600

Sign of the Dove, 1110 Third Ave. at 65th St., 861-8080. The ultimate in romantic, especially when seated in the garden. Try the prix fixe menu so you won't break the bank.

92nd Street Y, 1395 Lexington Ave., 427-6000.

This facility offers low-key working out options as well as a schedule of lectures and readings by eminent academics and writers, among others. Call for a schedule.

FAMILY FUN
IN THE UPPER EAST 'HOOD

When it comes to family fun in the hood, nothing beats Central Park. Check out the following:

CENTRAL PARK ZOO/WILDLIFE CONSERVATION CENTER
(Fifth Ave. and 64th St.), 439-6500. Yes, New York has it all, including an ill-adjusted polar bear (and who could blame her). Give your kids a thrill by showing them what these majestic and exotic animals look like when they're not portrayed as cartoons.

THE HANS CHRISTIAN ANDERSEN STATUE, at Conservatory Water. April through September, professional storytellers enthrall wee ones each Saturday at 11.

THE HECKSCHER PUPPET HOUSE, Central Park. Delight the kids with the magic of puppet shows. They are presented during the week, at 10:30 a.m. and 12 p.m. Call the Dairy (794-6564) for reservations.

THE CAROUSEL (Mid-Park at 64th St.), 879-0244. This old-fashioned carousel was relocated from Coney Island, and charms with its fanciful horses. Open every day in the warmer seasons, on weekends in the winter. Small fee.

HOW TO FIND OUT ABOUT SCHOOLS ON THE UPPER WEST SIDE

For information on the public schools on the Upper West Side, contact COMMUNITY DISTRICT NO. 3, 300 West 96th St., 678-2800. This district's theme is "in pursuit of excellence." You can either walk in or call first. Do try to speak with Ms. Pat Romandetto, Director of Curriculum and instruction. There are many options in this district, and she is a pro at evaluating your child's needs and recommending the best one.

Private Schools to look into:
THE CATHEDRAL SCHOOL, 1047 Amsterdam Ave., 316-7500.
DWIGHT SCHOOL 291, Central Park West, 724-2146.
ETHICAL CULTURE SCHOOL, 33 Central Park West, 874-5200.
PROFESSIONAL CHILDREN'S SCHOOL, INC., 132 West 60th 582-3116.
ST. HILDA AND HUGH'S SCHOOL, 619 West 114th, 932-1980.
TRINITY SCHOOL, 139 West 91st, 873-1650.

THE UPPER WEST SIDE

The **Upper West Side** is the Upper East Side's more laid-back brother across the park, with much of the same entrancingly beautiful residential buildings and historical institutions, but a sprawling, liberal sensibility and an ethnically and culturally infused energy. It is bounded on the West by the West Side Highway, Riverside Park, and the Hudson River. The eastern boundary runs along Central Park West to 125th Street, and then juts northwest along the extension of 125th Street now known as Martin Luther King Boulevard.

This neighborhood is home to many writers, journalists, and other media types, as well as Columbia academics and students. Celebrities are also drawn to it.

Far from espousing the radical chic of its neighborhoods to the south, the Upper West Side likes to be trendy but not avant-garde. Although lumped together somewhat dismissively with the Upper East Side by downtown denizens as "uptown," this neighborhood is great for families who don't quite identify with the grandness across the park but do value the area's proximity to museums, the staunch residential feel of the cross streets, the northern influence of Columbia University, and the scrumptious array of delicious eats, geared not only to the diner-outer but to the stay-in-and-preparer.

There are an extraordinary number of restaurants, bars, and shops of all kinds, from those that sell New Age stones and gourmet spices and just about everything else that might appeal to the locals. Many of the new establishments come and go, but there are still a few traditional old places, like **Barney Greengrass and Sturgeon King,** on Amsterdam between 86th and 87th, a vintage 1908 deli where a salmon-and-scrambled-eggs breakfast is a Sunday morning must. **The Museum of Natural History** (Central Park West at 79th St.) houses the to-scale dinosaur skeletons that are a must-see for kids interested in all things Jurassic.

HIDDEN COSTS OF THE NEIGHBORHOOD

Getting back uptown after bar-hopping or a late dinner downtown—taking the subway after midnight is never advisable, and the cab runs around $10-$15.

Services in general—Because it's a nice neighborhood, the services are priced accordingly, which makes little things pricier.

In much of New York, the smaller cross-town streets are primarily residential, while the wider north-south avenues are more commercial. That's largely true on the Upper West Side, though there are three north-south thoroughfares that are primarily residential as well: **Riverside Dr.** and **West End Avenue** on the west side of the neighborhood, and **Central Park West** on the east side. All three avenues are distinguished by large, old pre-war buildings with big—and usually expensive—apartments. The avenues running up and down the middle of the Upper West Side—**Columbus Avenue, Broadway,** and **Amsterdam Avenue**—are more commercial, lined with storefronts that sometimes have smaller, cheaper apartments above.

The main cross-town streets are **W. 72nd Street, W. 86th Street, W. 96th Street,** and **W. 110th Street,** which tend to be noisier. Most of the other side streets are quiet, lined with five-story brownstones that were originally single-family homes but now have as many as ten apartments each.

INSIDER TIP: *Broadway is a line down which the personality of the Upper West Side seems to divide. For the most part, west of Broadway lies a deeply quiet residential area, whereas that which is east of Broadway, going towards the park, is much more "happening." Boutiques, restaurants, nightlife, and crowded sidewalks are the rule more often than not. Although it's a little noisier, the plus is that there are more people around, which might make you feel more secure.*

Morningside Heights, is a sub neighborhood that lies between 110th and 125th Streets, and is significant mostly because Columbia University and Barnard College lie within its grasp. The collegiate atmosphere/college town feel has made it a natural place for cafes, bookstores, and restaurants to flourish. Rents are lower here than they would be a few blocks south, if you don't mind not being in the thick of the Upper West Side proper.

If You're Looking to Rent:

In **Morningside Heights** and in the low 100s, near Columbia University, **studios** start around $650 a month, **one-bedrooms** around $800 a month, **two-bedrooms** around $1,200 a month, and **three-bedrooms** around $1,500 a month. For a nice apartment in a good location, boost those rent estimates by at least 50 percent.

Below 96th Street, prices are often higher as you get closer to 59th Street and Midtown. In general, **studios** begin at $950 and range up to $1,400. **One bedrooms** typically range from $1,200 to $2,000. **Two-bedrooms** usually go for $1,800 to $3,000.

Three-bedrooms, which are relatively rare, typically start at

$3,000. Again, you can boost those rents at least by half again for nice places in good locations, particularly in the lower blocks of the Upper West Side.

If You're Looking to Buy:
For **condos, studios** typically start at $100,000, while **one-bedrooms** at $200,000 and up. For **co-ops, studios** typically start at $60,000, **one-bedrooms** at $100,000, and **two-bedrooms** at $200,000.

BAGELS IN THE 'HOOD

H&H BAGELS, 2239 Broadway (at 80th St.), 595-8003. You'll never do Lender's again. Has managed to snag "Best of New York" laurels left and right.

Essential Neighborhood Resources

Area Code: (212)

Zip Code: 10019, 10024, 10025

Police:
26th Precinct, 520 W. 126th St., 678-1311
24th Precinct, 151 W. 100th St., 678-1811
20th Precinct, 120 W. 82nd St., 580-6411

Hospitals:
St. Luke's Hospital, 419 W. 114th, 523-4000
Roosevelt Hospital, 428 W. 59th St., 523-4000

Post Offices:
Ansonia, 40 W. 66th St., 362-7486
Cathedral, 215 W. 104th St., 662-9191
Columbus Circle, 27 W. 60th St., 365-7858
Columbia University, 1123 Amsterdam Ave., 864-1874
Morningside, 232 W. 116th St., 864-6968

Park West, 693 Columbus Ave., 866-7322

Planetarium, 131 W. 83rd, 873-3701

Libraries:

Columbia University, 521 W. 114th St., 864-2530

Bloomingdale, 150 W. 100th St., 222-8030

St.Agnes, 444 Amsterdam Ave., 877-4830

Riverside, 190 Amsterdam Ave., 870-1810

Lincoln Center, 111 Amsterdam Ave., 870-1630

Community Resources:

CHURCHES:

Cathedral of St. John the Divine, W. 112th St. and Amsterdam
  Ave., 316-7540. Under construction for over a century, with
  decades still to go, this will be the largest cathedral in the world.
  Imposing, but with a fine lineup of righteous events linked to
  peace groups and causes.

Riverside Church, W. 120th and Riverside Dr., 222-5900. Gothic
  design, good observation deck. Theater and dance performances.

First Universal Spiritualist Church of N Y C, 216 W. 78th St.,
  877-6937

All Angels Church, 251 W. 80th St., 362-9300. Episcopal.

Church of the Holy Spirit, 152 W. 66th St., 595-2596.
  Anglican Catholic.

Pentecostal Church of God Emmanuel, 941 Columbus Ave.,
  866-2250

SYNAGOGUES:

Congregation B'Nai Israel Chaim, 353 W. 84th St., 874-0644

Congregation Habonim, 44 W. 66th St., 787-5347

The Jewish Center, 131 W. 86th St., 724-2700

West End Synagogue, 190 Amsterdam Ave., 579-0777

Congregation Morya, 650 W. End Ave., 724-6909

Landmarks:

American Museum of Natural History, W. 65th and Broadway,
  769-5000. One of the largest and best museums anywhere for

researching and displaying knowledge about the Earth and its life forms. For recorded information, call 769-5100.

Lincoln Center for the Performing Arts, 140 W. 65th St., 875-5000. For all your opera, ballet and philharmonic needs.

The Dakota Apartment Building, W. 72nd and Central Park West. There's no chalk outline of John Lennon's body at the 72nd St. entrance, but there are still people looking for it every day.

Riverside Church, W. 120th and Riverside Dr., 222-5900. Gothic design, good observation deck. Theater and dance performances.

Grant's Tomb, W. 122nd at Riverside Dr., 666-1640. Good 19th century design extravagance inside, good mosaics and skating tricksters outside. Inspiration for the old joke, "Who's buried in Grant's Tomb?" Supposedly, old Ulysses S. and his wife Julia, or what's left of them, are here. But the correct answer is nobody; the tombs are technically above ground, so they're not "buried."

Columbia University, W. 114th-120th Sts., between Broadway and Amsterdam, 854-1754. The Ivy League's urban outpost.

Main Drags:

The avenues are mobbed on the weekends in nice weather by people, local and not, who enjoy the experience of walking up and down **Columbus, Broadway,** and **Amsterdam,** to scope and be scoped, pop into different bars and cafes, and maybe catch a movie if their timing is right. Large cross-streets like **72nd** and **52nd streets,** seem like avenues due to their cross-town boulevard feel, and serve as routes to get from one avenue to another.

The Great Outdoors:

Central Park , of course, is the primary green space for residents of the Upper West Side. It is 840 acres, bounded on the north by 110th St., on the South by 59th St., on the West by Eighth Avenue, and on the East by Fifth Avenue. There are many activities and features, including: softball and occasional concerts on the Great Lawn; Shakespeare in the Park on summer evenings; ice skating at Wolman Rink; sunbathing on the Sheep Meadow; in-line skating around the park or in the dance, acrobatic and slalom areas; jogging around the Reservoir or the full six-mile loop; biking; dogwalking; horseback riding on the trails; taking kids to playgrounds; directing remote-control toy boats or rowing real ones; the zoo; the carousel, and much more—including that most favorite Central Park activity: watching other New Yorkers, and sometimes getting to know them. The main West Side entrances are at 66th, 72nd, 79th, 85th and 96th Streets.

Many committed Westsiders, however, actually prefer **Riverside Park,** a ribbon of woods, gardens, playgrounds, and promenades along the Hudson River, from W. 72nd St. up into Harlem. It includes the 79th St. Boat Basin, and the Soldiers and Sailors Monument at 89th St. It's often easier to get on the basketball courts, tennis courts, and softball fields at Riverside Park, especially on nice weekend days when Central Park is over-run.

Community gardens can be found at Amsterdam and 88th St. and at 104th St. between CPW and Manhattan

AND FOR DOG RUNS:

Theodore Roosevelt Park, Central Park West to Columbus Ave., from W. 77th to 81st Sts.

Riverside Park, Riverside Dr. to the Hudson River. 2 dog runs located here, one at W. 87th St., another at W. 105th St.

Parking:

Parking is tough, particularly on weekday evenings. Around Columbia University is usually one of the best places, but if you live below 100th St., be prepared to invest a lot of time if you intend to park on the street. Garages on the Upper West Side typically charge at least $300 a month to keep a car. The further west you go, the easier it is. It's relatively safe, but do invest in a visual deterrent like the Club for your steering wheel.

GARAGES:

Rapid Park, 1-800-804-7275. 101st St. (Broadway and Amsterdam) $275.

Kinney System, 1-800-KNY-PARK; 93rd St. (Columbus St. and Central Park West), $325; 95th St. at West End Ave., $350; 88th St. (Broadway and Amsterdam), $350; 89th St. (Broadway and Amsterdam), $350.

Garage Management Corporation, 888-7400; 2000 Broadway, $413.88; 267 W. 87th, $402.05.

West Side Parking Garage Corp. 157 W. 83rd St. (Amsterdam & Columbus), 362-2800, $360; 147 W. 83rd St. (Amsterdam & Columbus), 362-3900, $360; 150 W. 83rd St. (Amsterdam & Columbus), 877-6300,$360; 234 W. 108th St. (Broadway & Amsterdam), 222-8800, $340.

Banks and ATMs:

Apple Bank for Savings, 2100 Broadway, at 73rd, 472-4545.

Chase Manhattan Bank, 1-800-AT-CHASE; 2099 Broadway (W. 73rd St.); 307 Columbus Ave. (W. 75th St.); 540 Columbus Ave. (W. 87th St.).

Chemical Bank, 935-9935; 1934 Broadway (W. 65th St.); 2045 Broadway (W. 71st St.); 2219 Broadway (W. 79th St.); 2681 Broadway (W. 102nd).

Citibank, 627-3999, 162 Amsterdam Ave. (W. 67th); 175 W. 72nd (Amsterdam Ave.); 700 Columbus Ave. (W. 94th).

Grocery Stores:

Fairway, 2127 Broadway (between 73rd and 74th streets), 595-1888. Amazing produce, delicious raisin-studded rice pudding by the pint, and famously quick checkout lines.

Associated Supermarkets, 2680 Broadway, 932-2687

D'Agostino Supermarkets, 200 W. 60th St. 581-1070; 2131 Broadway, 362-2667; 633 Columbus Ave. (91st), 362-2692; 755 Amsterdam Ave. (97th St.), 864-9930. Good selection and decent prices.

Fischer Brothers & Leslie, 230 W. 72nd, 787-1715. Gourmet kosher food.

Food Emporium. Upscale, but clean, with great selection. 2008 Broadway(69th St.), 787-0012; 2431 Broadway, 873-4031.

West Side Supermarket, 2171 Broadway (77th St.), 595-2536

Pharmacies:

Anthorp Pharmacy, 2201 Broadway (78th St.), 877-3480.

Duane Reade Drugs, 2307 Broadway, 501-8355. Discount prices and good selection.

Love Health & Beauty Stores, 1873 Broadway, 222-3700;

2330 Broadway, 362-6558; 2513 Broadway, 222-2900;
156 W. 72nd, 799-6550. Inexpensive, with a good selection
of pharmacy, cosmetic, and other health products.

Gas Stations:
Stratford Service Center/Mobil, 323 W. 96th St.
Atlas Garage, 303 W. 96th St., 865-3311

Dry Cleaners:
Berger Service, 4 W. 63rd St. (near Central Park West), 265-1670
Columbus Valet Service, 61 W. 74th St., 721-6028
Merit Cleaners, 102 W. 79th St., 724-9140
Tower West Cleaners, 161 Amsterdam Ave., 724-5370

Laundromats:
Video Town Laundromat, 217 W. 80th St., 721-1706.
This place takes the pain out of laundry day. While your soiled
clothing gets washed and dried, you can hop on a tanning bed,
rent and watch a flick, or just watch TV in the lounge.
Economat, 140 W. 72nd, 362-2300. Environmentally friendly
washing and drying.
Chi Laundry, 2484 Broadway, 874-7450
Park West Laundromat, 101 W. 84th St. 721-7712. Pick-up
and delivery, 50 cents/pound.
Tidal Wave, 722 Amsterdam Ave., 283-0505
Westside Laundromat Corp., 165 W. 74th St. 721-5760.
No pickup/delivery, 70 cents/pound.

Hardware:
Gartner's Hardware, 134 W. 72nd St. (Columbus & Amsterdam),
873-1050
AJO Lumber Home Center, 817 Amsterdam Ave., 866-1050
Amsterdam Hardware, 147 Amsterdam Ave., 721-7804
Aquarius Hardware & Housewares, 552 Amsterdam Ave.,
362-4173
Beacon Paint & Wallpaper Co., Inc., 371 Amsterdam Ave.,
787-1090. Also rents tools.

True Value Hardware and Variety, 466 Columbus Ave.,
874-1910

Video Stores:

Blockbuster Video, 199 Amsterdam at 69th St., 787-0300.
552 Amsterdam at 87th St. 580-8822. To start a membership,
you need a major credit card and photo ID. If you don't have
a credit card, you need to bring in 2 utility bills. There's a $5
fee. $4.35 per rental for 1-3 evenings.

Channel Video, 472 Columbus Ave., 496-2759. Membership
policy: Free membership, need major credit card or $50 cash
deposit per movie. $3.49/one night. They carry a wide variety
of movies, including foreign, drama, classics and musicals.

Kahn Video, 2841 Broadway, 663-7780. Credit card needed.
Lifetime membership is $10, $2.77 per movie. Mon-Thurs $4
for 2 movies.

Movie Place, 237 W. 105th St. 864-4620

Joe's Video Store, 850 Amsterdam Ave., 678-1102

Cafes, Delis, Coffeeshops, and Diners:

Cafe des Artistes, One W. 67th St. (Columbus and CPW),
877-3500. Even surly Zagat's is reduced to raves when it comes
to describing this gem. Suffice it to say that it's truly romantic,
with French fare that will gently bring you back to earth.

Cafe Lalo, 201 W. 83rd St. (Amsterdam and Broadway), 496-6031.
This Toulouse-Lautrec inspired cafe offers high-ceilinged
elegance mixed with a dense concentration of tables. When
faced with the menu's pastry heaven, don't choose the earthbound frozen yogurt.

Cafe Luxembourg, 200 W. 70th St. (Amsterdam and West End
Aves.), 873-7411. Upscale cafe, offering solid fare and a chance
to throw some attitude (if you're into that).

French Roast Cafe, 2340 Broadway (85th St.), 799-1533. You
can feel slightly Dada at this 24-hour cafe, and when you're
tired of that, I recommend ordering their egg-white omelet.

Centerfold Coffee House, Church of Paul and Andrew,
263 W. 86th St., 362-3328. Coffee and poetry readings.

OTHER GOODIES:

Taste of the Apple, 283 Columbus (at 74th), 873-8892.
This li'l burger joint is a hop, skip, and a jump from the Dakota and Central Park's Strawberry Field.

Andy's Deli, 295 Amsterdam Ave., 580-2892

Cozy Gourmet Deli, Inc., 317 Amsterdam Ave., 799-7766

Records & Convenience Stores, Inc., 1467 Amsterdam Ave., 283-7440

BEST PIZZA:

V&T's, Amsterdam and 110th, 663-1708, for a whole pie.

Sal's, Broadway and 102nd, 663-7651, for a slice.

DINNER THE FIRST NIGHT

MAIN ST., 446 Columbus Ave. (West 81st), 873-5025. Features all-you-can eat mashed potatoes and other American comfort food served family-style, with main courses working out to about $10 a person. Desserts are homemade pies, chocolate cake, Heathbar crunch cake, puddings, splits and sundaes. The room has a clean, solid look, with brick walls and a sturdy bar near the entrance.

Fun Family Eats for the First Night:
ROYAL CANADIAN PANCAKE HOUSE, 2286 Broadway (at 82nd St.), 873-6052. Goofy, oversized food that'll make you and your kids feel safe, homey and full.

Miscellaneous Neighborhood Fun:

On the night before Thanksgiving, stay up late and go with friends (and any children that are available) to **W. 81st St.** and **Central Park West,** where the giant balloons are being blown up for the Macy's Thanksgiving Day parade the next morning.

The Museum of Natural History, W. 65th St. and Broadway, 769-5000. One of the largest and best museums anywhere for researching and displaying knowledge about the Earth and its life forms. For recorded information, call 769-5100.

Lincoln Center for the Performing Arts, 140 W. 65th St. (Broadway), 877-1800. Pick up a schedule of events for this temple of the performing arts. Home of the Metropolitan Opera, the New York Philharmonic, the New York City Ballet, the New York City Opera, and the Juilliard School, for starters. Inquire about their discount ticket policy.

Central Park, Get into a pickup softball, volleyball, basketball or soccer game in the park. Jog or walk around the Reservoir, entering Central Park at W. 85th.

West Side Community Garden, 89th St. between Columbus and Amsterdam. This wonderful little treasure is maintained lovingly by the West Side Community Garden Association, and is open to the public from dawn to dusk. Highlight: the rock garden.

Tom's Kitchen, 1172 Amsterdam Ave., 865-6590 (of Seinfeld fame) Where the gang eats virtually every meal. "Monk's" on the show.

Merchants, New York, 521 Columbus (85th & 86th), 721-3689. Crowded, lounge-y, good wine selection.

FAMILY FUN IN THE 'HOOD

SONY IMAX THEATER, 1198 Broadway, 336-5000. This larger-than-life, Disney-esque movie theater offers virtual reality immersion at its best. Call for current flicks.

THE MUSEUM OF NATURAL HISTORY AND HAYDEN PLANETARIUM, West 65th St. and Broadway, 769-5000. Give the kids a Jurassic thrill at this awe-inspiring institution. And then take a humbling gander at our solar system For recorded information, call 769-5100.

CHILDREN'S MUSEUM, 212 West 83rd St., 721-1223. Music and theater programs every weekend.

GOODS & GOODIES, 240 West 98th St. (Broadway and West End Ave.), 932-7965. This fantasia-full shop has imaginative toys, from trains to dress-up glad rags.

MIDTOWN EAST

Midtown East, from 34th to to 59th Streets, and stretching from the FDR (the highway that runs the length of Manhattan, parallel to the East River) to Fifth Avenue, has quite the split personality. Its vibe is markedly different during different times of the day. From 9 to 5, it's invaded by busy worker bees—milling around in their suits, or standing around near the entrance of various buildings smoking a clandestine cigarette. Everyone spills out into the streets at lunchtime, especially in the spring, to shop, have a three-martini lunch, catch some smoggy rays, and dodge traffic as they cross the streets.

The actual residents of this area hardly recognize their neighborhood by day. When home sick from work, if they go out foraging for orange juice or a videotape, they may feel as if they were under attack by the pod people. Suddenly, their sleepy, immaculate neighborhood had been transformed into another Financial District, complete with suits and high hair.

After six, the neighborhood reverts back to being quiet and residential, with just enough storefronts to impart a feeling of security. The frenzy which permeated the area just a couple of hours ago gives way to a welcome lull (especially on the weekend). Residents will indulge in such suburban activities as walking the dog, taking a jog or picking up groceries for a quick dinner. This neighborhood attracts a variety of people, ranging from young singles, who take advantage of Murray Hill's (bounded roughly by Madison and Third Avenues, 34th and 42nd Streets) lower rents, to older couples and seniors, who appreciate the feeling of safety and proximity to all the areas of the city. Despite the area's lack of outdoor recreation areas, families with children inhabit many of the residences.

Between the banks, global corporations, the United Nations, and the nearby embassies, a relatively high percentage of the residents are diplomats or international business types for whom money is not much of an object."Convenient" is a word often used to describe Midtown East by residents who feel that they have the best of both worlds: a safe and quiet neighborhood to live in—and the rest of Manhattan to play in.

Sub-neighborhoods (of which this area has its share) include **Kips Bay, Murray Hill, Turtle Bay, Tudor City, Beekman Place** and **Sutton Place.**

Midtown East falls under COMMUNITY SCHOOL DISTRICT 2, *330 West 18th St., 337-8700. This includes all of Manhattan on the East Side below 96th St., and on the West Side below 59th St., excepting the part of the Lower East Side that's covered by District One. Do make an appointment with Ms. Marjorie Robbins, Director of Pupil Personnel, or Mr. Michael Dance. You can also request printed material about their schools.*

Private Schools to look into:

CATHEDRAL HIGH SCHOOL, *Catholic School of the Archdiocese of NY (Girls) 350 E. 56th St., 688-1545 (Grades 9-12)*

THE FAMILY SCHOOL, *323 E. 47th St., 688-5950*
(18 mos.-12 years)

INTERNATIONAL PRESCHOOL, *330 E. 45th St., 371-8604*
(Ages 1-6)

THE MULTIMEDIA PRESCHOOL, *40 Sutton Place, 593-1041*
(Ages 2-6)

The exclusive nature of Places Beekman and Sutton have earned this area the moniker "Upper East Midtown." **Beekman Place** (49th through 51st Streets between the East River and First Avenue) takes its name from the Beekman family mansion, which was used as a British headquarters during the American Revolution. After 1920, the Beekman Hill Association was formed, with the goal of making Beekman Place into an upper-class, luxury-living area, which it is today. **Sutton Place** (York Avenue between 53rd and 59th Street) is the ultimate in snooty addresses—a cluster of elegant prewar buildings populated by the ultra-affluent.

Tudor City (40th and 43rd Streets between First and Second Aves.) is a private, cooperatively owned residential development, and takes its name from the Tudor architecture of its twelve original buildings. It faces a park next to the United Nations.

Turtle Bay (43rd to 53rd Streets, between the East River and

Lexington Avenue) has within its bounds the United Nations, its park, luxury apartments and renovated brownstones. This is an upscale, clean area.

Kip's Bay and Murray Hill are at the southern end of Midtown east. Kips Bay (27th to 34th Street, between the East River and Third Avenue) is just south of Gramercy, and serves as a site for many hospitals, including Bellevue and NYU Medical Center. The 2nd and 3rd Avenue elevated trains (now gone) had a negative influence on the area, and it still retains a vague feel of shabbiness, although the area is clean and well-maintained.

Murray Hill (35th to 39th Streets, between Third and Madison Aves.) is an area known for its former glory as the stomping grounds of J. Pierpont Morgan and other big deals. Now, it's a sleepy (for Manhattan) residential area much appreciated for its slightly lower rent and nice brownstones. Younger people, who are just starting out, often take advantage of the central location and economical cost.

If You're Looking to Rent:

Studios are all but impossible to find for under $900 a month in Midtown East, and a small, simple **one-bedroom** apartment typically rents for $1,200 to $1,600 a month—if you can find one. Midtown East has a higher percentage of what would be called "luxury" housing than other Manhattan neighborhoods. There are apartments in good locations, with amenities such as terrace and a dining room, and staff service that approaches that of a residential hotel, where one-bedroom and two-bedroom apartments rent for several thousand dollars a month.

If You're Looking to Buy:

Anything under $100,000 is like a needle in a haystack, and might provide about as much living space as a haystack. **One-bedroom** apartments, which are routinely listed for anywhere from $120,000 to $400,000, tend to be smaller than in other neighborhoods of Manhattan, unless they are "luxury" and have gourmet kitchens or rooftop patios or 20-foot living rooms with panoramic views. **Two-bedrooms** under $200,000 are rare, and **three-bedroom** apartments can easily range from $300,000 to $1 million.

Essential Neighborhood Resources
Area Code: 212

Zip Codes: 10016, 10017, 10022

Police:
17th Precinct, 167 E. 51st St., 826-3211
Mid-Town North, 524 W. 42nd St., 767-8400
Mid-Town South, 357 W. 35th, 239-8911

Hospitals:
Medical Arts Center, 57 W. 57th St. 755-0200
NYU Medical Center, 550 First Ave., 263-7300

Post Offices:
Murray Hill, 115 E. 34th St. 679-9127
Rockefeller Center, 610 Fifth Ave. (49th St.), 265-3854
FDR, 909 Third Ave., at 54th St. 330-5549
Mailboxes Etc., 847A Second Ave., 573-8360

Libraries:
58th Street, 127 E. 58th St. 759-7358
Cathedral, 560 Lexington Ave., 752-3824
Mid-Manhattan, 455 Fifth Ave., 340-0849

Community Resources:
Vanderbilt YMCA, 224 E. 47th St., 755-2410
Young Audiences New York (Arts and Culture Service),
     1 E. 53rd St., 319-9269
Fight for Sight, Inc. (Blind and Visually Impaired
     Organization), 150 E. 56th St., 751-1118
Concern Worldwide USA, 104 E. 40th St., 557-8000
Big Brothers Big Sisters of NYC, 223 E. 30th St., 686-2042

Landmarks:
Trump Plaza, 167 E. 61st (Third Ave.). The waterfall
     and public open space are the attraction, not The Donald.

Trump Tower, E. 56th and Fifth Ave., 832-2000

Plaza Hotel, W. 59th at Fifth Ave., 759-3000. Still synonymous with class despite the Trump connections, the hotel has become more famous than the Grand Army Plaza, which it overlooks. Have a drink in the Oak Bar.

Grand Central Station, E. 42nd St., at Park Ave. The entire complex exudes the notion of motion, and the clock in the main terminals remains one of the most-used, and most romantic, meeting places anywhere.

United Nations, E. 45th at First Ave., 963-7713. Tours are popular, and it's possible to sit in on sessions.

Citicorp Center, E. 53rd, between Lexington and Third Aves., 559-1000. This distinctive angle-topped skyscraper is a popular gathering place for lunch in the casual restaurants and shops in the plaza between ground level.

Sony Building, Madison Ave. between E. 55th and 56th St., 751-7272. Some New Yorkers call this the "Chippendale" building for its scroll-design top worthy of a giant pink-granite cupboard. Also called the AT&T Building, its original name when opened way back in 1992.

Waldorf-Astoria Hotel, 301 Park Ave. (between E. 49th and 50th), 355-3000. Still perhaps the most famous hotel in the world, at least for visiting diplomats and royalty.

Helmsley Building, 230 Park Ave. (between E. 45th and 46th). A good art-deco lobby.

Met Life Building, 200 Park Ave. (between E. 44th and 45th). Still called the Pan Am building by many New Yorkers, a landmark because it's next to Grand Central, and sits astride Park Ave., so it's visible from afar both uptown and downtown.

Chrysler Building, 405 Lexington Ave. (E. 42nd). New Yorkers' favorite skyscraper, for its remarkable art-deco architecture and spire that shines like a bright beacon to excess.

St. Patrick's Cathedral, Fifth Ave. (between 50th and 51st), 753-2261. Famous for its gothic spires, which are lighted to good advantage at night. The archbishop's home church, it's opulent inside, too. Visitors welcome.

Main Drags:

57th is known for its art galleries and restaurants, from refined French bistros to the raucous "theme" restaurants, such as Planet Hollywood and the Hard Rock Cafe, which serve as Pied Pipers to slavishly devoted, souvenir-chomping tourists.

42nd Street still deserves much of its reputation for the sleazier aspects of New York, including hookers of both sexes and a broad age range. With its many bars and restaurants, the area around Grand Central Station is always busy, even during non-commuting hours.

The Great Outdoors:

There's not much of it, here. Pretty much the public open spaces provided at the base of big office buildings are what you're going to find. Here are a few recommendations:

Paley Park, on 53rd St. (between Madison and Park). A nice place to bring lunch on a sunny day, or sit and lose yourself staring at the little waterfall.

Greenacre Park, on 51st between Second and Third Aves. Another good place for lunch. Popular with cigarette smokers.

Citicorp Plaza, Lexington Ave. between 53rd and 54th. With many tables and benches, this small outdoor area is a lunch destination for many of the area's business people. Underused aside from lunch time.

Dag Hammarskjold Plaza, 46th St. and Second Ave. Small outdoor area, with benches, trees, a little fountain, and a few homeless people. The corner is quiet and feels very residential.

AND FOR DOG RUNS:

Peter Detmold Park, West of FDR Dr., between E. 49th and 51st Sts.

Parking:

Garages in Midtown typically charge at least $300 a month to keep a car. For those who can afford it, the price is worth the hassle of driving around looking for places on the street, and then moving the car—or paying someone else $100 a month—to move the car every day from one side of the street to the other, to conform with the alternate-side parking rules that allow street sweepers to come through.

GARAGES:

Twentieth Century Garage, 320 E. 48th, 755-9253.

Home Parking Corporation, 405 E. 56th St., 750-4274,
$354.70/month

Kinney, $325/month 53 E. 33rd St., 679-8111, 340 E. 34th St.,
213-6929 315 E. 40th St., 697-7773

Horizon Garage Corp., 415 E. 37th St., 725-8640,
$385.51/month

Marlborough Garage, 237 E. 40th St., 599-9485, $310/month

Banks and ATMs:

Citibank, 1044 First Ave. (between 57th and 58th Sts.), 627-3999

East NY Savings Bank, 401 E. 57th St. (First Ave.),
1-800-724-3697

Chase Manhattan Bank, 241 E. 42nd (Second Ave.),
1-800-282-4273

EAB, 800 Third Ave. (49th St.), 688-0992

Chemical, 349 Fifth Ave. (34th St.), 935-9935

Grocery Stores:

Todaro Brothers Grocers, 555 Second Ave., 532-0633. Since
1917, Todaro Brothers has imported gourmet italian specialties
and provided a wide array of fresh, prepared and packaged
product to discerning New Yorkers.

Pisacane Midtown, 940 First Ave. (between 51st and 52nd), 752-
7560, are the purveyors of fresh fish to many of Manhattan's finer
restaurants but also sell their salmons and soles at retail prices.

Food Emporium, 1052 First Ave. (between 57th and 58th Sts.),
688-5640

Sloan's, 748 Second Ave. (40th St.), 599-4615

Pharmacies:

Third Avenue Pharmacy, 552 Third Ave. (36th St.), 447-6111

Plaza Pharmacy, 1091 Second Ave. (between 57th and 58th Sts.),
755-8685

Kaufman Pharmacy, 557 Lexington Ave. (50th St.), 755-2266.
Open 24 hours.

Duane Reade, 122 E. 42nd (Third and Lexington Aves.), 682-9586

Corby Chemists, 988 First Ave., 755-6632

Gas Stations:

Don't count on finding any in Midtown East. Gas up elsewhere.

Dry Cleaners:

Meurice Garment Care, 245 E. 57th St., 751-5138. This establishment seems more like a spa for your fine unwashables, what with
its professional hand cleaning and pressing, environmentally safe
methods, and radio dispatched pick-up and delivery.

Symphony Cleaners, 927 Second Ave. (49th St.), 826-5066.
Reasonable rates and no charge for pickup and next day delivery.

LaMoll Fashion Award Cleaners, 944 Second Ave. (50th St.),
753-2650. Monthly accounts available ($75 minimum) for
slaves to dry cleaning

Lido Cleaners, 990 First Ave. (between 54th and 55th Sts.),
688-6789. Been there since 1905. Free pickup and delivery.

Gold Star Dry Cleaners, 249 E. 45th St., 856-0836

Laundromats:

East 51st Street Launderette, 305 E. 51st (Second Ave.), 759-
5430. This is one of the few self-service laundromats in Midtown East.
Many others offer "service" washes—you drop your clothes off, and
pick them up washed and folded. Most Midtown East buildings have
laundry facilities. If not, ask neighbors or your doorman for a good tip.

Hardware:

Kramer's Hardware, 952 Second Ave., 758-2694

Gasnick Supply, 992 Second Ave., at 52nd, 758-2953

Video Stores:

Video Express, 1093 Second Ave. (between 57th and 58th Sts.),
752-3456. Free delivery and pickup.

Blockbuster Video, 155 E. 34th St. (Third Ave.), 686-0022
To start a membership, you need a major credit card and photo ID.
If you don't have a credit card, you need to bring in 2 utility bills,

and there's a $5 fee. $4.35 per rental for 1-3 evenings.

Video Couch, 715 Second Ave. (39th St.), 972-1076. Special
selection of Kung Fu and action movies. Delivery.

DINNER THE FIRST NIGHT

*SMITH & WOLLENSKY'S STEAK HOUSE, 205 E. 49th St.,
753-1530. Its famously well-cooked boeuf and fabulous wine
selection (which will set you back a bit) have made it a stand-out
with lovers of a good, old fashioned gnaw.*

Fun family eats for the first night:
*JACKSON HOLE BURGERS, 521 Third Ave. (at 35th St.), 679 3264.
Comforting, greasy spoon burgers and old-fashioned egg creams.*

Cafes, Delis, Coffeeshops, and Diners:

Sarge's Deli and Restaurant, 548 3rd Ave. (between 36th
and 37th Sts.), 679-0442. Specializes in Kosher delicacies such
as generous pastrami and corned beef sandwiches, as well as
knishes and a matzoh ball soup which puts Mom's to shame.

Midtown Tunnel Gourmet, 322 E. 34th St. (First and Second
Aves.), 689-7610. Delicious specialty items delivered around
the clock.

660 Lexington Farm, 660 Lexington Ave. (between 55th and
56th Sts.), 838-9466. Open 24 hours.

Regency Gourmet, 801 Second Ave. (between 42nd and 43rd),
661-3322. Accepts credit cards.

Green Garden Deli, 919 Second Ave. (49th St.), 838-1144

Jackson Hole, 521 Third Ave., 679-3264. Giant burgers. $
Kid-friendly.

Madison Restaurant, First Ave. and 53rd, 421-0948. $ Kid-friendly.

Beekman East Diner, 886 First Ave., 223-2716. $ Kid-friendly.

Star's Deli & Restaurant, 593 Lexington Ave. (52nd),
935-9480. Open 24 hours. $ Kid-friendly.

Scotty's, 336 Lexington Ave. (39th St.), 986-1520. This Greek diner is the solution to a 4 a.m. jones for souvlaki; they have 24-hour delivery.

Moonstruck Restaurant East, 449 Third Ave. (31st St.), 213-1100. The American/Greek fare is so good here, there is often a line out the door—great omelets and burgers.

FAMILY FUN IN THE 'HOOD

FAO SCHWARZ, 767 Fifth Ave., 644-9400. This hyper-real toy store will give your kids a huge series of thrills, as well as a huge holiday wish list. This will, however, guarantee their good behavior for a few hours.

WARNER BROTHERS STUDIO STORE, 1 E. 57th St. (Fifth Ave). For lovers of all things Tweety-ish and Bugs-y, as well as minor characters like the Martian. A fantasy come to life.

SONY PLAZA, Sony Building, 55th and Madison. Home to the Sony Wonder Technology Lab, a free amusement park, which lets your little smarties design their own video games, see their faces on huge video screens, and max out their techie selves.

<u>Miscellaneous Neighborhood Fun:</u>

Tiffany & Co, 727 Fifth Ave., 755-8000. Whether the mention of Tiffany evokes the haunting strains of Moon River or your itchy ring finger, breeze in and dream a little dream.

The Waldorf-Astoria, 310 Park Ave. (at 50th St.), 355-3000. Swoop into this grande dame of hotels, and alight at the Peacock Restaurant for a cocktail.

Barnes & Noble, E. 54th at Third Ave., 750-8033. Has become the new hot spot for singles on the weekend with the addition of the cafe and couches all over the store. I hear that the stacks for existential literature and meditation have proved awfully lucky for some-others luck out in self-help and stress management.

Sparks, 210 E. 46th St., 687-4855. For businessmen on expense accounts or for anyone with a craving for red meat, this is arguably the best steakhouse in all of NYC.

Chin Chin, 216 E. 49th St., 888-4555. Swanky midtown Chinese restaurant, frequented by celebrities.

Beer Bar, 200 Park Ave. (45th and Vanderbilt), 818-1222. This Brooks Brothers crowd pleaser offers a variety of micro-brews and a beer tasting menu.

Ginger Man, 11 E. 36th St., 532-3740, has more than 60 beers on tap. It's the newest and most promising entry into Manhattan's microbrew scene.

MIDTOWN WEST

Midtown West runs from 34th Street on the south to 59th Street on the north, and from Fifth Avenue on the east to the Hudson River on the west.

Midtown West is certainly not the first area that comes to mind when you think residential. If the Upper East Side is a lady who lunches, Midtown West is a flamboyant, aging actress who smells faintly of mothballs and *Je Reviens*. She won't tell you her age, but she will tell you her life story, and you can figure it out from there. She's also just received a facelift, and is a little bruised around the ears. In other words, a tough old broad who's still standing.

INSIDER TIP: *One thing you should pass on is celebrating NEW YEAR'S EVE in Times Square. It might have looked fun on the telly in Normal, Illinois, but in reality it's a petrie dish of public idiocy. You're liable to get your posterior pinched, along with your wallet, and the booze you so cleverly hide in your vest will be snagged by the cops as you get frisked on your way in. Much better to find a cozy little restaurant or a party.*

Midtown West encompasses both **Clinton** (previously known as Hell's Kitchen, hence the facelift) and the **Garment District.**

The glitz of Broadway and off-Broadway shows mingles with the underworld of peep shows, triple-X rated movies, and street hustlers,

HOW TO FIND OUT ABOUT SCHOOLS IN MIDTOWN WEST

For public schools, Midtown West belongs to COMMUNITY SCHOOL DISTRICT 2, 330 West 18th St., 337-8700. Do make an appointment with Ms. Marjorie Robbins, Director of Pupil Personnel, or Mr. Michael Dance. You can also request printed material about their schools.

Private Schools to look into:

THE LYCEUM KENNEDY FRENCH SCHOOL, 20 West 44th St., 730-0868. K-12, an international school with many French and Japanese students.

THE COOKE FOUNDATION (SPECIAL EDUCATION), 456 West 52nd St., 245-3376 (Ages 5-13)

THE FAMILY SCHOOL WEST, 308 West 46th St., 582-1240 (2.5 mos.-7 years)

HOLY CROSS, (CATHOLIC SCHOOL OF THE ARCHDIOCESE OF NY), 332 West 43rd St., 246-0923 (Nursery-8th Grade)

SACRED HEART OF JESUS (Catholic School of the Archdiocese of NY), 456 West 52nd St., 246-4784 (Nursery-8th Grade)

creating an impression of what most people picture the Big Apple to be—over-the-top, neon, and larger than life. Times Square is a big rhinestone in Midtown West's crown, with its mile-high neon murals, theaters, and tourist klatches. Big musical faves *(Phantom, Grease, Showboat, Les Miserables)* alternate with LIVE NUDE GIRLS. However, recent efforts to clean up Times Square have already taken effect, and by the day, it becomes more and more sanitized, almost Californian. Disney has purchased a large tract of land, and this will no doubt spruce up the area further.

Living here is something to get used to, especially if you're fresh off the proverbial boat. And if your lodgings happen to have a blinking sign that flashes into your bedroom via the window, it's hard to shake the sensation that you're in a movie. Make that a film noir.

Many people in the theater world make this 'hood their home, as it's close to many auditions and to the restaurant jobs that, pardon the cliche, pay the rent. As tourism is king here, it's a perfect place to benefit from heavy-tipping guys in leisure suits. Close to half the people living here are in the 20 to 40 age group, which is relatively young, vibrant, moving, and shaking. It's not exactly a retirement destination.

The dark side of all the flash and dash is the grim rep this area has for crime. Away from all the lights, blocks are often deserted and creepy. It's very important that if you look into living here, you come back at night to see how the atmosphere changes. Because both Clinton and the Garment district are heavily commercial, they get a little fearsome after the sun goes down.

Ninth Avenue has of late become renowned as a foodie outpost. Every May, its annual Ninth Avenue Food Festival offers many global ways to stuff your face. Check May listings in *Time Out New York* for the exact dates.

Below Hell's Kitchen, 'er, Clinton, that is, is the **Garment district.** A daytime hustle-and-bustle hive, filled with 9 to 5ers running to work, running home, or running themselves ragged, it's a study in corporate culture. The Fashion Institute of Technology is just south of here, which jives with the high-style vibe of the streets when it's spiked with the presence of sartorially splendid fashion assistants en route to their fabulous designer's headquarters. Pennsylvania Station is the main conduit for commuters from Long Island and the outer boroughs. Although Penn Station doesn't possess the cavernous grandeur of Grand Central Station, it's undergone some redecoration lately, and provides a convenient pathway to the beach in the sweaty summertime. It's very Gotham City, which means dramatic during the day, and somewhat foreboding at night. The glut of skyscrapers is pure Manhattan.

Another area that has become famous is **57th Street.** Well into Midtown East, the street has been known for decades as a home to many prestigious art galleries and art dealers. In recent years, however, 57th Street and the area around it between Fifth Avenue and Broadway have become perhaps even more famous as the home to so many glitzy "theme" restaurants, including the Motown, Fashion, Jekyll & Hyde, and Hard Rock cafes, among others. Other notable features of Midtown West include Rockefeller Center, the gleaming retail and office complex between Fifth and Sixth Aves. in the high 40s and low 50s. Check out the skating rink and Christmas tree in winter, and the art-deco architectural flourishes any time. It's a far cry from the dirt and noise that plagues much of Midtown West.

If you will be working in Midtown, this might be the perfect place to settle. It's always a plus to have little or no commuting time. However, it is short on charm, and lacks the gloss of Midtown East. At night, it gets desolate.

INSIDER TIP: *If you've decided to live in Midtown, look for apartments listed on flyers posted on telephone poles, bus shelters, and bulletin boards at neighborhood grocery stores, deli's, coffee shops, gyms, bars, laundromats, etc. Also check bulletin boards in offices, schools, community associations, and other public places.*

If You're Looking to Rent:

It's still possible to find a **studio** apartment for under $800 a month in Midtown West, though they are not exactly plentiful. The further west you go, the cheaper the apartment. For a **one-bedroom** $900 to $1,300 a month is typical. However, like other areas of the city, it's possible to spend a lot more.

INSIDER TIP: *For neighborhood classified listings, a company called RESIDENT PUBLICATIONS publishes the WEST SIDE RESIDENT. It is available in streetcorner boxes, or in local shops.*

If You're Looking to Buy:

As with rentals, prices go down as you go west. There isn't a lot of housing for sale in Midtown West, but if you are patient and lucky, you can find a **studio** for around $50,000, a **one-bedroom** for $100,000 and a **two-bedroom** for $150,000.

Essential Neighborhood Resources:

Area Code: 212

Zip Codes: 10018, 10019, 10036

Police:

Mid-Town North, 524 W. 42nd, 767-8400

Mid-Town South, 357 W. 35th St. 239-8911

10th Precinct, 230 W. 20th St. 741-8211

Hospitals:

Roosevelt, 428 W. 59th St., 523-4000

Medical Arts Center, 57 W. 57th St., 755-0200

Post Offices:

New York General Post Office, Eighth Ave. and W. 33rd, 967-8585. Limited Sunday and holiday services. Despite being south of 34th St., the main Post Office is nonetheless usually regarded as part of Midtown.

Midtown, 223 W. 38th St., 944-6598

Radio City, 322 W. 52nd, 265-6677

Libraries:

Columbus, 742 Tenth Ave., 586-5098

Donnell, 20 W. 53rd, 621-0618

Community Resources:

Westside YMCA, 5 W. 63rd St., 787-4400

J A C S Foundation (Alcoholism Service), 426 W. 58th St., 397-4197

Covenant House Crisis Center, 460 W. 41st St., 613-0300

Landmarks:

New York Public Library, Fifth Ave. between W. 40th and 42nd, 661-7200. Besides being such a great library, the expanse of front steps make this one of the best places in America for people-watching on a sunny day.

Times Square, between W. 42nd and 47th, between Seventh Ave. and Broadway. Not really a square, but really the touchstone for the theater world, and the big electric advertisement world. Bad idea for New Year's Eve.

Rockefeller Center, between Fifth and Sixth Aves., and W. 48th and 51st, 632-3975. This gilded structure is most alluring around the holidays, when glowing gift-shoppers take a break and absorb the effect of the Christmas tree, as well as the circling skaters on the sunken ice rink.

Radio City Music Hall, 1260 Avenue of the Americas (Sixth Ave.), 632-4000. Musicals, concerts, and special events, especially the Christmas spectacular, make this a real gem. Take the tour if you're interested in the history and the art-deco architecture.

Port Authority Bus Terminal, between W. 40th and 42nd, and Eighth and Ninth Aves. There's no reason to go here unless you're taking a bus to New Jersey or other points on the continent, or unless you want to go roll a few lines with Floyd in the upstairs bowling alley.

Museum of Modern Art, 11 W. 53rd, between Fifth and Sixth Aves., 708-9480. The authority on art from 1880 to the present. New Yorkers often call it "Moma," with a long o.

Ed Sullivan Theater, 1697 Broadway, between W. 53rd and 54th. Home to the David Letterman show. Tourists flock around, even without tickets, to chat with the neighboring shopkeepers, glimpse guests and hang out on W. 53rd St. hoping Dave will dash out during shooting and bring them back to sit on his fire escape on stage.

Empire State Building, Fifth Ave. at W. 34th St., 736-3100. This is still the most famous skyscraper in the world, and a real NYC icon. It caught the world's imagination in the 1930s, and never let go. The Observation Deck offers a great view of Manhattan. Just say no to dropping a penny off the ledge. Do you want to mess up your karma for life?

Madison Square Garden, Seventh Ave., between W. 31st and 33rd, 465-6741. Knicks, Rangers, college basketball, the circus, horse shows, boxing matches, track meets, tennis tournaments.

Everything from little dogs jumping through hoops to political conventions with presidential candidates.

Penn Station, beneath Madison Square Garden, Seventh Ave. at W. 33rd. Amtrak and the Long Island Rail Road. Like Madison Square Garden, it is south of 34th St. and technically not part of Midtown, but virtually everyone regards both Penn Station and the Garden as Midtown fixtures.

Carnegie Hall, 154 W. 57th St. (Seventh Ave.), 247-7800. Practicing isn't the only way to get here. Still one of the world's pre-eminent performance halls, particularly since the tons of concrete poured under the stage by incompetent workmen a few years ago has been discovered and removed, thereby restoring the famous "warmth" of the acoustics.

FAMILY FUN IN THE 'HOOD

THE INTREPID, Pier 86m West 46th St. and the Hudson River, 245-0072. This former aircraft carrier is now a floating museum.

MUSEUM OF TELEVISION AND RADIO, 25 West 52nd, 621-6880. In this vast, at-your-fingertips archive, you can requisition the very cartoons you watched as a child, and share them with your own kids. Hey, it's not my fault if they prefer Barney. An extra treat: many of the shows come with the ancient commercials they first aired with.

<u>Main Drags:</u>

57th is known for its art galleries and restaurants, from refined French bistros to the raucous "theme" restaurants, such as Planet Hollywood and the Hard Rock Cafe, which serve as Pied Pipers to slavishly devoted, souvenir-chomping tourists.

42nd St. still deserves much of its reputation for the sleazier aspects of New York, including hookers of both sexes and a broad age range. Times Square and the few surrounding blocks north of 42nd St. can be more crowded with people at midnight on a Saturday night than at noon on a Wednesday, with people going to movies, sex shows, theater, bars, restaurants or souvenir shops, or just cruising.

The Great Outdoors:

Bryant Park, 40th to 42nd St., between Fifth and Sixth Aves. This park serves as the palatial back yard to the majestic main branch of the New York Public Library, and offers quite the swanky park experience, from the kiosks selling gelato and latte to the descent of semi-annual, tent-protected fashion shows. For more earthbound pleasures, take in one of their free outdoor summer evening movies (bring a blanket and munchies), take advantage of the tkts booth selling half-price concerts, opera, and dance events (call 382-2323 for hours) for the day of the show, or just take time to smell the flowers in the perennials garden.

    DeWitt Clinton Park, Tenth Ave. between 52nd and 53rd. Basketball courts offer the brave possibilities for shootin' hoops. On nice Sunday mornings, residents toting coffee and a newspaper sit and read for a bit.

    Grand Army Plaza, Fifth Ave., between 58th and 59th. Mainly a gathering place for tourists, the plaza is the gateway to Central Park. The Joseph Pulitzer fountain is one of the main focal points.

Parking:

Garages in Midtown typically charge at least $300 a month to keep a car. Some garages also charge a fee, usually about $3, for every time you take it out of the garage. For those who can afford it, the price is worth the hassle of driving around looking for places on the street, and then moving the car—or paying someone else $100 a month—to move the car every day from one side of the street to the other, to conform with the alternate-side parking rules that allow street sweepers to come through. There are many garages and parking lots in Midtown West, particularly in and near the Theater District.

Edison, 13 W. 56th St., 397-4440
Garage Maintenance Corp., 148 W. 48th St., 888-7400
52 W. 36th Street Parking, 59 W. 36th St., 502-5188

Banks and ATMs:

Chemical Bank, Worldwide Plaza, Eighth Ave. (between 49th and 50th), 935-9935

Citibank, 1740-48 Broadway (56th St.), 627-3999. This is one of
   the few ATMs that gives out $10, which is convenient when
   the checking account balance hovers around $14.79.

Republic National Bank, 1180 Avenue of the Americas
   (46th St.), 718-488-4050

Grocery Stores:

Z Deli Discount Supermarket, 803 Eighth Ave. (48th and
   49th), 315-1659. This market not only has a wide variety of
   stuff for sale, it also delivers around the clock. Just don't tell
   this little fact to your 2 a.m. ice cream jones.

Ernst Klein, 1366 Sixth Ave. (53rd), 245-7720. More expensive
   than most grocery stores, but very nice meat and produce.

Food Emporium, 452 W. 43rd (Tenth Ave.), 714-1414

Red Apple, 907 Eighth Ave. (54th St.), 582-5873

Pharmacies:

Metropolis, 721 Ninth Ave. (49th St.), 246-0168.
   What makes pharmacies magical isn't the meds behind
   the counter. It's the 64-packs of Crayola, the greeting cards,
   school supplies, and other takes-you-back flotsam. And
   it's nice to feel this way in hardened Clinton.

Carewell Pharmacy, 767 Ninth Ave. (between 51st and 52nd),
   265-8110; 564-7127

Duane Reade, 110 W. 34th St. (between Sixth and Seventh Aves.),
   268-5330

Duane Reade, 224 W. 57th St. (Broadway), 541-9708.
   Open 24 hours.

Westerly Pharmacy, 911 Eighth Ave., 247-1096

Gas Stations:

Mobil 21, 842 Eleventh Ave. (57th St.), 582-9269

Dry Cleaners:

Carlton Dry Cleaners, 805 Eighth Ave. (48th and 49th Sts.),
   489-0468. You can put your fine unwashables in Bruce Kim's
   able hands—he hems and alters, too.

Jin's French Cleaners, 260 W. 52nd (between Seventh and Eighth Aves.), 582-8313

Strand Valet, 500 W. 43rd, 268-2710

Sparkle Cleaners, 888 Eighth Ave. (between 52nd and 53rd), 397-4093

Laundromats:

Great American Wash, 704 Ninth Ave. (49th St.), 974-8353. They'll wash it for you, and you pay by the pound. How much?

Hardware:

Lopez Sentry Hardware, 691 Ninth Ave., 581-8019

Scheman & Grant, Inc., 575 Eighth Ave., 947-7844

Video Stores:

Video Cafe, 697 Ninth Ave. (48th St.), 765-6165. This is a total rental experience, right down to available popcorn and movie candy.

RKO Warner Video, 1608 Broadway (49th St.), 581-6260

57th Street Video and Photo, 332 W. 57th St., 586-5400

Beer and Wine:

Manhattan Plaza Winery, 589 Ninth Ave. (42nd and 43rd Sts.), 695-8710. A good selection and a convenient home-delivery service.

Cafes, Delis, Coffeeshops, and Diners:

Mangia, 50 W. 57th St. (Fifth and Sixth Aves.), 582-5882. This upscale, foodie eatery offers a multitude of tasty treats, sure to satisfy those with fussy palates.

Hero Boy, 492 Ninth Ave. (37th and 38th), 947-7325. Only in New York would hero-making be elevated to such an art form. For the uninitiated, hero means hoagie or sub, macho style. Whether you want to feed 40 people with a six-footer or just nibble on your very own, do it here.

Smiler's, 637 Ninth Ave. (45th St.), 582-5550

Joy II Deli, 162 W. 56th St., 757-2930

Joy's Gourmet Deli, 887 Eighth Ave., 974-9066

Applejack Coffeeshop, 230 W. 55th St., 586-6075. $ Kid-friendly.

Westway Diner, 614 Ninth Ave. (43rd), 582-7661. $
Kid-friendly.

Art Cafe, 1657 Broadway, at 52nd, 246-6790. $

Ellen's Stardust Diner, 1377 Avenue of the Americas, 307-7575.
$$ Kid-friendly. This very neighborhood-esque joint has a
special thrill-depending on you, the diner's luck, you could
end up in front of everyone yodeling a showtune. C'mon.
We've all got it in us.

DINNER THE FIRST NIGHT

MANHATTAN CHILI, 1500 Broadway (43rd), 734-8666. Cheap,
cheerful and good—rare for Times Square these days. Popular
with families, couples and singles, Manhattan Chili also draws
crowds of "kids," both from the chorus and backstage, who work
in the nearby theaters. It's possible to have a good meal for under
$10. Ask if the owner, Bruce, is around. He's a true New Yorker
who knows and loves the city as well as anyone, and will be happy
to tell you about it if you tell him this is your first night in town.

Miscellaneous Neighborhood Fun:

TKTS, called "tickets" by New Yorkers, offers half-price theater
tickets on the day of the performance at two boths, one at 47th St.
and Broadway, the other on the ground floor of 2 World Trade
Center. The line is always longer on Broadway. Cash and traveler's
checks only. No phone reservations. You never know what shows
are going to be listed for that day, so be flexible. The most popular
shows will never be on the board. Sales start at noon for matinees
and 2 p.m. for evening performances. Some people get in line well
before that, especially at the Broadway booth, while flexible,
experienced theatergoers stop by in late afternoon, when the line
is shorter, to see if any bargains are still available.

Virgin Megastore, 1540 Broadway, 921-1020. This humongous music-listening experience is like the Barnes & Noble of tune-hawking-multimedia bravado you'll have to see to believe.

Virgil's Barbeque, 152 W. 44th St. (Sixth Ave. & Broadway), 921-9424. A dubious treat for your arteries, but unbeatable for that slutty BBQ high.

Rudy's Bar and Grill, 627 Ninth Ave., 974-9169. This ur-dive in the heart of Hell's Kitchen is nonetheless frequented by gleefully slumming collegiate types and the occasional boozy editor. Alternately, you'll be drinking next to down-and-outs as well as hardened off-duty (one hopes) cops on the make. Jump on the cheap, fancy-beer pitchers. Pass on the wizened weiners.

McHale's, 750 Eighth Ave. (46th St.), 997-8885. The other divey bar.

Circle Line, at Pier 83, W. 42nd and the Hudson River, 563-3200. Get a grip on wily Manhattan by taking this three-hour cruise around it.

Ninth Avenue Cheese Shop, 529 Ninth Ave. This foodie outpost imparts not only a wealth of toothsome treats, but a bargain-basement bunch of great coffee by the pound.

GRAMERCY AND STUYVESANT SQUARE

Gramercy is a pretty little pocket of a neighborhood, worn around the edges but undeniably refined. It is bounded by 23rd and 18th Streets on the North and South, between Park and Third Aves. Its namesake, Gramercy Park, is not open to the public, but gives off a rarefied air that also infects the handsome prewar residential buildings that surround it on four sides. The park is manicured, immaculate, and somewhat sterile, everything that public parks aren't. Only residents facing the square who pay a yearly maintenance fee have possession of the park's keys.

This area, historically, is known more for its art patrons than its artists. Henry Frick (as in The Frick Collection) and Jules Bache were the original members of the **National Arts Club** at 15 Gramercy Park South, a lovely old building which houses a gallery and a very swanky lounge, which is open during NAC events and private parties. Upstairs is the Poetry Society of America, a literary organization responsible, in conjunction with the MTA, for the auspicious presence of Poetry in Motion posters in subway cars. Streets around the park retain the park's grand, sedate feel, which is also a good way to describe the majority of the inhabitants, who are wealthy and between the ages of 35-60+.

A main artery of the Gramercy area is **Park Avenue South,** which is notable for its linear, Gotham City architecture. A two-way avenue, Park Avenue South is surprisingly narrow and elegant, particularly in comparison to parallel **Third Avenue,** with its pragmatic, uninspired array of delis, dry cleaners, bars, and shops.

Just south and east of Gramercy is **Stuyvesant Square,** between 14th and 18th Streets, and First and Third Aves. Due to its proximity to Beth Israel and Bellevue hospitals, it has a tendency to be noisy. As a neighborhood, its personality is overshadowed by its neighbors, but it is imbued with the sedate charm of Gramercy. The area has been enlivened since its 1975 designation as a historic district.

Stuyvesant Town is a housing development worth mention, although there's a waiting list of thousands of people who want to live in this inexpensive, safe, and roomy high-rise development. Between 14th and 18th Streets, and Third Avenue and Avenue C, this complex offers such amenities as a jogging circle and regular security patrols.

If You're Looking to Rent:

Rents in Gramercy generally range from $800 to $2,700 per month, though it's easier to find a place at the higher end of that range than at the lower. Gramercy typically is more expensive, and, being small, has fewer rental properties on the market than say, Chelsea. In either Gramercy any **studio** under $1,000 a month is a bargain, while **one-bedroom** apartments cover a wide range, usually between $1,000 and $2,000 a month. A **two-bedroom** for under $2,000 is probably a bargain, and most likely a dream—or a nightmare.

If You're Looking to Buy:

Buying in Gramercy, as opposed to further downtown, often means that you have a little more space. However, because the area is so small and lovely, fewer places are on the market at any one time.

Studios ....$ 80,000
One-Bedroom $100,000
Two-Bedroom $300,000

HOW TO FIND OUT
ABOUT SCHOOLS IN GRAMERCY

Gramercy belongs to Community School District 2, 330 West 18th St., 337-8700. Do make an appointment with Ms. Marjorie Robbins, Director of Pupil Personnel, or Mr. Michael Dance. You can also request printed material about the different schools.

Private Schools to look into:

THE ACORN SCHOOL, 330 E. 26th St., 684-0230
  (Nursery, Ages 2-5)

BELLEVUE SOUTH NURSERY, 10 Waterside Plaza (25th St.),
  684-0134, (Ages 3-5)

EPIPHANY SCHOOL, Catholic School of the Archdiocese of NY. 234
  E. 22nd St., 473-4128 (Nursery-8th Grade)

FRIENDS SEMINARY, 222 E. 16th St., 979-5030 (Grades K-12)

JACK AND JILL SCHOOL, 209 E. 16th St., 475-0855 (Ages 3-6)

U.N. INTERNATIONAL SCHOOL, 24-50 FDR Dr., 25th St.,
  684-7893 (Grades K-12)

Essential Neighborhood Resources

<u>Area Code:</u> (212)

<u>Zip Code:</u> 10003, 10010

<u>Police:</u>
Precinct 13, 230 E. 21st St., 477-7411

<u>Hospitals:</u>
NYU Medical Center, 550 First Ave., 263-7000
Bellevue, 462 First Ave., 561-4141
Beth Israel, 281 First Ave., 420-2000

<u>Post Offices:</u>
Madison Square, 149 E. 23rd St., 673-3771

Libraries:
Epiphany, 228 E. 23rd, 679-2645

Community Resources:
14th Street/Union Square Association, 4 Irving Place, 460-1200
23rd Street Association, 200 Fifth Ave., 255-3037
Flatiron District Business Association, 22 W. 19th St., 242-4231

Churches:
Calvary Episcopal Church, Tracy House, 61 Gramercy Park
  North, 475-1216
Church of the Good Shepherd, 236 E. 31st St., 689-1595
Church of the Transfiguration, 1 E. 29th St., 684-6770
Christ Lutheran Church, 355 E. 19th St., 475-5906
Aquarian Foundation, 320 E. 22nd St., 460-5820

Synagogues:
The Brotherhood Synagogue, 28 Gramercy Park South, 674-5750
Congregation Talmud Torah Adereth El, 135 E. 29th St.,
  685-0241
Congregation Tel Aviv, 155 E. 22nd St., 475-7081

Landmarks:
Flatiron Building, 175 Fifth Ave. (between E. 22nd and 23rd).
  A distinctive turn of the century skyscraper, whose point at the
  sharp intersection of Fifth Ave. and Broadway makes it look like
  a stately ocean liner.
Pete's Tavern, 129 E. 18th St. (Irving), 473-7676. A classic
  old saloon. Have lunch in the booth where O. Henry wrote
  "The Gift of the Magi."
Union Square, between Park Ave. South and University Place and
  E. 14th and 17th. One of the liveliest areas of Manhattan, where
  uptown and downtown mix and give way to each other.

Main Drags:
Gramercy is traditionally one of the quieter areas of Manhattan.
People stroll **Second Ave.** and other streets around Stuyvesant Park.

Another street popular for walking and looking is **Irving Place,** the extension of Lexington Ave. between 14th and 23rd, which is broken up by Gramercy Park between 20th and 21st.

The Great Outdoors:

Union Square Park, at Park Ave., Fourth Ave., and Broadway, between 14th and 17th Sts., Home to the Greenmarket, which happens every Monday, Wednesday, Friday and Saturday. 8 a.m.-6 p.m. Call 788-7900.

Gramercy Park, at Irving Place and 20th St., Private.

Stuyvesant Square Park, at 15th St. and Second Ave.

Madison Square Park, Madison Ave. and 23rd St.

AND FOR DOG RUNS:

Madison Square Park, at Madison Ave. and 23rd St.

Parking:

Gramercy has a healthy number of garages and parking lots, largely because the area has little on-street parking, and is heavily populated with people who aren't willing to give up their cars just because they live in Manhattan, and are able to afford to keep them. Garages in Gramercy typically charge around $300 a month, sometimes more, sometimes less, to keep a car. For those who can afford it, the price is worth the hassle of driving around looking for places on the street, and then moving the car—or paying someone else $100 a month to move the car every day from one side of the street to the other, to conform with the alternate-side parking rules that allow street sweepers to come through. Three to check out:

State Park Co., 329 E. 21st St., 473-0400, $266/month

Jeff Parking Corp., 328 E. 22nd St., 254-5444, $313/month

Precise Parking Corp., 150 E. 18th St., 254-3955, $325/month

Banks and ATMs:

Chase Manhattan Bank, First Ave. (23rd St.), 242-7333

Chemical Bank, customer service 935-9935; new accounts 1-800-243-6226; 201 Park Ave South (17th); 221 Park Ave South (18th); 131 23rd (Lexington Ave.)

EAB, 475 Park Ave. South (E. 32nd St.), 532-5202

East New York Bank, Peter Cooper Office at E. 20th St. and
First Ave., 1-800-724-3697

European American Bank, 1107 Broadway (24th St.), 645-3200.

Grocery Stores:

D'Agostino's, 532 E. 20th St., 777-9658; 341 Third, 686-0619

Garden of Eden, 310 Third Ave. (23rd & 24th). A Gramercy foodie
outpost, with gourmet goods and succulent produce to be proud of.

Gramercy Food Fair, 266 Third Ave., 260-0053. Good beer
selection, prepared foods.

Food Emporium, 215 Park Ave. South, 777-7010. More than
D'Agostino, less than Fairway.

Associated Supermarkets, 409 E. 14th St. 254-1509

BAGEL IN THE 'HOOD

*ESS-A-BAGEL, 359 First Ave., 260-2552, has the moistest, largest,
and most-topping-encrusted bagels downtown, not to mention
yummy cream cheeses loaded with veggies, fruit, or fish.*

Pharmacies:

Duane Reade, 360 Park Ave. South (26th St.), 685-6717.
Duane Reade is a Manhattan institution, a ubiquitous presence
where you can get everything from epsom salts and Advil to
Mint Milanos and discount pantyhose. But you're better off
filling your prescriptions at a mom-and-pop scrip shop, as
Duane Reade often has a heinous waiting time—like four hours.

Park East Pharmacy, Inc., 240 E. 23rd (between Second and
Third Aves.), 696-5410

Treatwell Pharmacy Inc., 115 E. 23rd (between Lexington and
Park Ave. South), 505-2788

17th Street Apothecary Inc., 11 E. 17th St., 255-6900

Gramercy Park Prescription Center, 180 Third Ave. (17th St.),
529-8899

Dry Cleaners:

Cameo Cleaners, 284 Third Ave. (22nd St.), 677-3949. This
husband-and-wife team has been doing it for 50 years. But they're
not afraid of new technology—in fact, the store is computerized
and garments are color-coded, to make you feel more secure.

New Cleaners & Tailors, 134 E. 17th St., 529-5926

Tower Cleaners, 106 E. 15th St., 477-0010

Lee's Cleaners & Tailors, 15 E. 21st, 254-8560

Laundromats:

Jan Sun Chinese Hand Laundry, 123 17th St. (Third Ave. & Irving
Place), 254-1850. Hand-finished details for the sartorially finicky.

East 29th Street Laundry, 212 E. 29th St., 679-7421

Gold Laundromat, 217 E. 26th St., 685-4280

H&T Laundry and Cleaning, 356 E. 19th St., 505-9497

Hardware: **Vercesi Hardware,** 152 E. 23rd, 475-1883

Video Stores:

The Video Stop, 367 Third Ave. (26th & 27th), 685-6199.
How wonderful is it that this place delivers? Now, when you're
depressed enough to want to watch Annie Hall for the fourteenth
time, but too depressed to venture outside, it can be brought to
your door. Make sure to get a pizza with that.

Blockbuster Video, 151 Third Ave. (15th St.), 505-7766

14th Video Haven, 220 E. 14th St., 475-4273

Libra Varieties, Inc., 483 Third Ave. (33rd), 481-9158

Palmer Video, 295 Park Ave. South, 982-4000

Liquor:

1st Avenue Wines and Spirits, 383 First Ave. (between 22nd and
23rd), 673-3600. A New York rarity: this store is staffed by special-
ists, and will consult with you on menu matches. Delivers.

Cafes, Delis, Coffeeshops, and Diners:

Lady Mendl's Tea Salon, at The Inn at Irving Place, 56 Irving
Place, 533-4600. $$ In the words of John, the innkeeper here,

Lady Mendl's feels like you went to your rich aunt's house to visit, after she stayed up late the night before making delicious pastries. This Victorian tea salon is flush with antiques and flanked by two working fireplaces. A total dream.

Eureka Joe, 168 Fifth Ave., 741-7500. $ Kid-friendly. This cappuccino spot/bar has inviting slipcovered chairs to sink into.

NY Bagel Espresso, 112 E. 23rd, 777-3200. $ Kid-friendly.

Espresso Coffee Roaster, 157 E. 18th St., 674-1702. $ Kid-friendly.

Provisions Coffee Bar, 24 Union Square East, 539-1532. $ Kid-friendly.

Sarge's Deli, 548 Third Ave., 679-0442

Lenz Delicatessen, 514 E. 20th St., 254-4130

Su Chin Kim, 1 E. 28th St., 725-0645

Bono Brothers, 35 E. 28th St., 532-9190

CHINESE DELIVERY

TANG TANG, 243 Third Ave. (at 20th St.), 477-0460. Recommended by Time Out New York *as the best Chinese delivery in Gramercy.*

Miscellaneous Neighborhood Fun:

Farmer's Market: Union Square Park buses in friendly agricultural types Monday, Wednesday, Friday and Saturday to help you countrify your urban kitchen. Walking through the verdant offerings will tempt you to purchase the necessary (fresh produce) as well as the suddenly necessary (maple syrup candy).

Friend of a Farmer, 77 Irving Place (between 18th and 19th), 477-2188. A cozy restaurant with a decor and a menu you might find in a little cottage restaurant in Wisconsin.

Irving Plaza, 17 Irving Place, 777-6800. This cavernous, multi-level, shabby-baroque venue serves as both a concert hall and a club with theme nights. Concert hotline: 249-8870

Poetry Society of America, 15 Gramercy Park South, 254-9628. Send a self-addressed stamped envelope to 15 Gramercy Park

South, New York, NY 10010 for a schedule of their events. Not only will you be giving yourself a soberly pleasant literary infusion; you'll also be able to sneak a peek at the interior of the august National Arts Club.

ABC Carpet & Home, Broadway at 19th, is a must stop if you're going to be doing any nest-feathering. Besides all manner of quality rugs and carpeting, ABC has six floors of home merchandise, ranging from centuries-old antiques to little plastic thingies for your fridge.

DINNER THE FIRST NIGHT

I TRULLI, 122 E. 27th St. (Park & Lexington), 481-7372. Named "Best New Restaurant" in New York Press's Best of New York issue, it charms with its outdoor garden in the temperate months, spacious dining room in the chilly ones. The pasta with lobster and clams is a must.

Fun Family Eats for the First Night:
CHAT-N-CHEW, 10 E. 16th St. (Fifth Ave. & Union Square). This comfort-food canteen, which has the temerity to feature a cheerfully obese woman in their print ads, serves up thick slabs of meatloaf, mounds of creamy, no-b.s. mashed potatoes, macaroni and cheese to merit the county fair's blue ribbon, and a healthy side of bacon. Definitely gives you that church picnic feeling, perfect for kids that have had it up to here with parenty, fussy food.

CHELSEA

Chelsea is an old-fashioned neighborhood, not as stately as Gramercy, and not as rowdy as the West Village. It's bounded on the North and South by 14th and 30-34th Streets (depending on who you ask) and runs west of Fifth Avenue to the Hudson River.

Many of its blocks are lined with beautifully kept brownstones, and its aves. are lined with tempting places to grab a cup of coffee, have dinner, or meet someone for a drink. It also offers the convenience of mega-stores like Bed, Bath & Beyond, Old Navy, and is also close to Bradlees, at Union Square.

Like the West Village, Chelsea is known for its diversity, as a

"DO YOU NEED ANY HELP WITH YOUR BAGS MR. VICIOUS?"

THE HOTEL CHELSEA, at 222 West 23th St. (between Seventh and Eighth Aves.), is a major landmark. It's played host to such luminaries as Mark Twain, Tennessee Williams, Arthur Miller, Dylan Thomas, and O. Henry, along with Bob Dylan, Jimi Hendrix, Frank Zappa, the Grateful Dead, Leonard Cohen, and the Sex Pistols' Sid Vicious, who offed Nancy Spungen here and then did the same to himself. Jack Kerouac finished On the Road *here, and William Burroughs did the same with* Naked Lunch. *It's also where Andy Warhol filmed "Chelsea Girls," and where Valerie Solanas stayed, right before she almost finished off Andy Warhol. If you want to be famous, stay here for a while and it'll probably happen. Just kidding. But you can get your glad rags dry cleaned here, at their very own CUSTOM ART LAUNDRY & VALET SERVICE (216 West 23rd, 532-8969).*

place that gay, straight, and multicultural residents call home. However, it has a more refined, quiet feel to it than its neighbor to the south, and many families settle here, appreciative of its calm vibe and proximity to uptown and downtown. Chelsea is definitely post-yuppie yuppie-ish, and is a bit smug about having a Barney's in its hood.

This neighborhood was developed as a residential area, which explains its lovely blocks of brownstones, with sidewalks punctuated by trees. It also owes its seedier western edge to the presence of the **Meat Packing District,** which is made up of warehouses and meat facilities, with some streets that literally run red with cattle blood at times, and naturally smell horrid. However, even in this area, restaurants and bars have cropped up, and give one reason to venture west. In addition, the Chelsea Piers, where the Lusitania and Mauretania once docked, have recently been transformed into a massive athletic complex on the Hudson.

The Flower District (along Sixth Avenue/Avenue of the Americas, between 27th and 30th Streets) is a lovely little concentration of botanical shops, which have an extraordinary range of flora, from delicate Japanese bonsai to thick, lush vegetation. It's definitely a good place to pick out some housewarming presents for your new apartment.

The Flatiron district, just east of Chelsea proper, is a newly defined area (it's those real estate developers again) between Chelsea and Gramercy/Stuyvesant Square. It's bounded on the North and South by 23rd and 14th Streets, and on the East and West by Park Avenue South and Sixth Avenue/Avenue of the Americas. The name comes from the imposing, surreal Flatiron Building, which is shaped like an acute angle. Flatiron has come to life with a new influx of restaurants, like Cafe Beulah, Flowers, Cal's, and Aja, as well as nightspots like System, Flamingo East, and Twilo. It's also close to Union Square's Greenmarket.

When Chelsea residents go out, they have a nice array of local things to do. **The Big Cup** (228 Eighth Avenue, 206-0059) is a whimsical, yet graphically punchy cafe, strewn with brightly colored couches. In the same vein, the **Bendix Diner** (219 Eighth Avenue, 366-0560) is a kitschy, over-the-top spot to have a burger and shake.

The Joyce Theatre (175 Eighth Avenue, 242-0800) a major center of dance, always has a wonderful schedule of performances, and **Kaffeehaus** (131 Eighth Avenue, 229-9702), with requisite Austrian gravitas, offers a nice selection of beers along with a delicious menu of salads and other light-to-heavy regional fare. When straying west, **La Lunchonette** (130 Tenth Avenue, 675-0342), a French restaurant, is known not only for its succulent bistro fare but for its fetching waitstaff.

If You're Looking to Rent:
Rents in Chelsea generally range from $800 to $2,700 per month, though it's easier to find a place at the higher end of that range than at the lower. In Chelsea, any **studio** under $1,000 a month is a bargain, while **one-bedroom** apartments cover a wide range, usually between $1,000 and $2,000 a month. A **two-bedroom** for under $2,000 is definitely a possibility.

If You're Looking to Buy:
Many families choose Chelsea because they can still get a **three-bedroom** apartment for $300,000 to $400,000.

Essential Neighborhood Resources
Area Code: 212

Zip Code: 10011, 10001

Police:
10th Precinct, 230 W. 20th, 741-8211
Mid-Town South, 357 W. 35th, 239-8911

Hospitals:
New York Foundling Hospital, 590 Sixth Ave./Avenue of the Americas, 633-9300
St. Vincent's Hospital and Medical Center of New York, 7th Ave. & 11th St., 604-7000
St. Vincent's Hospital and Medical Center of New York AIDS Center, 412 Sixth Ave./Avenue of the Americas, 228-8000

Post Offices:

New York General Post Office, Eighth Ave. and W. 33rd,
967-8585. Limited Sunday and holiday services.

Old Chelsea, 217 W. 18th, 675-2415

Libraries:

Muhlenberg, 209 W. 23rd, 924-1585

Community Resources:

Gay and Lesbian Alliance Against Defamation Inc.,
150 W. 26th St., 807-1700

Community Counseling and Mediation, 115 W. 31st St.,
925-9060

Far West 14th Street Association, Dedicated to the bettering of
their sub-neighborhood, check local listings.

Churches:

Bul Kuksa Temple of New York (Buddhist), 5 W. 31st St.,
643-9215

St. Peter's Episcopal Church, 346 W. 20th St., 929-2390

French Evangelical Free Church, 126 W. 16th St., 929-6312

St. John the Baptist Roman Catholic Church, 210 W. 31st St.,
564-9070

Synagogues:

Congregation Beth Israel, 347 W. 34th St., 279-0016

Congregation Emunath Israel, 236 W. 23rd St., 675-2819

Fur Center Synagogue, 230 W. 29th St., 594-9480

National Council of Young Israel, 3 W. 16th St., 929-1525

Landmarks:

General Theological Seminary, 175 Ninth Ave., 243-5150.
Notable for its Gothic architecture.

Jacob K. Javits Exhibition and Convention Center,
655 W. 34th St., 216-2000. This I.M. Pei-designed five-block
structure hosts many conventions and trade fairs.

Madison Square Garden, Seventh Ave., between W. 31st and 33rd,

465-6741. Knicks, Rangers, college basketball, the circus, horse shows, boxing matches, track meets, tennis tournaments.

Penn Station, beneath Madison Square Garden, Seventh Ave. (at W. 33rd.). A utilitarian structure which houses Amtrak and the Long Island Rail Road.

Union Square, between Park Ave. South and University Place, and E. 14th and 17th. One of the liveliest areas of Manhattan, where uptown and downtown mix and give way to each other.

Hotel Chelsea, 222 W. 23rd (between Seventh and Eighth Aves.), 243-3700.

THE BEST BAR IN CHELSEA

A downtown newspaper called CHELSEA COMMONS, 242 10th Ave. at 25th St. the Best Bar in Chelsea for a long string of years. In the summertime, the garden in the back is a cloistered oasis for quiet conversation sheltered by brick walls, classical music humming through like a cool breeze, and fans blowing in desperate times of heat flash, when you're just about to give up in New York City heat. On Wednesday evenings, for a five dollar cover, you can listen to a jazz ensemble in the dusty wooden comfort that this pub provides without any of the East Village jazz-dog pretensions. When there's not jazz, there's plenty of Rock & Roll classics on the somewhat mundane jukebox: Neil Young, Eagles, and Bonnie Raitt. For a quiet and friendly bar in Chelsea, nothing beats it.

Main Drags:

The crosstown streets in Chelsea—**34th** at the top, **23rd** in the middle, **14th** at the bottom-all have plenty of life. But like the Upper East Side and Upper West Side, which are also residential areas laid out on the grid system, most of the action is on north-south ave.s. In Chelsea, the farther western ave.s, such as **Ninth** and **Tenth,** are more respectable and more lively than they are in Midtown West. **Sixth Ave.** is another favorite of New Yorkers, however, largely because of the Flower District in the upper 20s.

The Great Outdoors:

Chelsea Park, Ninth to Tenth Ave. (between W. 27th and 28th Sts.)

Thomas F. Smith Park, 11th Ave. (between W. 22nd and 23rd Sts.)

Union Square Park, at Park Ave., Fourth Ave., and Broadway
(between 14th and 17th Sts.)

AND FOR DOG RUNS:

Thomas F. Smith Park, 11th Ave. (between W. 22nd and 23rd Sts.)

FAMILY FUN IN THE 'HOOD

WONDERCAMP, 27 West 23rd St., 243-1111. This indoor summer-camp themed park has super-fun stuff like a kid-sized maze, interactive science games, and video monitors. $4.95 per person.

Parking:

Chelsea has an extraordinary number of garages and parking lots, largely because the area has little on-street parking, and is heavily populated with people who aren't willing to give up their cars just because they live in Manhattan, and are able to afford to keep them. Garages in Chelsea typically charge at least $200.

Here are some garages, with monthly rates including tax:

15 Parking Corp., 422 W. 15th, 243-8989, $210/mo. Rumor has it
you might be able to swing a discount with the gemutlich manager.

Mutual Parking, 7 W. 21st, 243-6540, $275

Valet Parking, 7 W. 14th, 243-9112, $325

Champion Parking Corp., 41 W. 17th, 691-1474, $375

Champion Parking Corp., 28 W. 18th, 929-9463, $375

Banks and ATMs:

Chemical Bank, customer service 935-9935; new accounts
1-800-243-6226; 158 W. 14th (Seventh Ave.); 79 Eighth Ave.
(14th.), No ATM; 475 W. 23rd (Tenth Ave.)

Atlantic Bank, 253 W. 28th, 494-0400

Carver Federal Savings Bank, 261 Eighth Ave., 989-4000

Citibank, 322 W. 23rd, 627-3999. Full service branch.

Grocery Stores:

D'Agostino's, 315 W. 23rd, 989-5113

Chelsea Terrace Supermarket, 231 Ninth Ave., 929-7047

Western Beef Co., 403 W. 14th, 989-6572

BAKERIES IN THE 'HOOD

TAYLOR'S, 228-230 West 18th St., 366-9081. This place oozes charm, from the oversized muffins, cookies, and bread to the (gasp) front porch opposite an almost rustic fire station. It's a trip sure to please, especially if you have an Ethan Hawke sighting. Just don't let his latest trollop cut you in line.

Pharmacies:

Chelsea Bottom Line Pharmacy, 181 Eight Ave., 366-0321

Statlanders Pharmacy, 126 Eighth Ave., 807-8798

Love Stores/Health & Beauty Aids, 7 W. 14th, 242-0900

Gas Stations:

Brothers Sales & Service, Inc., 63 Eighth Ave. (13th),
    645-9578

D. Vitanza Repair & Service, 165 Tenth Ave. (20th), 242-6239

Power Test Gas Station, 239 Tenth Ave. (24th), 727-8793

Dry Cleaners:

New Cleaners & Tailors, 134 E. 17th, 529-5926

Custom Art Laundry & Valet Service, 216 W. 23rd, 532-8969.
    In the Chelsea Hotel.

Supreme Specialty Cleaning, 231 W. 29th, 695-5499.

Laundromats:

Alice's Laundromat Corp., 164 Eighth Ave. (between 18th
    and 19th), 645-0974

Chelsea Laundromat & Dry Cleaners, 156 W. 15th,
    929-0616

DINNER THE FIRST NIGHT

LA LUNCHONETTE, 130 Tenth Ave., 675-0342. A French restaurant, is a romantic, semi-formal place to indulge in rich fare, along with some delightful red wine. A great way to soothe newbie nerves and fall in love with Chelsea.

Fun family eats for the first night:
BENDIX DINER, 219 Eighth Ave., 366-0560. Kids and parents alike can appreciate this kitschy, over-the-top spot to have a burger, grilled cheese sandwich, shake or ice cream sundae.

Hardware:
AF Supply Corp., 22 W. 21st St., 243-5400
B&N Hardware Corp., 12 W. 19th St., 242-1136
Hardware Mari Inc., 151 W. 14th St., 243-0519
Hitchman Hardware, 246 Tenth Ave., 924-5535
Spreesaver Hardware Co., 132 W. 23rd St., 924-1550

Video Stores:
Blockbuster Video, 128 Eighth Ave. (17th), 924-4771
Video Blitz, 144 Eighth Ave. (17th), 645-6410

Cafes, Delis, Coffeeshops, and Diners:
Chelsea Bistro & Bar, 358 W. 23rd St., 727-2026. Can you say relaxed elegance? Fabu French fare and a lovely back garden room. $$
The Coffee Shop, 29 Union Square West, 243-7969. A temple of reconstructed middle America chic. Coltish, moonlighting model waitstaff and skewed, Brazilian-American fare. $$
140 Chelsea Coffee Co., Ninth Ave at 19th St., 206-7325. $ Kid-friendly.
Big Cup Tea & Coffee, 228 Eighth Ave., 206-3200. $ Kid-friendly.
MMTI, 245 W. 26th, 243-1007
23rd Street Delicatessen, 25 W. 23rd, 807-1713
Chelsea Square Restaurant, 368 W. 28th St., 691-5400. $

Kid-friendly. Fake ferns, french fries, oversized menus, and indestructible booths. Y'know, a diner.

Bendix Diner, 219 Eighth Ave., 366-0560, is a kitschy, over-the-top spot to have a burger and shake.

Miscellaneous Neighborhood Fun:

The Atlantic Theater Company, 336 W. 20th St. (Eighth and Ninth Aves.), 239-6200. This old church-cum-theater has a formally pleasing theater company which has a reputation for offering polished theatrical endeavors.

EAST VILLAGE

The East Village is a neighborhood that might instantly appeal to someone interested in the more glam-gritty aspects of New York. Running from Broadway to East River and Houston to 14th Street, the East Village has absorbed the bohemian runoff of those who fled the west when the rents skyrocketed in Greenwich Village.

INSIDER TIP: *The East Village's Aves are Third, Second, First, A, B, C, and D, west to east. This number-to-letter switch can be confusing for the uninitiated.*

It's a very young neighborhood, home to students and recent graduates of a hipsterish bent. Latino families, older couples, and students live side by side, with the Latin community more concentrated the further east you go. Near the western border (Broadway), it enjoys a certain slickness, from influences of the West Village and SoHo. **Lafayette Street,** just east of Broadway, gets a culinary and image kick from the presence of pricey restaurants such as **Toast** (428 Lafayette Street, 473-1698), **L'Udo** (432 Lafayette Street, 388-0978), **Riodizio** (411 Lafayette Street, 529-1313), and **Indochine,** as well as the Lafayette branch of **Crunch Fitness,** (404 Lafayette, 614-0120) a health club that got its boost from being popular with the young, hip and village-y set, including Henry Rollins.

As you travel east, the mood changes somewhat to take in the

HOW TO FIND OUT ABOUT SCHOOLS IN THE EAST VILLAGE

For information on the public schools for the East Village, contact
COMMUNITY DISTRICT NO. 3, 300 West 96th St., 678-2800. This
district's theme is "in pursuit of excellence." You can either walk
in or call first. Do try to speak with Ms. Pat Romandetto, Director
of Curriculum and instruction. There are many options in this dis-
trict, and she is a pro at evaluating your child's needs and
recommending the best one.

Private Schools to look into:

(These all happen to be Catholic Schools of the Archdiocese
of New York.)

CORNELIA CONNELLY CENTER, 220 E. 4th St., 982-2287,
  (Grades 6-7)

HOLY CHILD MIDDLE SCHOOL, 220 E. 4th St., 982-2287,
  (Grades 6-8)

IMMACULATE CONCEPTION, 419 E. 13th St., 475-2590,
  (Nursery-8th Grade)

LASALLE ACADEMY, 44 E. 2nd St., 475-8940, (Grades 9-12)

MARY HELP OF CHRISTIANS, 435 E. 11th St., 254-2537.
  (Nursery-8th Grade)

NOTRE DAME (GIRLS), 104 St. Mark's Place, 982-0740.
  (Grades 9-12)

ST. BRIGID, 185 E. 7th St., 677-5210. (Nursery-8th Grade)

ST. GEORGE ACADEMY, 215 E. 6th St., 473-3130
  (Grades K-8), High School, 473-3323

presence of **Cooper Union,** the **Astor Place cube** (a large sculpture on a traffic island, where skateboarders rule) and **St. Mark's Place.** St. Mark's is the main drag of the East Village, with the most tourist t-shirts per square foot, and a plethora of good restaurants and groovy cafes staffed by the natives.

Just south of St. Marks is **Little India,** on Sixth Street between First and Second Aves. It consists of about a zillion Indian restaurants crammed onto one block, giving you quite a choice or too many choices, depending on your perspective. The skinny: go to **Panna** (330 E. 6th Street, 475-9274) for ultra-cheap eats, **Mitali** (334 E. 6th Street, 533-2508) for a more elaborate spread. You can also buy Indian spices and ingredients for your own feast at nearby shops, like **Bombay Bazaar** (85 First Ave., 529-1815).

Avenue A is where the real fun starts, and where the faint of heart beg off. Of course old-school hipsters would scoff at this—for them, the East Village has been hopelessly softened by years of subtle gentrification. **Alphabet City** (the area bounded by avenues A through D) has a bad rep for drugs, crime, and the like, and its battle scars are not hidden behind shiny new facades. Avenue A has the highest concentration of cafes, restaurants, record stores, bars, and clothing shops, and its proximity to mostly tamed **Tompkins Square Park** makes it a popular choice for living and chilling.

The park, once famous for squatter's riots and 24-hour illegal behavior, is now frequented by a diverse crowd of more domesticated squatters, weekend punk rock hangers-on, young guys playing pick-up basketball and twentysomething hipsters playing pick-up-each other, as well as moms and dads with their kids in the playground area. It also has doggy moms and dads in the dog run. Every summer, this park plays host to the **Charlie Parker Jazz Festival,** and the main lawn is covered by locals and travelers alike, spread out on their blankets, with a picnic lunch packed for the occasion. Avenue B between 7th and 9th Streets was christened Charlie Parker Place recently, to honor Charlie Parker, who once lived at 151 Avenue B.

People who live in the East Village have a wealth of local things to do. You can eat anything under the sun in the East Village, from $2 falafel sandwiches to $34 prix fixe French cuisine at **Delia's Supper Club** (197 3rd Street between A and B). Japanese? Take **Takahachi** (85 Avenue A, between 5th & 6th, 505-6524), for an aromatic and succulent sushi event. Mexican? **Benny's Burritos** (93 Avenue A at 6th Street, 254-2054) will fill your tummy and their margaritas will get you goofy. Italian? **Ci Vediamo** (85 Avenue A, between 5th & 6th Streets, 995-5300) or **Il Bagatto** (192 E. 2nd Street, between A & B, 228-0977). Soul food is here too. Go upscale to **Mekka** (14 Avenue A, 475-8500). If you're planning to cook dinner (often a foreign concept in Manhattan), you can snag organic produce at **Prana Foods** (125 First Avenue, 982-7306), and pick up mouth-watering, inexpensive authentic Italian pastry at century-old **Veniero Pasticceria** (342 E. 11th Street at First Avenue, 674-7264) for dessert. Mmm. Indulgence is the only option with these cannoli and tarts, so don't buy too many, as you'll end up finishing off every one of them that very night.

The pros of this neighborhood include somewhat low rent, a bohemian atmosphere, and inexpensive restaurants and bars. The cons are the absolute lack of anything approaching, well, luxury living. For that, get thee to **Sutton Place.** Any East Villager worth their salt spits on Sutton Place. Or they would if they ventured above 14th Street, where the oxygen gets a bit thin. Also, this neighborhood east of Astor Place is woefully subway-deficient.

Bars and nightspots are present in such a variety, from dives to high-stepping hot spots. The very Catskills **Holiday Cocktail Lounge's** (75 St. Mark's Place) celebrity cachet is for the most part, posthumous-poet W .H. Auden was often seen here for a rousing breakfast scotch, as it was convenient to his former residence, next door at **no. 77.** You can appease your fussy beer palate at **d.b.a.,** a specialty beer bar at 41 First Avenue. They have old-fashioned hand-pumps for the cask-conditioned English ales, and offer a wide variety of American microbrews and European imports in bottles and on draft. The date that each keg was opened is on a blackboard above the bar.

E. 7th Street is a magnet for beer lovers. After having a couple quick mugs (they sell them two at a time) at **McSorley's** (15 E. 7th), the venerable tavern literally with the history of the city on its walls (immortalized by Joseph Mitchell in his "McSorley's Wonderful Saloon"), walk down a few doors to 43 and 41 E. 7th to **Burp Castle,** a temple of beer where "monks" worshipfully take your order for prized imported beer, and Brewsky's, which specializes in American micros.

The East Village also has some secret, very zen pockets worth investigating (as long as you clean up after yourself and talk quietly amongst yourselves, I won't mind sharing them too much). For starters, there's the **community garden** at 6th Street and Avenue B, a big corner plot that's a good example of ordered, floral chaos. It's also often the site for dance, music, and poetry performances, especially in the summer. On 7th Street between B and C is a tiny amber jewel called the **Jacklight Gallery,** where the artist and coordinator, Walter, paints and displays his work, when he's not having a group show. Walter paints on extant wood, salvaged from old doors or embellishments, so if you happen to find a good slab, bring it by and he'll be quite appreciative. **Mama's Restaurant** (on the corner of 3rd Street and Avenue B) is a cheapie soul food spot, brimful of garlic mashed potatoes, sinful macaroni and cheese, and fried chicken. Mmm. Rough-hewn tables are packed in close, so don't plan on having a private conversation, although you might overhear one. And the walls are plumb with framed paintings and photos of peoples' moms. Aww.

HIDDEN COSTS

Although common services like dry cleaning and luxuries like eating out are much more inexpensive in this part of the city than in parts elsewhere, the dearth of subways makes last-minute cabbing a bit of a reality. This can really add up. How to counter this: get down with the bus schedules and routes. They run up and down all the avenues on a regular basis, with the First Ave. bus uptown being especially frequent.

If You're Looking to Rent:

The good news is, you can almost definitely get a **studio** for under $1,000, if you apply yourself. Most landlords charge between $700 and $1,000 for a studio, unless there are amenities like a doorman or concierge, which is as much as a rarity as a hair-helmeted socialite sighting. You can often snag a **one-bedroom** for $900, and from there they run up to about $1,500. Oddly enough, Avenue A is the most expensive, with prices decreasing as you run both east and west from there. **Two-bedrooms** are from $1,100 to around $2,200.

If You're Looking to Buy:

Most of the people drawn to the East Village are young, don't have a lot of money, and are renters. Without the same sort of demand for housing for sale, there isn't as much as in the West Village or other, wealthier, parts of the city. This can work to your advantage, though, as there are often **studios** and **one-bedrooms** for as low as $45K. Comb the *New York Press* classifieds for real deals, as well as super-cheap foreclosures. They recently listed a 3rd floor walk-up studio for $49,000, $361 maintenance.

INSIDER TIP: *A typical East Village resident's idea of "movin' on up" would be to land a pad in the Red Square apartment building on Houston between A & B. This 13-story structure, with its russkie pastiche and whimsical, surreal clock tower, offers such bourgeois treats as spacious rooms, a concierge, doorman, and terraces upon which to chill in the temperate months . . . to the tune of $1,050 for a studio, $1,400 for a one bedroom, and $2,000+ for two bedrooms. Still, when you consider what that would run you uptown, it's a steal.*

Essential Neighborhood Resources

<u>Area Code:</u> 212

<u>Zip Codes:</u> 10003, 10009

<u>Police:</u>
9th Precinct, 321 E. 5th, 477-7811

<u>Hospitals:</u>
St. Vincent's, 153 W. 11th, 790-1000
Beth Israel, 281 First Ave., 420-2000

<u>Post Offices:</u>
Cooper, 93 Fourth Ave., 254-1389
Tompkins Square, 244 E. 3rd, 673-6415
Peter Stuyvesant, 432 E. 14th St., 677-2112
Ottendorfer, 135 Second Ave., 674-0947
Hamilton Fish, 415 E. Houston, 673-2290

Libraries:

Tompkins Square, 331 E. 10th, 228-4747

Hamilton Fish Park, 415 E. Houston, 673-2290

Churches:

San Isidro y San Leandro Orthodox Church of the Hispanic Rite, 345 E. 4th St. (C&D). Swing around the back to see the startlingly beautiful back of the church, covered with a mosaic of mirror and tile.

Trinity Lower East Side Lutheran Parish, 602 E. 9th St. (Avenue B)

Damascus Christian Church, 289 E. 4th St., 228-5544

Emmanuel Presbyterian Church, 737 E. 6th St., 228-0431

Collegiate Reformed Dutch Church, 2nd Ave. and 7th St., 477-0666

Synagogues:

Community Synagogue Center, 325 E. 6th St., 473-3665

Town and Village Conservative Synagogue, 334 E. 14th St., 677-8090

Village Temple, 33 E. 12th St., 674-2340

Landmarks:

St. Marks Place, an extension of E. 8th from Fourth Ave. and Astor Place to Tompkins Square Park. Famous for being the New York version of Haight Ashbury during the hippie years, it's still the heart of the East Village.

St. Marks-in-the-Bowery Church, Second Ave. at E. 10th, 674-6377. A true community center, not only for religion (it's an Episcopal church), but also for neighborhood arts and poetry. This church houses The Poetry Project, a world-famous group dedicated to preserving and promoting poetry. Check out their New Years Day Marathon Reading, which features everyone from Patti Smith to Allen Ginsberg to Eric Bogosian to Penny Arcade.

McSorley's Old Ale House, 15 E. 7th (between Second and Third Ave.), 473-9148. The most famous and oldest beer bar in New York, with McSurly waiters and the city's history on its walls.

Too bad the beer isn't as good as the atmosphere. But it's worth
the trip. Try the Liverwurst sandwich.

Cooper Union, 7 E. 7th (Fourth Ave.), 353-4195. A private
college with a tradition of historic meetings and speeches in its
Great Hall.

Little India, 6th St. (between First and Second Aves.). One of the
fastest-growing ethnic enclaves in the city, spilling out onto the
avenues and onto neighboring streets.

Main Drags:

Avenue A and **St. Marks Place** both reign as East Village's Main
Drags. They are chockablock with boutiques, eateries, boites, and
sidewalk sales.

The Great Outdoors:

Tompkins Square Park, 7th to 11th Sts. (between A & B). Lawn,
b-ball courts, old Ukrainian men playing chess, pick-up soccer
games with toothsome, shirtless lads.

The East River Park lies between the FDR Highway and the
East River, and has a track with a soccer field in the center.
A jogging/strolling esplanade runs along the river in both
directions. Do this one in full daylight.

Community Garden at 6th St. and Avenue B. A lovely,
non-municipal retreat.

Parking:

Street parking isn't bad, here for Manhattan, although weekend nights
can be a nightmare. Garages in the East Village typically charge at
least $200 a month to keep a car, although they're more often open
lots than enclosed buildings. Small garages scattered throughout the
neighborhood:

Consolidated, 146 Third Ave., 475-9159

Brevoort, 21 E. 12th, 924-1604

P T Parking Corp., 303 E. 6th St., 598-9821

Banks and ATMs:

NatWest, 72 Second Ave. (E. 4th), 628-9378

Chemical Bank, 255 First Ave. (E. 15th), 935-9935

EAB, 50 Avenue A (E. 2nd), 533-3087

Lower East Side People's Federal Credit Union,
   37 Avenue B, 529-8197

Grocery Stores:

Unfortunately, the East Village's supermarkets are highly undistin-guished. But try these:

Farm Grocery, 146 Second Ave. (between E. 9th & 10th), 475-7521

Key Food, Avenue A (between 3rd & 4th Sts.). Kosher food to be
   had, especially around Passover.

Sloan's, 81 First Ave., 995-5147; 196 Third Ave., 674-9599

Grand Union, 130 Bleeker, 674-5997

Commodities East, 165 First Ave., 260-2600

FAMILY FUN EATS

LUCKY DOG DINER, 167 First Ave. (10th & 11th), 260-4220. This airy, cheerful "diner" is all good. High ceilings, retro touches, and a clean nineties vibe make this both fun and uplifting for kids and parents alike. A simple, oversized menu offers hearty burgers, milk-shakes, and for dessert: a rousing banana split that's perfect for sharing. You'll love the perky staff, homey food and fifties vibe.

Pharmacies:

East Village Prescription Center, 72 Avenue A, 260-4878.
   This mom-and-pop establishment are great for quick
   prescription turnaround and delivery.

Block Drugstore, 101 Second Ave., 473-1587

Estroff Pharmacy, 138 Second Ave., 254-7760

Gas Stations:

There are several on Houston St., from Broadway east to the river. Also:

Eastside Service Station, 253 E. 2nd, 529-9320

Westfield, 24 Second Ave., 475-9397

Dry Cleaners:

East Village Cleaners, 239 E. 5th, 673-5007

Hattan House Cleaners, 145 Third Ave., 477-1740

Laundromats:

E V Launderama, 286 E. 10th, 473-7760

Laundrobot, 202 E. 6th, 533-0704

Laundry Boys, 246 E. 14th, 254-6078

Avenue A Laundry King, 97 Avenue A, 673-6886

Hardware Stores:

H Brickman & Sons, 55 First Ave., 674-3213

AARDENT Hardware Co., 15 Avenue A, 473-6050

Lucky Home Center, 100 Lafayette, 925-4008

Allied Hardware, 59 Second Ave., 477-0507

Video Shops:

Kim's, 85 Avenue A, 529-3410. Perhaps the best video store in
  New York. Super-stocked with art films.

Tompkins Square Video Club, 170 Avenue B, 979-8709.
  This little nook of a shop was the subject of a chapter in Lisa
  Jones' book, *Bulletproof Diva.* It also has a healthy amount of
  cult films, art films, and a Black film section.

Tower Video, 383 Lafayette St., 505-1166

Blockbuster, 151 Third Ave., 505-7766

Cafes, Delis, Coffeeshops, and Diners:

The East Village is glutted with Ukranian or other Eastern European
diners, whose food becomes more and more miraculous the colder the
winter wind blows. Most are open 24 hours, all serve hot, homemade
soups and fresh bread, as well as standard eggs, bacon and hash
brown fare. Among the best:

Kiev, 117 Second Ave. (E. 7th), 674-4040. $ Kid-friendly.

Leshko Coffee Shop, 111 Avenue A, 473-9208. $ Kid-friendly.

Odessa, 117 Avenue A, 473-8916. $ Kid-friendly.

Veselka, 144 Second Ave., 228-9682. $ Kid-friendly.

2nd Avenue Deli, 156 Second Ave., (10th St.) 677-0606. (kosher)

Come for the matzoh ball soup. Stay for the noodle pudding.

Katz's Deli, 205 E. Houston St., 254-2246, (not kosher). Almost as much as an institution as what Meg Ryan faked here famously in When Harry Met Sally. "I'll have what she's having" ring a bell?

Russ & Daughters, 179 E. Houston, 475-4880. If in this delightfully named bagelry and hors d'ouvre shop, we recommend the scallion tofu cream cheese. They also sell dried pineapple rings.

Yonah Shimmel's Knishes, 137 E. Houston, 477-2858. Knishes so genuine, they don't even resemble the ones sold in carts.

B & H Dairy, 127 Second Ave., 505-8056. Terribly cheap and delicious soup and challah bread, but skip the weird carrot cake.

Miscellaneous Neighborhood Fun:

The Russian and Turkish Baths, 268 E. 10th (between First and Avenue A), 473-8806, is an authentic old steam house, like you'd find in Moscow or Istanbul. Formerly a rejuvenating hangout for mobsters, this strange little world is frequented by everyone from old Ukrainian men to Wall Streeters to the occasional celebrity, who come here for a schvitz (Yiddish for sweat). Do I have to say this? It's not an illicit sex spot. Totally on the up and up.

INSIDER TIP: *To feed your friends who help you move the first night, call:*

VILLAGE EAST PIZZERIA, 180 Avenue C, 477-1926.
  Cheap, fast, and good.
TWO BOOTS TO GO, 36 Avenue A, 505-5450. Pricier,
  elaborate, and scrumptious.

DINNER THE FIRST NIGHT

CI VEDIAMO (85 Avenue A, 995-5300) This charming little underground eatery has a perfect mixture of: attentive, unobtrusive service, uncomplicated, yet tasty fare, whimsical decor, and low prices. Plus, you get a free glass of port with your check.

WEST VILLAGE

The **West Village** (also known as Greenwich Village) is one of the most attractive living options in Manhattan. It's aptly named, because it really does give off a village-y and "college town" feel. Many NYU students make it their home, as well as older professionals who can afford the high rent because they've "made it." The cozy, clean feel of the areas around Bank Street, where brownstones line the quiet streets, gives off a calm, secure vibe, and just a few streets away, nightlife reigns for those of all different stripes. The Village takes the best aspects of uptown and marries them to a young, adventurous and open-minded mood, where gay is as normal as straight, art is something people make as well as buy, and boutiques don't (usually) sell items that would put you back a year's salary.

Bleecker Street is a main drag of the West Village, and has a multitude of bars, restaurants, and action. It embodies the younger self of the West Village, when rents were lower and residents were more bohemian. **Seventh** and **Eighth Aves.,** as well as **Hudson Street** are quite wide, and have a multitude of shops and restaurants, from the pedestrian to the unique. Side streets like **Macdougal** and **Sullivan** house little cafes, each one a world unto itself, where people-watching and cappuccino-savoring are the main sports, not to mention having an intimate conversation (or eavesdropping on one) with a soul mate or close friend.

It seems like virtually anyone who ever had anything to do with American art lived and worked in the Village, including Eugene O'Neill, John Dos Passos, journalist John Reed, sculptor Gertrude Vanderbilt Whitney (founder of the Whitney Museum of American Art), Gertrude Stein, and Upton Sinclair. The Village was also home to the Abstract Expressionist painters Jackson Pollock, Larry Rivers, and Franz Kline, and the Beat Poets, including Alan Ginsberg and Jack Kerouac.

Still a left-wing bastion, the Village today is, like much of Manhattan—also home to doctors, lawyers, publishing executives, and other professionals; its once-quiet side streets are gradually being overtaken by ever-burgeoning cafes and bars ranging from hole-in-the-wall student dives to Euro-chic; there are dozens of health clubs, health food stores, and herbal medicine shops, and, of course, cafes.

If you want to live here, the one main thing to keep in mind is that despite its rep for providing sanctuary to successive generations of struggling artists and intellectuals, the Village is not cheap.

HOW TO FIND OUT ABOUT SCHOOLS IN THE WEST VILLAGE

For public schools, the West Village belongs to COMMUNITY SCHOOL DISTRICT 2, 330 West 18th St., 337-8700. Do make an appointment with Ms. Marjorie Robbins, Director of Pupil Personnel, or Mr. Michael Dance. You can also request printed material about their schools.

Private Schools to look into:

THE CITY & COUNTRY SCHOOL, 146 West 13th St., 242-7802. (Ages 2-13)

FIRST PRESBYTERIAN NURSERY, 12 West 12th St., 691-3432. (Ages 2.9-5)

GRACE CHURCH SCHOOL, 86 Fourth Ave. (10th St.), 475-5609. (Grades K-8)

ELIZABETH IRWIN HIGH SCHOOL, 40 Charlton St., (Sixth Ave.), 477-5316. (High School)

OUR LADY OF POMPEII, 240 Bleecker St., 242-4147. (Nursery-8th Grade) (Catholic School of the Archdiocese of New York)

VILLAGE COMMUNITY, 272 West 10th St., 691-5146. (Grades K-8.)

ST. BERNARD/FRANCIS XAVIER, 327 West 13th St., 243-6368. (Nursery-8th Grade) (Catholic School of the Archdiocese of New York)

If you choose to live in the West Village, your neighbors will be somewhat youngish, often gay, and very polished. Many will be toting the expensive-but-chic bag of the moment, while wearing comfortable jeans and the shoes of the season. This is the neighborhood of choice for Trustafarians (young Manhattanites buoyed by a trust fund) as well as people who are quite successful at their often creative careers.

Families here are usually made up of thirtiesh parents, who either started out here or in the East Village and don't want to give up the mod, progressive atmosphere for the more remote and comparatively conservative Uptown. Its proximity to SoHo, Chelsea, and the East Village is also a plus, as these neighborhoods tend to feed off each other in complementary ways.

Drawbacks include a touristy/Bridge-and-Tunnel influx on weekends, with weekend warriors roving the streets in search of some kind of celebrity sighting or urban high. It's hard to feel at home when secluded or insidery Friday and Saturday night options are hard to come by, and being jostled along the sidewalk is a matter of course. That's when it's good to know of an overlooked dive in the East Village, or to be on the list at a chichi watering hole below Houston. Other negatives are a commercialized feel—businesses, bars and restaurants here are geared towards the gawking tourist with a wallet full of cash, and not you, the person who actually lives there. Luckily, there are lots of wonderful little hideaways undiscovered by the masses, and we'll try to give you a sense of them, although it's always wonderful to discover some yourself.

HIDDEN COSTS OF THE VILLAGE

Everything is often a little more expensive here than it would be to the East, just because it's the West Village. Prepare to shell out more for everything from toothpaste to laundered shirts. However, you have wonderful access to the subways, so you'll save on taxis.

INSIDER TIP: *The best classified ads for housing in the Village are in the* NEW YORK TIMES *and the* VILLAGE VOICE. *Some people argue that the* TIMES *offers better quality places, others say the* Voice *does. The* VILLAGE VOICE, *which recently became a giveaway paper, comes out each Wednesday. Be sure to get it Tuesday evening at Astor Place.*

If You're Looking to Rent:

Consider yourself lucky if you can find a Village studio for under $1,000. Even a tiny sixth-floor walkup is likely to cost $900, and a nice-sized **studio** or **small one-bedroom** will probably go for $1,200 or more a month. Buildings with a doorman or an elevator usually get $1,500 or more a month for one-bedrooms. Anything around $2,000 is probably a bargain for a **two-bedroom** apartment, and $3,000 isn't unusual.

INSIDER TIP: *If you've decided to live in the Village, NYU has a great housing office that can help find good places that aren't in the classifieds. But you must know someone to get in there, or be a student yourself. The bulletin boards of local supermarkets, health clubs and laundromats are also good bets—particularly for shares.*

If You're Looking to Buy:

There's a good market for buying and selling apartments in the Village. It's possible to find a clean little **studio** for less than $100,000, but the emphasis is on *little*. Don't plan on having any big dinner parties in any of them, and don't plan on turning sideways in some of them. For studios ranging between $75,000 and $100,000, typical monthly maintenance fees range from $500 to $700. There are also a great many **one-bedroom** apartments, mostly cooperatives but some condominiums, in the Village.

There are small **two-bedroom** places available for under—a very little bit under—$200,000, but most nice two-bedroom places sell for between $250,000 and $400,000. Some of the apartment buildings in the Village feature an in-house garage, a rare luxury in Manhattan.

Essential Neighborhood Resources
<u>Area Code:</u> 212

<u>Zip Code:</u> 10011, 10014

Police: **Sixth Precinct,** 233 W. 10th St., 741-4811

Hospital: **St. Vincent's,** 153 W. 11th St., 790-1000

Post Offices:
Village, 201 Varick, 989-9741
Patchin, 70 W. 10th St. 474-2534

Libraries:
Jefferson Market, 425 Sixth Ave., 243-4334
Hudson Park, 66 Leroy St., 243-6876

Community Resources:
COMMUNITY GROUPS:
Lesbian and Gay Community Services Center,
    208 W. 13th St., 620-7310

Churches:
St. Luke's in the Fields, 487 Hudson, 924-0562
St. Joseph's Church, 371 Avenue of the Americas. The city's
    oldest Roman Catholic Church and one of its earliest Greek
    revival church buildings.
Church of the Ascension, Fifth Ave. and 10th St. Gothic Revival.
First Presbyterian Church, Fifth Ave. (between 11th and 12th).
    Gothic Revival.

Synagogues:
Greenwich Village Synagogue, 53 Charles St., 242-6425

VILLAGE LITERATURE

*The Village isn't only known for great writers—it's also known for its
great bookstores. Check out THE STRAND, 832 Broadway (at 12th
St.), 473-1452. New York fixture Fran Lebowitz's haunt, and frequented by many other less quoted as well, due to the variety, new
and used, of discounted books of every type and stripe.*

Landmarks:

New York University, between Waverly Place and W. 3rd, scattered around Washington Square to MacDougal, 998-1212. A private university known for its urban setting as much as for its prestigious curricula, including business, public administration and the arts, notably the film school.

Washington Square, between W. 4th, Waverly Place, University Place and MacDougal. Its ornate arch is the gateway to the Village, and to many symbolic of the free-spirited expressionism that has become a hallmark of Village life. A popular public gathering place, for all manner of public and all manner of gatherings.

Peculiar Pub, 145 Bleecker, at Thompson, 353-1327. A famous college bar, now also famous for its vast selection of beers— nearly 400 at last count.

The Blue Note, 131 W. 3rd, between Sixth Ave. and MacDougal, 475-8592. A jazz mecca.

Christopher Street. The historic heart of Manhattan gay life, and scene of the 1969 riot that many view as the birth of the gay pride and gay rights movement.

INSIDER TIP: *Get your slice from FAMOUS RAY'S PIZZA, 465 Sixth Ave. (at W. 11th), 243-2253. Many pizza joints claim to be famous, original and Ray's, but this is the real McCoy. Or, rather, the real Ray's. Get a slice to go, or sit at the tables.*

Main Drags:

There are few streets in the Village that are action-less. For action. try any of the following: **West 4th** for—on second thought, West 4th is busy but not specifically for any reason, except for near Christopher St., where it becomes gay and lesbian ground zero. It's more of a thoroughfare. But W. 8th is primo shoe and trendy shopping territory—**Christopher** for cafes, **Waverly Place** for NYU folks, **Broadway** for shopping, **7th Ave. South** for nightlife, **Bleecker** for trendspotting, **Hudson** for cafes and restaurants. Virtually everywhere in the Village there are people walking and talking.

The Great Outdoors:

The West Village is not known for its flora and fauna. There are no parks, in the run-of-the-mill, grass-and-tree sense. **Washington Square Park,** however, is something to see: one of the city's great meeting places, a convergence point for street musicians, artists, NYU students, and other village residents. Known for its Arch, which marks the entrance to the park at the foot of Fifth Ave., Washington Square is also getting famous for its dog run-a local hangout for downtown dog-lovers and their pets. There are also jungle gyms and a sandbox for the kids, designated grassy patches for sunning and reading, outdoor chess tables, and an abundance of benches. (For more information, call **Manhattan Parks & Recreation** at 408-0100.)

For parents, **Abingdon Square,** located on Eighth Ave., just north of Hudson St., near the start of Bleecker, is kid-central on Saturday, Sunday and most weekday afternoons: a plethora of jungle gyms, swings and sandboxes. Naturally, there are many good coffee bars nearby.

AND FOR DOG RUNS:

Washington Square Park, South Side (behind the building)

Parking:

There are quite a few lots and some garages in the far West Village, and a few near Fifth Ave. But there have to be, because on-street parking is so tough.

Garages in the Village typically charge at least $200 and sometimes more than $300 a month to keep a car.

A few to try:

York Parking Corp., 17 E. 12th, 243-5900

Eighth Street Parking Corp., 11 Fifth Ave., 254-2760

Dover Garage 2 Inc., 534 Hudson, 929-8308

Apple West 11th Street Garage, 332 W. 11th, 741-9079

Express Parking, 575 Washington, 645-1132

Travelers, 160 W. 10th (Seventh Ave. South), 888-7400

FAMILY FUN EATS FOR THE FIRST NIGHT

COWGIRL HALL OF FAME, 519 Hudson St. (10th St.), 633-1133. This kitschy Tex-Mex restaurant is a popular spot for children's birthday parties, so a family dinner should be a breeze. Margaritas for the big kids only.

Banks and ATMs:

Chase Manhattan, 718-962-3060; Abington Square, 302 W. 12th; 2 Fifth Ave. (W. 8th).

Chemical Bank, 935-9935; 158 W. 14th (Seventh Ave.); 32 University Place (Ninth); 204 W. 4th (Grove).

Citibank, 627-3999; 75 Christopher (near Sheridan Square); 72 Fifth Ave. (W. 13th).

Grocery Stores:

Balducci's, 424 Sixth Ave. (9th St.), is a foodie paradise. They have delicious everything, and it's all quite attractive, to boot. The fruit is concupiscent, the challah is voluptuous, and the cheese is not Velveeta.

D'Agostino, 375 Hudson. Three locations, with a thoughtful ATM on the premises. Open 8 a.m.-10 p.m, seven days. 666 Greenwich St. in The Archives, 463-0801; 790 Greenwich St., 741-9080 64 University Place, 674-7101.

Sloan's, 585 Hudson (Bank), 229-3656

Grand Union, 130 Bleecker, 674-5997

Integral Yoga Natural Foods, 229 W. 13th, 243-2642

Pharmacies:

C.O. Bigelow Chemists, Inc., 414 Avenue of the Americas/Sixth
   Ave., 533-2700. Fancy-schmancy aroma-therapeutic products
   available here, along with, ahem, ostomy supplies and your other
   necessities. All deliverable.

Action Pharmacy, 254 W. 10th (Hudson), 627-8888

McKay Drugs, 55 Fifth Ave., 255-5054

Value Drugs, 77 Seventh Ave., 243-2446

Gas Stations:

Amoco, 610 Broadway (Houston). A good place to catch a
   cab, actually, because they come here to get some juice
   before hauling us all over town.

A&I Service Station, 1 Seventh Ave. South, 242-9872.

Singh Harvinder, 140 Avenue of the Americas, 925-6392

Brothers, 63 Eighth Ave., 645-9578

Dry Cleaners:

Dino's Cleaners, 17 Eighth Ave., 647-0756. Dino offers
   his West Village compadres free delivery and no minimum.
   But don't be a meanie and send out his schlepper for one
   measly shirt, okay?

L&S Chinese Laundry and Dry Cleaners, 643 Hudson,
   255-6067

Lafayette Laundry and Cleaners, 31 University Place, 473-4548

J&J Harmony Cleaners, 71 University Place, 420-9574

Laundromats:

Only the West Village would have cutesy names for laundromats. If it
was up to me, they all would.

Suds Cafe Laundromat, 141 W. 10th, 741-2366

The Clean Bean, 166 Christopher, 242-3912

Greenwich Laundromat: 112 Greenwich Ave., 691-2713;
   177 Thompson, 673-8161

Village Laundercenter, 146 W. 4th, 777-2801

L&S Chinese Laundry and Dry Cleaners, 643 Hudson,
   255-6067

Hardware:

Blaustein Paint, 304 Bleecker St. (between Grove and Seventh Ave.), 255-1073. This place has been around since 1908. In a city that always seems to be turning over a new leaf (unless you're in the Upper East Side) it's nice to shop for hammers, nails, and the turquoise paint for the living room (surprise your new roommates!) at a place with some serious experience.

Alternative Houseware & Hardware, 242 W. 10th, 924-6545

Hardware Mart, Inc., 151 W. 14th, 243-0519

Shapiro Hardware, 63 Bleecker, 477-4180

Video Shops:

Mrs. Hudson's Video Library, 573 Hudson, 989-1050

Kim's Video & Audio, 350 Bleecker, 675-8996

RKO, 93 Greenwich Ave., 691-2200

DINNER THE FIRST NIGHT

CAFE DE BRUXELLES, 118 Greenwich Ave. (West 13th), has a good little bar and a great restaurant specializing in Belgian cuisine—grilled meat, stews, mussels and french fires, in other words. If you're not up for beef or lamb, try the seafood stew or one of the vegetarian dishes. In a neighborhood full of terrific eating establishments, this is the "home" restaurant for many West Villagers. Thierry, the chef, may come by the table, but ask his wife Patricia, the hostess, to send him around if he doesn't show up by the time you're ready for one of his amazing desserts. They're both French, so they know what it's like to move to a new place.

Cafes, Delis, Coffeeshops, and Diners:

Corner Bistro, 331 W. 4th St., 242-9502. Perfect for a juicy burger, yummy pints, and an Ethan Hawke sighting.

Caffe Reggio, 119 MacDougal St., 475-9557. Baroque furniture, delicious bruschetta, well-pulled espresso, and understated rococo atmo.

French Roast, 78 W. 11th, 533-2233. $ Kid-friendly.

Bus Stop, 597 Hudson, 206-1100. $ Kid-friendly.

Village Den, 225 W. 12th, 255-2444. $ Kid-friendly.

University Place Restaurant, 101 University Place (W. 12th), 475-7727. $ Kid-friendly.

Silver Bullet, 759 Broadway (8th St.), 254-9755. Not only do they serve amazing hot roast beef sandwiches and entire meals with mashed potatoes and gravy to boot, they also deliver cases of beer to your door. For the boozy carnivore in you.

Zampognaro, 262 Bleecker, 929-8566

University Place Gourmet, 116 University Place, 243-3139

Six Avenue Deli, 136 Waverly Place, 989-2053

Pyramid Delicatessen, 174 Christopher, 691-8211

Miscellaneous Neighborhood Fun:

Washington Square Park—My friend Nina's mother, in her boho days, once witnessed a man writing in a notebook in Washington Square Park, and shamelessly looked over his shoulder. A few weeks later, she heard those same words in a song coming out of the radio. That man was Bob Dylan. Although the same caliber of artist may no longer come to this park to seek his muse (hey, you never know), there are plenty of funky youth-culture-killed-my-dog types, as well as curmudgeony NYU professors having a sit and a puff on their pipes.

INSIDER TIP: *If you get a knish or soda from a vendor in WASHINGTON SQUARE PARK, it will often be 25-50 cents more expensive than outside the park's limits. The famous ARCH, although fenced in, is certainly a reminder of things Parisian, just to give you that feel of cognitive dissonance.*

SOHO AND TRIBECA

Soho and Tribeca are regarded as slick addresses, as they shuffle the cultural sheen of an area steeped in art with the sweet smell of success. Although Soho (and by logical extension, Tribeca) has been dubbed a Eurotrash shopping mall, what with its reams of pricey boutiques, sniffy galleries, and attitudinous boites, it still retains a prettiness not usually found in Manhattan.

Soho is bounded on the north, by Houston Street, on the south by Canal Street, on the east by the Bowery, and the west by the Hudson River. Soho's buildings are primarily converted warehouses, when warehouses still prioritized attractive facades. The tall windows, open spaces and high ceilings are uncharacteristic of the rest of the city, and give Soho and Tribeca a real atmospheric advantage. Both neighborhoods had modest beginnings, starting out first as warehouse districts and then as artist communities. Now, although the art's still here, only commercially successful artists can afford to live in what was started out as a real bargain. Although these neighborhoods espouse the trappings of a dedication to art, young artists strapped for cash are better off in cheapie neighborhoods like Williamsburg, Brooklyn, and the Lower East Side of downtown Manhattan.

However, if you're not a young artist sans trust fund, and you love big lofty spaces, high ceilings, large windows, and hardwood floors, as well as a wealth of chic shopping options and fabulous, voguey restaurants (where the only thing free is the attitude), Soho and Tribeca are worth looking into. It's a real scenester's paradise, and offers such chichi nightspots as **Spy Bar** (101 Greene) and Robert de Niro's very own **Tribeca Grill** (375 Greenwich), lest you feel your celebrity-spotting quotient is falling below sea level.

Soho is home to **Dean and Deluca** (560 Broadway) and **Gourmet Garage** (453 Broome), two foodie paradises, as well as scads of galleries and artists spaces. It is also a great place to have a shopping spree, as you can alternate between breaking the bank at Soho outposts of **Agnes B.** (116 Prince), **Todd Oldham** (123 Wooster), **Anna Sui** (113 Greene), and **Dolce & Gabbana** (532 Broadway) and being a bargain hunter at **L'Atmosphere $10 store** (Broadway between Prince & Spring), sample sales, and seasonal markdowns. During the week it's quite pleasant, as the mixture of gallery assistants, artists, and residents mingle on the streets. On the weekends, it's a turisto nightmare, as everyone from everywhere comes to trample the sidewalks, tricked out in their over-the-top, "I want to blend in" Soho costumes. Taking on Soho, whether by foot or by car, can be daunting, particularly on weekends in the fall and spring, the art world's two major seasons. Galleries do most of their business Saturdays and Sundays, leaving West Broadway, Soho's main drag, gridlocked nearly all day.

"Save Soho" purists have begun to complain at the new presence on Broadway of Banana Republic, Eddie Bauer, Williams-Sonoma, and other mall chains. This, combined with its overall expensiveness and universally acknowledged commercialization, has spawned a movement of many galleries to Chelsea. However, Soho still brims over with unique, expensive boutiques. Due to the abundance of Soho modeling agencies (Next, Hunt, and Ford), the sidewalks are very good for gaping, as long as you're not having a "bad hair day." This neighborhood is popular with the sprockety international set (in not-so-nice local parlance: Eurotrash), as well as with actors, and artists. Most nights, bars

HOW TO FIND OUT ABOUT SCHOOLS IN SOHO

Soho is in COMMUNITY DISTRICT NO. 2, *330 West 18th St., 337-8700. Do make an appointment with Ms. Marjorie Robbins, Director of Pupil Personnel, or Mr. Michael Dance. You can also request printed material about their schools.*

Private Schools to look into:

ST. ANTHONY, *60 MacDougal St., (at Prince St.),
477-1297. (Nursery-8th Grade)*

ST. PATRICK, *233 Mott St. (Prince), 226-3984.
(Nursery-8th Grade)*

WASHINGTON MARKET SCHOOL, *55 Hudson St., 233-2176.
134 Duane St., 406-7276, (Ages 18 months-6 years).*

To find out more about Tribeca's COMMUNITY SCHOOL DISTRICT 1, *call 602-9700. They are located at 80 Montgomery St. Here are some people you might want to contact.*

Director of Elementary Education: Ms. Celenia Chevere

Director of Parent Programs: Ms. Myrna Soto

Director of Pupil Personnel:

   Dr. Jacqueline Peek-Davis.

and restaurants are packed to the gills. The neighborhood has excellent and pricey Japanese, Italian, Thai, and French restaurants.

INSIDER TIP: *Houston St., by the way, is pronounced not like the city in Texas, but like this: HOW-ston. If you pronounce it HEW-ston, boy, do you sound like a yokel.*

Soho stands for "south of Houston," the east-west main drag that marks the southern border of the Village.

Tribeca ("the TRIangle BElow CAnal Street"), bounded on the north by Canal Street, on the south by Chambers Street, on the east by Broadway and on the west by the Hudson River, is a neighborhood below Soho and above the Financial District, which has an artsy, spacious allure. It has a healthy gallery and restaurant scene, as well as a hip bunch of residents, including Harvey Keitel and Robert DeNiro, whose Tribeca Film Center and Tribeca Grill give the area a Hollywood-goes-gritty vibe. There is a surprisingly neighborhood-y feel to Tribeca, which has made it popular with families as well as a slightly more down-to-earth established artist and professional crowd.

This area was dubbed Tribeca in the 1970s by real estate developers who wanted to boost this warehouse district's residential cachet by giving it a new image. It soon became popular with alternative galleries that wished to escape the heightening commercialism of Soho, and enjoyed the more modest rental costs. Eighties trustcore novelists like Jay McInerney and Bret Easton Ellis immortalized its then-nightlife by recording the scenes at Odeon and Area, which were big pit stops on the much-disparaged eighties excess circuit.

Now the things to do in Tribeca are more in keeping with a nineties minimalist gloss, whether it's partaking of civilized Sushi at **Nobu** (105 Hudson Street at Franklin), attending well-honed, yet vibrant poetry readings at **Biblio's Bookstore & Cafe** (317 Church Street, between Lispenard and Walker Streets), or having a nice chat and pint with the personable fellows behind the bar at **riverrun,** cummings-ish small "r" notwithstanding (176 Franklin Street, between Hudson and Greenwich).

Tribeca is no longer a bargain, but certainly an attractive option, due to its larger living spaces (often converted from warehouse and loft space), tall windows, off-the-beaten-track feel, and proximity to the Financial District. As it's quieter than most neighborhoods, you might not like the deserted feel, which could seem menacing at night. However, what you get in return is lovely quiet, a true rarity in this city that never seems to sleep (but does so quite soundly in Tribeca).

Many Tribeca residents work in or near City Hall, the downtown courts and the Financial District. Many who work in or near the World Trade Center and Wall Street walk back and forth to work from this area. Soho and Tribeca are also convenient for the Village, and for Little Italy and Chinatown. They have excellent subway and bus links to the rest of New York City. And if you have a car, the Holland Tunnel provides a nearby (though not always quick, especially during rush hour) escape to New Jersey. I can personally think of better places to escape to . . .

INSIDER TIP: *If you've decided to live in SOHO or TRIBECA, look for apartments listed on supermarket bulletin boards. For Soho, comb NEW YORK UNIVERSITY hangouts— bars, restaurants, campus-for ads posted on bulletin boards. Occasionally you will see an ad pasted on local signposts and utility poles, or in delis or laundromats.*

If you're considering an apartment in Soho, make sure it's not one that requires "artist certification." Unless you're a real working artist, of course.

If You're Looking to Rent:

The average price for a **studio** or **one-bedroom** is roughly $1,200-$1,500 in Manhattan's more desirable neighborhoods—and both SoHo and TriBeCa are definitely desirable neighborhoods. If you're lucky, you may find a studio for under $1,000, but you'll probably be 1 of at least 25 people in line for it. Your odds, needless to say, are slim. Most people pay in the $1,000-$1,500 range, although it's not unusual for a prime one-bedroom apartment to rent for $1,800 or more a month. A **two-bedroom** can easily cost $3,000 a month, and $4,000 or more is common. Lofts, whether one or two or an unspecified number of bedrooms, are often more—not only because of the high ceilings and tall window exposures, but also because they are suited to "live and work" situations. Any loft for $2,000 a month is probably a bargain, and $3,000 or more a month is not uncommon.

If You're Looking to Buy:

There's not much for sale in SoHo or TriBeCa for under $200,000, plus several hundred dollars a month in maintenance.

HIDDEN COSTS OF THIS NEIGHBORHOOD

You'll have to work double-time to find inexpensive markets for grocery shopping-the downside of being inundated with gourmet foodie paradises like DEAN & DELUCA and GOURMET GARAGE. The trick is to get your basics delivered by SLOAN'S above Houston, and pick up the bells and whistles at nearby temples of the perfect tangelo.

Essential Neighborhood Resources

Area Code: 212

Zip Codes: 10012, 10013, 10014

Police:
1st Precinct, 16 Ericsson Place, 334-0611

Hospitals:
St. Vincent's, 153 W. 11th St., 790-1000
Gouverneurs, 227 Madison St., 238-7000
Beekman Downtown, 170 William, 312-5000

Post Offices:
Canal Street, 350 Canal St., 925-3378

Church Street Station, 90 Church, 330-5247

Prince Street, 103 Prince, 226-7868

Libraries:
Hudson Park, 66 Leroy, 243-6876

Landmarks:
As Soho has been designated a historic district, the whole place is a bit of a landmark. Side streets like **Crosby** and **Mercer** are cobblestoned, and the buildings' famous cast iron facades have an archetypal Soho allure.

OTHER LANDMARKS:

Guggenheim Museum Soho, 575 Broadway (at Prince). This downtown satellite offers a very Soho selection of permanent and traveling exhibits, including Chagall and Lichtenstein. Great gift shop, too.

Pop Shop, 292 Lafayette (at Jersey St.), 219-2784. This Haring tributorium and shop contains a wealth of Haring designs on everything from backpacks to watches.

Main Drags: **Broadway, West Broadway**

Mini Drags: **Prince St., Spring St.**

The Great Outdoors:
Battery Park, at the southern tip of Manhattan, bordered by the Hudson River, the East River, Battery Place and State St. is where SoHo and Tribeca residents most often go to hang out, play Frisbee,

FAMILY FUN IN THE 'HOOD

THE CHILDREN'S MUSEUM OF THE ARTS, 72 Spring St., 941-9198. This is a great place to get your kids involved in a hands-on appreciation of their own artistic abilities. Workshops available. Call for information.

KEITH HARING'S POP SHOP, 292 Lafayette (at Jersey St.), 219-2784. Kids will love this graphically bold shop, overrun with Haring's signature cartoony creatures.

jog, and people-watch. There is a long promenade along the Hudson, ideal for roller-blading and jogging.

Parking:

Garages in SoHo and Tribeca typically charge at least $200 a month to keep a car, and sometimes closer to $300 or even more. The neighborhood abounds with parking lots. Most are located in TriBeCa, or slightly north of SoHo:

Clara Parking Corp., 243 Hudson, 989-7374

Marna Parking Corp., 20 Varick, 925-1149

Reade Parking Corp., 75 Reade, 577-9039

Broome-Thompson St. Garage, 520 Broome, 226-9130

165 Mercer Garage, 165 Mercer, 226-8911

Banks and ATMs:

Chemical Bank, 525 Broadway (at Spring), 935-9935

Citibank, 108 Hudson (at Franklin), 627-3999; 160 Varick (at Vandam), 627-3999

Chase Manhattan, 623 Broadway (at Houston), 242-7333

NatWest, 528 Broadway, 628-9378

Grocery Stores:

Food Emporium, 316 Greenwich, 766-4598

Commodities Natural Foods, 117 Hudson, 334-8330

Dean & Deluca, 560 Broadway, 431-1691. A Manhattan institution, with a wide range of gourmet food and gear, a shopping destination for people from all over New York. Great presentation. If for no other reason, go just to look, and sniff.

Grand Union, 130 Bleeker, 674-5997

Whole Foods in SoHo, 117 Prince St., 982-1000

Pharmacies:

SoHo Pharmacy, 23 Sixth Ave., 219-0095

Duane Reed, 598 Broadway, 343-2567; 305 Broadway, 227-6168; 225 Broadway, 587-0662

The Health Shoppe Pharmacy, 579 Broadway, 966-4945

Gas Stations:

Singh Harvinder, 140 Sixth Ave., 925-6392

A&I Service Station, 1 Seventh Ave. South, 242-9872

G.S. Service Station, 90 W. Broadway, 226-8626

INSIDER TIP: *When you drive out of town, fill up before coming home. The gas is cheaper, particularly across the river in New Jersey, which has lower gasoline taxes.*

Dry Cleaners:

American Thread Dry Cleaners, 260 W. Broadway, 431-8760.
  Also tailoring.

Memphis Cleaners, 679 Washington, 627-3646

SoHo Dry Cleaner, 529 Broome, 431-0115

Ramon's Tailor Shop and Dry Cleaner, 275 Greenwich,
  962-4185

Laundromats:

Mercer Launderette, 208 Mercer, 505-2440

Laundromat Broome Street, 512 Broome, 966-2400

Tai Looney Laundromat, 299 Broome, 941-5830

Hardware Stores:

Metropolitan Lumber & Hardware, 175 Spring, 966-3466

Vesey Hardware Corp., 60 Reade, 267-0336

CNL, 378 Canal St., 274-8630

Video Stores:

Tower Video, 383 Lafayette, 505-1166

Thunder Video, 100 Greenwich, 227-8888

Mrs. Hudson's Video Take-Away, 200 Varick, 620-7020

Greenwich Street Video, 368 Greenwich, 732-7007

Cafes, Delis, Coffee Shops and Diners:

Bubby's, 120 Hudson, 219-0666. $ Kid-friendly.

Moondance Diner, 80 Sixth Ave. (just north of Canal), 226-1191.

$ Kid friendly.

Franklin Station Cafe, 222 W. Broadway, 274-8525.

$ Kid-friendly.

TriBeCa Cafe, 74 Leonard, 431-0211. $ Kid-friendly.

Miscellaneous Neighborhood Fun:

SoHo Antiques Fair and Flea Market, Broadway at Grand, 682-2000. On a corner parking lot, there are often good bargains—and often not—among the mix of quality antiques and piles of junk that look like they just came out of somebody's attic. Open on Saturdays and Sundays, this is a good change of pace from the SoHo galleries.

Dean & DeLuca, 560 Broadway (at Prince), 431-8350, is a knockout food hall where the high-tech gadgets and great aromas play second fiddle to the fantastic presentation of the luscious-looking food. This is food as presentation art, and also a great place to stock up for dinner or especially brunch.

Fanelli's, the corner of Mercer and Prince, a staunch, establishment that gives a hint of its charm from the outside, but until you step up the few stairs and open the door, you won't get the full effect of red checkered tablecloths, a dark wood bar, and a serious feeling of having been beamed into an Irish village public house. It's a perfect vacation from the unrelenting glammy gloss of Soho.

You may be overwhelmed by the plethora of galleries in SoHo, so here's a li'l Baedeker to get you started.

Exit Art, 548 Broadway, 966-7445

Gen Art, 145 W. 28th St., 290-0312

Sperone Westwater, 142 Greene St., 431-3685

Dia Center for the Arts, 155 Mercer St., 431-9233

Mary Boone Gallery, 417 W. Broadway, 431-1818

Gagosian Gallery, 136 Wooster St., 228-2828

PaceWildenstein Gallery, 142 Greene St., 431-9224

Poets House, 72 Spring St., 431-7920. Devotees of the poetic arts will feel like they've died and gone to heaven in this peaceful structure dedicated to the cultivation of both poets and poetry. You can browse among the extensive small press collection, type up an impromptu sonnet at one of their waiting typewriters, or stop by for one of their readings or discussion panels, featuring the best and brightest poets, pundits and lecturers.

Ear Inn, 326 Spring St., 226-9060. This Fanelli's-esque, maritime-themed bar/performance space has comforting atmosphere all the time, as well as a wonderful Sunday poetry brunch, where you can grab a table, order up a storm, and listen to wonderful poets like Eileen Myles and Lee Ann Brown ply their glossolalia.

Housing Works Used Books Cafe, 126 Crosby St., 334-3324. This newish bookstore/cafe is more reminiscent of a baronial library, with its balcony and liberal groupings of handsome furniture. The profits from these used books, furniture (often including a Naked Lunch-y typewriter or two), and sundry other offerings all go towards helping homeless Manhattanites regain homes, jobs, and self-confidence.

DOWNTOWN
(The Lower East Side, the Financial District, Chinatown, and Little Italy)

"Downtown" usually refers to the vast, villagey land below 14th Street, famous for its bohemian and irreverent rep. But just for the purposes of simplification, we're narrowing this term's territory to lump together the **Lower East Side,** the **Financial District, Chinatown** and **Little Italy.**

The **Lower East Side** is a sprawling neighborhood where gentrification dare not speak its name. It's still brimful of multicultural personality—English is a second language here, for the most part. Previously a Jewish immigrant mecca, it's now primarily a vibrant Latino community. Ratner's, the historical bagel nosh of the early 20th century, still remains on Delancey, in the shadow of the Williamsburg Bridge, flanked by big, cheapie Woolworth-type stores where you can buy flip-flops, washcloths, and ceramic picture frames for a song (and a few pesos). The narrow streets that flow south from Houston, extensions of Alphabet Avenues, are Essex, Suffolk, Clinton, and Attorney, to name a few. These streets have tenement-style housing, the storefronts occupied with bodegas, Caribbean/Cuban/Puerto Rican restaurants, bridal shops, and second-hand furniture stores.

Many people do not view the Lower East Side as a great place to live, because it's grimy and crowded, the polar opposite of the whitebread Upper East Side. But for those with adventurous souls and low budgets, it's a cheap, viable way to live in the city, despite its detractions.

Many young artists have taken advantage of the low rent in this area, and use their apartments as a combination living/working space, almost like what Soho used to be, without the loft dimensions and huge windows. East Village nightlife and cafes are mere blocks away. Orchard Street, a few blocks west of Essex, is closed off to cars on Sunday, when its famous bargain market takes place on the sidewalks. You can get braided leather belts, fashionable knockoffs of popular clothing, toys, perfumes, and leather bags for way below regular prices. Bring your bargaining cap, though, as you're expected to haggle with the merchant. And do pass on the screamingly bogus Prada handbags.

South of Delancey are huge housing projects, both low-income and middle-income. The area's residents are predominantly Jewish (from Orthodox to non-practicing) and Latino families. Kosher food is available at many restaurants and markets. Many now-elderly people live in the middle-income housing, and have for the last fifty years.

The **Financial District,** or **LoMa** (Lower Manhattan) is the polar opposite of the Lower East Side: a monument to urban commerce. Skyscrapers soar and rat-racers scurry—to work, to lunch, to meetings, to get the brass ring, to succeed in business. More popularly regarded as a place to work than a place to live, the architecture spans from the cool, open modernism of the World Trade Center and World Financial Center to the Dickensian, slumping offices of narrow lanes like Fulton Street. Although you wouldn't guess it, this area is rich in colonial history. George Washington read the Declaration of Independence on the site where City Hall now stands, which initiated the Revolutionary War, and many buildings are centuries old. The true beauty of the area is revealed when you happen upon it at night, when the gigantic buildings, from sleek to heavily ornamented, are lit up with a starry brilliance.

INSIDER TIP:

Here is your guide to kooky new mini-neighborhood terms.
BOHO: Bowery-Houston Area. Below Houston on the
Bowery, you might be able to snag some significant
loft space for a little less cash than in . . . Soho.
LOMA: Lower Manhattan. Basically referring to Tribeca,
the Wall Street Area, etc.
LOHO: The Lower East Side, but below Delancey . . .
sort of . . . it's not really precise.

Although living space is scattered throughout the area, the Battery Park City condominiums are the penultimate downtown residential choice. At the southern tip of Manhattan, this complex rises up in solidarity, flanked on the west with a handsome esplanade that runs along the Hudson. When you live in Battery Park City and have a great view, your window always seems like a postcard depicting the Statue of Liberty or the World Trade Center and its lesser brothers, depending on the exposure. Battery Park City has a great rep for raising a family, as it's safe, secluded and quiet, and unlike any other NYC neighborhood. Its public school district is highly regarded, and nearby Stuyvesant High School (a public magnet high school) is near. The South Cove, a park on the southernmost tip of Battery Park City, is lovely, a verdant jumble of wooden piers, footpaths and greenery, meant to resemble the Hudson's shoreline in the 18th and 19th centuries. Disadvantages of this area are that after 5-6 p.m. and on weekends, LoMa is a ghost town, and dining and shopping options are limited.

At night, pretty much everything closes up in the Financial District, though there are signs of a residential revival with the development of **Silicon Alley,** the New Media industry in Manhattan. The Financial District is the southern tip, and some would say the heart, of the New Media boom in New York. Take, for example, 55 Broad Street, once the home of now defunct financial house Drexel Burnham Lambert and its disgraced junk-bond king, Michael Milken. The building, shuttered for several years, has been refitted and rewired to

HOW TO FIND OUT ABOUT SCHOOLS IN THE DOWNTOWN AREA

To find out more about Downtown's COMMUNITY SCHOOL DISTRICT 1, call 602-9700. They are located at 80 Montgomery St. Some people you might want to contact:

Director of Elementary Education: Ms. Celenia Chevere

Director of Parent Programs: Ms. Myrna Soto

Director of Pupil Personnel: Dr. Jacqueline Peek-Davis

Private Schools to look into:

ST. JAMES, 37 St. James Place, (212) 267-9289.
   (Nursery-8th grade)

TRINITY PARISH PRESCHOOL, 74 Trinity Place, (212) 602-0802.
   (6 mos.-5 years)

WASHINGTON MARKET SCHOOL, 55 Hudson St., (212) 233-
   2176/134 Duane St., (212) 406-7276. (18 mos.-6 years)

become a high-technology mecca for New Media tenants that live and work on the Internet. As the New Media artists, Web-page designers, software engineers, virtual-reality film producers and Internet providers move in, some of the idled office buildings are also being renovated to become residential apartments. Coffee shops, book stores, restaurants, and bars are opening—and staying open 'till late at night to serve the new residents of downtown.

In addition to Battery Park, other residential options are cropping up as a growing trend is commercial buildings convert some or all space to residential units. If you live in the Financial District, your neighbors are most likely going to be corporate types and affluent families, with both mom and dad working nearby.

Chinatown is a joyful exercise in disorienting cultural immersion. It's a great place to lose your bearings. But as for finding an apartment there, as the old adage goes, you either have to know someone, be Chinese, or both. But that doesn't mean you can't enjoy all it has to offer. Whereas most cities' Chinatowns are a little over a block long, Manhattan's is a veritable mini-city of 35 blocks, where once again, English is a second language. During the day, the sidewalks teem with frenetic seas of people, and stores' merchandise spills over into your path while food carts douse your nostrils with pungent, mouth-watering aromas. You can get all manner of exotic accoutrements inexpensively, from jade elephants to hand-painted plates, all while wearing your new kimono and heading for your foot reflexologist. Needless to say, the array of restaurants is staggering, and if you want authentic Chinese cuisine, look no further. You can also get your fortune at Chinese temples that are open to the public. Beyond this rundown, there's always something going on here that will thrill and excite, especially if you catch their Chinese New Year Parade.

Little Italy is also low on housing options, but definitely another exercise in cultural immersion. Located between Houston and Canal Streets on the north and south, and on the East and West by Mulberry and Lafayette Streets, it exudes an old world charm, with low buildings and narrow streets accentuating the sense of intimacy. Restaurants and pastry shops offer delicious traditional fare, with a goodfella atmosphere that could make you feel like you're an extra in The Godfather. The Festival of San Gennaro is an annual carnival, replete with freak shows, traditional musicians, and funnel cakes. It's a definite Manhattan must-do.

People who live downtown have a wealth of neighborhoody options, as they're a stone's throw from cultural outposts of every sort. They can eat authentic Chinese, Italian, and Caribbean food, or go west to Tribeca for a trendy, slick dining or drinking experience. Because the neighborhoods are relatively close to each other, traveling from one to another for different kinds of fun is fairly common. It's truly a global jumble, with Tribecan Wall Streeters chowing smugly at their favorite Chinese restaurant, while young pierced artists from the Lower East Side do the same one table over.

If You're Looking to Rent:

Renting in Downtown is a mixed bag, with **studios** in the $500-$800 range in the Lower East Side (no doorman, learn to love stairs, drug dealers on the corner) and $1,350 for a studio in the sanitized enclave of Battery Park City. But you never know what's out there unless you comb the classifieds regularly and keep an ear out. If you wish to live downtown because your new job is in the Financial District, spread the word amongst your colleagues, as they may know of a good situation. If you're drawn to the economical Lower East Side, there's a $20 roommate service on 5th Street right between A & B that often has listings for that area: **Roommates NYC,** 543 East 5th Street (A&B), 982-6265.

According to the Alliance for Downtown New York's A Report on the Downtown Manhattan Residential Market, "downtown units tend to rent at a 10% to 20% discount from comparably amenitized units on the Upper West or East Sides." What this boils down to is that your typical downtown **one bedroom** is around $1,400, in a converted building previously used for commercial purposes.

If You're Looking to Buy:

For most people who want to buy Downtown because they work in the Financial District, the obvious place to begin looking is in the condominiums of Battery Park City, with its small but tidy shops and parks built as part of the planned community. Around Wall Street, it's possible to get a **one-bedroom** for $100,000, with monthly maintenance under $1,000.

HIDDEN COSTS OF DOWNTOWN

When it comes to transportation issues downtown, hidden costs arise. The Financial District is remote from popular areas like Midtown and Uptown, and so you must either take public transportation or a taxi to get there. Luckily, this area is blessed with an abundance of subway lines to take you most anywhere.

The same holds true for Chinatown and Little Italy, although they are not as far from "civilization." The Lower East Side, however, along with the East Village, is subway challenged, and so taxis become more of a necessary evil, however optimistic you may be about planning ahead.

Another big Financial District expense is the day-to-day stuff. Most standard services have hiked prices, as they suspect every hapless muffin-buyer or dry cleaning schlepper is a leveraged buyout king more than happy to pay through the nose. This is particularly obvious at the shopping center near Battery Park City.

Chinatown suffers from no such indignities, and you may do well to base your buying power here, as it's somewhat proximate. Little Italy suffers from Soho inflation overspill, but people rave about the inexpensive, meticulous tailors who make the Lower East Side their base of operations, and have for decades. A benefit of Downtown is that one nabe's ripoff is another one's bargain.

Essential Neighborhood Resources
<u>Area Code:</u> 212

<u>Zip Codes:</u> 10002, 10004, 10005, 10006, 10007, 10013, 10038, 10041, 10047, 10048

<u>Police:</u>
LoMa: 1st Precinct, 16 Ericcson Place, 334-0611
Little Italy/Lower East Side: 7th Precinct, 19½ Pitt, 477-7311
Chinatown: 5th Precinct, 10 Elizabeth St., 334-0711

Hospital:

Gouverneurs, 227 Madison St., 238-7000

Beekman Downtown, 170 William St., 312-5000

Post Offices:

Bowling Green, 25 Broadway, 363-9490

Chinatown, 6 Doyers, 267-3510

Church Street, 90 Church, 330-5247

Wall Street, 73 Pine, 269-2161

Peck Slip, 1-19 Peck Slip, 964-1054

Libraries:

Seward Park, 192 E. Broadway, 477-6770

Ottendorfer, 135 Second Ave., 674-0947

Chatham Square, 33 E. Broadway, 964-6598

Community Resources:

Alliance for Downtown New York Inc., 120 Broadway,
566-6700

Churches:

St. Paul's Chapel, at Broadway and Vesey

Trinity Church, at Broadway and Wall St.

Synagogues:

Bialystoker Synagogue, 7 Bialystoker Place (Willett St.),
475-0165

First Roumanian-American Congregation, Shaarai Shamoyim
(Gates of Heaven), 89 Rivington St.

**Eldridge Street Synagogue (Congregation K'hal Adath
Jeshurun),** 12-16 Eldridge St., 219-0888. Gothic, Moorish and
Romanesque style.

Landmarks:

LoMA

Statue of Liberty: You can grab a ferry at Battery Park to this
popular attraction, and see what all the fuss is about. Even

the jaded will have to admit that it's kind of cool to stare back at the skyline from of all things, an oversized torch.

World Trade Center, 1 World Trade Center's 107th floor, 938-1100. You can take the A, C, E, 4, 1, and 9 to the World Trade Center subway stop. This imposing, dual structure has bounced back from its little terrorist event in record time, and offers everything from tours to a nosebleed dining experience at Windows on the World, the pricey restaurant.

World Financial Center, 1 World Financial Center (at West Highway between Vesey and Liberty Sts.). Most notable here are the shops, eateries, and Winter Garden, a glassed-in pink marble hall where many freebie concerts and dance performances take place. The glass west wall overlooks the beautiful yacht basin. Call 945-0505 for a schedule of events.

Trinity Church, at Broadway and Wall St. This site dates back to 1697, although the original structure was burned down in the Revolutionary War. Rebuilt and reconsecrated in 1846, its features include Gothic flying buttresses, stained glass windows, and vaulted ceilings. In the ancient and well-groomed cemetery, with stones dating back to 1681, you can pay your respects to Alexander Hamilton and others.

City Hall and City Hall Park, bounded by Broadway, Park Row, Chambers and Centre Sts. This august complex is a must-see for those interested in municipal history, federalist architecture, and politics. You may even happen upon a news conference. City Hall houses a museum which displays George Washington's writing desk, his inaugural flag, and art by John Trumbull.

New York Stock Exchange, 20 Broad St., 656-5168. This Corinthian-columned Beaux Arts structure contains all the stock-trading mayhem you might imagine it would. View it from the glassed-in observation platform.

South Street Seaport, Water St. between Dover and Fletcher, 669-9400. Museums, shops, restaurants and entertainment, in good weather, make the Seaport a quaint quay to frequent, when it's not over-run by tourists.

LOWER EAST SIDE/LITTLE ITALY

Ratner's Dairy Restaurant, 138 Delancey St., between Norfolk and Suffolk Sts., 677-5588. Ratner's, the oldest Jewish dairy restaurant in Manhattan, has a mouthwatering array of blintzes, bagels, potato latkes, and desserts.

The Lower East Side Tenement Museum, 90 Orchard St., 431-0233. This unique museum has preserved the memory and life experience of immigrants who lived in 97 Orchard St. around the turn of the century.

Umberto's Clam House, 129 Mulberry (at Hester), 431-7545. Notorious as the place where mobster Joey Gallow was rubbed out in a hail of bullets, blood and sauce in 1972.

CHINATOWN

Statue of Confucius, Confucius Plaza, Division and Bowery Sts. This bronze statue with its green marble base was a gift of the CCBA.

Eastern States Buddhist Temple of America, 64 Mott St., 966-6229. This storefront shrine serves both as a spiritual and social meeting place, and you can receive your fortune for one dollar.

Main Drags:

Canal Street, The ultimate Chinatown thoroughfare, bustling with people, merchandise, and carts.

Delancey Street, This is another wide, "avenue-ish" street that runs east and west. On the east, it runs into the Williamsburg Bridge. Many large markets offer everything from discount sneakers to appliances, and Woolworth-type stores provide a way for you to pick up the necessities for very small change. Broadway: In the Financial District, Broadway is jammed with stores, office buildings, and sidewalk vendors, not to mention pedestrians.

The Great Outdoors:

Ellis Island Park, Ellis Island. Circle Line ferries leave Battery Park hourly at 15 minutes past the hour from 9 to 4. Call 269-5755 for info.

Statue of Liberty, Liberty Island. Reachable by ferry from Battery Park. Call 269-5775 for information.

Battery Park, Battery Place, State St. and the Hudson River. Take the 1 or 9 train to South Ferry, or the 4 or 5 train to Bowling Green.

City Hall Park, bounded by Broadway, Chambers St., and Park St. Watch out for the ghosts! In years past, this park has served as a burial ground for the poor, a site of public executions, and protests. But it's also a lovely place to eat your sandwich, believe it or not.

Columbus Park, Bounded by Worth and Bayard Sts. on the north and south, Mulberry and Baxter Sts. on the east and west. This is one of the few parks in the Lower East Side/Chinatown area.

Orchard Street Outdoor Market, Sunday is bargain day on Orchard St., one of New York's favorite outdoor shopping bazaars.

South Street Seaport, entrance at Water St. (between Fulton and John Sts.). This tourism-loving maritime-themed complex does tend to woo one with its selection of luxe shops, pricey restaurants, and lovely boardwalk. A great destination on hot summer nights during the week.

FAMILY FUN IN THE 'HOOD

Kids will love BATTERY PARK CITY'S SOUTH COVE, with its nautical/tropical theme. (take the 1 or 9 train to South Ferry, or the 4 or 5 train to Bowling Green). It's the part of Manhattan that is closest to the Statue of Liberty.)

Parking:

It's not so hard to park in the Lower East Side, but your car may not be there when you come back, due to good old crime. Ideally, for your own peace of mind, get a rusty old can of a car for use in the city and park your pride and joy in a suburban relative's garage. Chinatown and the Financial District are both pretty abominable when it comes to parking, as they are very congested most of the time.

Below is a sampling of local garages, with monthly rates (tax included).

Area Garage Corp., 275 Delancey St., 228-9200, $178.16
Amal Parking Corp., 321 Bowery, 420-0753, $200
Downtown Parking Corp., 56 Fulton St., 227-5185, $338

57 Ann Street, 57 Ann Street, 732-2942, $300

Garage Management Corp., 333 Rector Place, 945-0028, $355

Banks and ATMs:

Chemical Bank, 935-9935; 16 Wall St. (Nassau St.);
5 World Trade Center; 231 Grand Ave. (Bowery)

Citibank, 627-3999; 1 Broadway (Battery); 55 Wall St.
(near William); 30 Fulton St. (Water St.); 111 Wall St.
(near Water St.); 2 Mott St.

Emigrant Savings Bank, 110 Church St., 349-2150;
465 Grand St., 797-5550

Republic National Bank of New York, 100 Maiden Lane
(Pearl), 809-4400; 1276 Broadway (Maiden Lane),
227-2000

Bank Leumi Trust Company of New York, 120 Broadway,
343-5343

Atlantic Bank of New York, 15 Maiden Lane, 608-6430

Grocery Stores:

C Town, 500 Grand St., 677-7722. Notable for their large selection
of kosher foods.

Gristede's, 71 South End at Battery Park, 233-7770. This quiet
market is not as overpriced as it could be, and has a nice selection of healthy produce and packaged foods.

Chung Hing Food Corp., 141 Mott St., 966-2810. A lively
Chinatown market. You may want to bring a Chinese foods guide
there with you, if you're feeling adventurous.

Italian Food Center, 186 Grand St., 925-2954. This gourmet
market offers specialty meats imported from Italy, like prosciutto
and capicola, as well as fresh mozzarella and sausage made on
the premises. Lunch specials, too.

Associated Food, 77 Fulton St., 227-4109. Known for their good
fruit selection.

Pharmacies:

Duane Reade, 1 World Trade Center, 775-0005. This Duane Reade
location caters to the commuters, so you'll find a healthy stash of

train-munchable food like chips and pretzels, as well as makeup, grooming products, and some beverages.

Other Duane Reade locations: 95 Wall St., 363-5830; 80 Maiden Lane, 509-8890; 37 Broadway, 425-8460; 1 Whitehall St., 509-9020.

Gas Stations:

GS Service Station, 90 E. Broadway, 226-8626

335 Bowery Operating Corp., 335 Bowery, 253-7790

Park on Auto Service Inc., 75 Kenmare, 431-7618

Dry Cleaners:

Chou Yai Fung, 54 Mulberry St., 964-5566

Pearl Cleaners, 7 Hanover Square, 509-1490

Silky Fashion, 132 Mulberry St., 941-0075

Subway Cleaners, 150 Fulton St., 566-1959

Taylor Cleaners, 88 Fulton St., 693-1400

Chow Kee Dry Cleaners, 30 Ann St., 233-7433

Laundromats:

101 Allen Laundromat, 101 Allen St., 925-2791

Long Giang Dang Laundromat, 168 Elizabeth St., 966-5191; 121 Elizabeth St., 925-7476

Hardware Stores:

Dick's Hardware, 205 Pearl, 425-1070

Fulton Supply and Hardware, 74 Fulton, 587-4088

Whitehall Hardware, 19 Rector, 269-2698

Metropolitan Lumber and Hardware, 175 Spring, 966-3466

Grand Trends, 70 Canal, 941-9548

General Hardware, 80 White, 431-6100

Video Stores:

J & R Music World, 23 Park Row, 238-9000

D & M Video City, 73 Catherine, 732-9805

Friendly Video Center, 4 Allen, 343-2916

Wah Men Video, 33 Catherine, 406-0632

Ann Adult Entertainment Center, 21 Ann, 267-9760

Cafes, Delis, Coffee Shops and Diners:

Little Italy Coffee Shop, 151 Mulberry, 925-7812. $

Sambuca's Cafe and Desserts, 105 Mulberry, 431-0408. $$

Coffee Arts, 124 Fulton, 227-5857. $

Ely's Coffee Shop, 63 Orchard, 966-4530. $

Java Works, 3 Hanover Square, 425-7600. $

New World Coffee, 80 Broad, 742-2199. $

Beaver Deli & Grocery, 60 Beaver, 425-4080

Petaks of Wall Street, 80 Wall, 558-6000

M & H Manna Deli, 125 Chambers, 233-1701

N & N Gourmet, 69 Liberty, 227-2100

324 Bowery Food Co., 324 Bowery, 598-0628

Water Street Gourmet, 12 Water, 785-5220

DINNER THE FIRST NIGHT

*SFUZZI, in the Winter Garden of 2 World Trade Center, 385-8080
Not only succulent pasta concoctions and a bit of continental
elan, but a dazzling proximity to the wharf and archetypal New
York views of the Statue of Liberty and the World Trade Center
(you'll have to crane your neck to see the latter).*

Miscellaneous Neighborhood Fun:

Century 21, 22 Cortlandt St., 227-9092. If you can psyche yourself
up to do battle against the hordes of bloodthirsty bargain mavens who
descend upon this humble department store, it's certainly worthwhile.
They've got everything from $50 Betsey Johnson halter dresses to $30
Fila crosstrainers to discount Le Creuset dutch ovens—in short, the
requisite New York labeled signifiers that prove you're in the know.
Frequented avidly by fashion editors and fashion idiots alike. But
you're local. Hit it at odd times, like 10 a.m. and 3:30 p.m., for opti-
mum elbow room.

Little Italy's Festival of San Gennaro is an annual carnival,
replete with freak shows, traditional musicians, and funnel cakes. It
takes place in June.

Chinatown Ice Cream Factory, 65 Bayard St., 608-4170. Head here for inventive flavors including green tea, mango, red bean and ginger.

Chinese New Year Celebration. Watch traditional lion dancers and stay clear of volatile, no-regulation firecrackers Takes place in February.

Windows on the World, One World Trade Center, 938-1100. Nosebleed dining at its best.

Cafe Gitane, 242 Mott St., 334-9552. This precious, francophile, easy-on-the-eyes cafe is the perfect place to appear soive while lighting up or eating one of their savory salads.

OTHER NEIGHBORHOODS TO CONSIDER

The detailed listings of neighborhoods focus on the areas of New York that attract the most newcomers: the bottom half of Manhattan. But there are many other places where people live in and around New York. Here are some brief capsule descriptions of other neighborhoods.

Upper Manhattan

Harlem is one of the most famous neighborhoods in Manhattan. Or infamous, depending on whether the only thing you know about it is that parts of it are high-crime. Harlem is also one of the most historic areas of the city, and probably has the absolute best residential architecture. Its capacious brownstones are a well-kept secret, and many Columbia University students take advantage of all it has to offer. However, if you don't have a sense of what area is safe and what isn't, it may not be wise to make this neighborhood your first home. If you have friends or relatives that are familiar with the area, then you're much better off. Harlem is one of those areas—like Staten Island, or Queens—where most of the newcomers are moving there because they already have friends or family in the neighborhood.

Washington Heights, north of Harlem from 151st St. to the George Washington Bridge, has long been a residential neighborhood with a typical New York ethnic mix. In recent years Washington Heights has suffered more than some neighborhoods from drugs and gangs, but it remains a housing bargain with good subway connections to the rest of Manhattan.

Brooklyn

Brooklyn is a large, historic, and distinctive city in its own right, and many Brooklynites believe it is infinitely more interesting, and more livable, than Manhattan. There are many neighborhoods, but two that attract a good share of people moving to New York are Brooklyn Heights and Williamsburg.

Brooklyn Heights is the area just south of the Brooklyn Bridge, a neighborhood that is not that much different than Manhattan, but is nonetheless noticeably quieter and more laid-back. Easily accessible by subway, or by walking across the Brooklyn Bridge on nice days, Brooklyn Heights is famous for its Promenade, great for walking, jogging, skating, or just sitting and staring across at the Manhattan skyline. It's a neighborhood with many trendy shops and restaurants, mixed in with the old mom-and-pop places. Housing is maybe a little more affordable than Manhattan, and there are many big old prewar buildings with family-friendly apartments. The area is famous for writers (Norman Mailer, Arthur Miller) and artists, but is now mostly given over to people who commute to Manhattan.

Williamsburg today is sometimes compared to Soho thirty years ago, before Soho became malled and trendy. The first stop in Brooklyn on the L train from 14th St. in Manhattan, Williamsburg is a neighborhood with warehouses, industry, small shops, restaurants, and a remarkable ethnic mix. The industrial lofts are just being taken over by artists, and there's a thriving community of young and not-so-young people working in media as diverse as stone sculpture and Web page design. It's a vibrant scene, with housing that offers more space for less money than Manhattan.

If you want more space for the money, if you don't mind riding crowded subway cars to and from work every day, and if a slightly slower pace and less crowded atmosphere is appealing, Brooklyn might be the place for you.

New Jersey

Hoboken, a few minutes from the Financial District on the PATH (Port Authority) train under the Hudson River, has become a very popular settling place for young singles and couples who work in

Manhattan. Naturally, housing prices have crept up with the coming of microbreweries, coffee bars, gelato shops, and other landmarks of Manhattan civilization. Oddly, unlike some Manhattan neighborhoods, Hoboken has not given itself over to family life. The typical pattern is for a young couple to meet in Manhattan, move to Hoboken, and then retreat further into New Jersey when it's time for the kids to go to school.

Bergen County, the area of New Jersey across the George Washington Bridge, is one of the wealthiest areas of the United States. It is a network of suburbs, some strictly bedroom communities and some their own distinct little villages, but all featuring single-family homes that typically range from $200,000 into the millions. Many newcomers to New York who choose Bergen County are corporate types who bring their families with them, and want to have a house and a yard and a school system that they feel is comparable to whatever they left behind. And shopping malls. Even New Yorkers who scorn the idea of living in Bergen County drive over to hit the many shopping malls and giant grocery stores, and to fill up the car with gas while they're there.

If you don't mind taking at least one and maybe two or more trains and/or buses every day, or if you're going to brave the traffic and drive through rush hours, the appeal of cheaper housing and the possibility for a suburban lifestyle might make New Jersey appealing to you.

NEW YORK'S TV LAND

Many TV shows have been filmed in and around Manhattan. Here's where to find a few of the actual venues:

THE COSBY SHOW
10 St. Lukes Place, New York, NY. The front of this brownstone in Greenwich Village was used as the Huxtable's Brooklyn Heights home.

FAME
The Old High School of the Performing Arts, 120 West 46th St., New York, NY. This is the building that was featured on the show, but it's only used for alternative school programs. The real High School of the Performing Arts is the LaGuardia High School of the Performing Arts, 108 Amsterdam Ave.

THE JEFFERSONS
The High Rise Apartment Building, 85th St. and Third Ave., New York, NY. Here's where they moved on up to.

MAD ABOUT YOU
The Apartment Building, 12th St. and Fifth Ave., New York, NY. Paul and Jamie Buchman supposedly live here.

The Old Town Bar, 45 E. 18th St., New York, NY. Paul and Jamie eat here—if they can get Ursula to serve them.

THE ODD COUPLE
The Apartment Building, 1049 Park Ave., New York, NY. Felix and Oscar argued here.

SEINFELD
Tom's Restaurant, 112th St. and Broadway, New York, NY. This is the place the gang spends just about all of their waking hours in.

TAXI
Dover Garage, 534 Hudson, New York, NY. This former cab garage doubled as Louie's garage in the show.

ALL IN THE FAMILY
The House, 89-70 Cooper Ave., Queens, NY. Archie bigoted and Edith whined here, supposedly.

Chapter Four

MOVING IN AND SETTING UP THE ESSENTIALS

SO YOU'VE SIGNED YOUR LEASE, and you think you're home free. Guess what? You're not. Ahead lies the oft-baffling maze of getting settled in. For most people, it can prove to be a series of mishaps, but not for you. Put away your Sherlock Holmes cap—we've done the sleuthing for you. Below is an exhaustive collection of all your Manhattan moving in needs, from getting the juice turned on in time to watch "X-Files" to finding a storage spot for the other two TVs you suddenly realize you don't need.

THE MOVE ITSELF

Moving is never fun, but of course it has to be extra challenging in Manhattan. Here are some tips.

Survival Tips

- If you can afford it, hire movers!
- Make sure you have extra cash for tips.
- Check your building's policy regarding moving hours, elevator use and freight elevator use.
- Landlords are required to repaint the apartment between tenants.

- If possible, you may want to clean the apartment before you move in. Better yet, call a cleaning service. (This obviously does not apply to some places, but I have seen too many to which it does.)

If You're Moving Yourself:

Bribe everyone you know, especially if you're moving into an apartment above the first floor of a walk-up. Buy beer, coffee, soda or whatever to keep them there. Don't forget to lock the truck between trips into the building, or leave a "helper" in the truck to watch it. Remember to turn off hazard lights on the truck when the move is completed, because the battery will die.

INSIDER TIP: *Look on bulletin boards (at the grocery store, bus shelter, etc.) for "Guy with truck" ads, which are often cheap easy ways to move big non-fragile items and boxes, etc.*

If you're hiring help to make the move, have a friend stay with the movers and the truck at all times. Better safe than sorry.

Local Moving Companies
Padded Wagon, 1569 Second Ave., 222-4880
Reliable Moving and Storage Corp., 1-800-769-4679
Shleppers, 1386 2nd Ave., 472-3820
West Side Movers, 644 Amsterdam Ave., 874-3800

Self Hauling Companies
U-Haul, 620-4177
Hertz/Penske, 741-9800, 1-800-222-0277
Ryder, 397-2893, 1-800-297-9337

Truck Rentals
Manhattan Rent-A-Van, 59 W. 53rd St.,
   1-800-348-3133

GETTING THINGS UP AND RUNNING: BANKS

You'll need a bank account before you can get anything done, and conveniently, Manhattan is home to a zillion banks, including the Bank of Kinki (I kid you not). Below are a few nice, stable banks that you can feel secure about, with their new account information numbers. Chemical Bank is merging with/ becoming Chase, so treat them as one entity.

Chemical Bank, 935-9935
Chase Manhattan Bank, 1-800-282-4273
Citibank, 974-0900
EAB, 557-3700

GAS AND ELECTRIC

Call **Con Edison**, 338-3000. In most circumstances, you will pay Con Edison for both services, although some leases specify that the landlord pays for gas. There is no initial installation charge for residential customers. Unless the former resident neglected to turn off his electricity (very rare), a Con Edison representative will have to come to your building to turn it on. Minimum monthly charges: $5.15 for electric; $11.84 for gas.

INSIDER TIP: *When you call to schedule a turn-on, make sure you get the customer service person's name and confirm the scheduling with her or his superior. Unfortunately, Con Edison is famous for not showing up, and the more accountable they feel, the better your results. If you don't have a doorman or a daytime super, you will need to stay home to buzz them in.*

TELEPHONE

You can open up a Nynex account (local service) by calling 890-1550. You may need to give a credit card number and your landlord's phone number to the service representative. The standard plan offers you a fixed monthly charge of $10.10, and 10.6 cents for each local call. Additionally, you may want to consider Regional Calling, which charges around $18 for unlimited calls in the city as well as to neighboring counties like Nassau, Suffolk, Westchester, and Ulster. If you have relatives, friends, or business contacts nearby, it's a worthwhile service.

Long Distance:
AT&T, Business, 1-800-222-0400. Residential, 1-800-222-0300.
  Maintenance and Repair,
  1-800-222-3000
MCI, Business 1-800-888-0800
  Residential 1-800-950-5555
Sprint, Business 1-800-366-2370
  Residential 1-800-877-4646
Nynex, Business 890-2700
  Residential 890-1550

Cellular
Nynex, 1-800-696-3955
Motorola, 643-0368
Payless Mobile Electronics, 747-0800

CABLE
Contact **Manhattan Cable** (Time Warner) at 674-9100. They service all of Manhattan. It usually takes 2 to 5 business days from the day you call to get cable service started. There is a $56.00 initial installation charge—not including tax. There is also a $25.00 deposit on the Cable Box. There are three types of cable: Basic, Standard, and Premium. Basic, which includes two or three public stations, is $14.86 monthly. Standard includes channels like CNN, American Movie Channel, and Nickelodeon, and charges $30.22 monthly.

  Premium includes channels like HBO and Showtime. It charges $12.95 for first channel, $9.00 for the second channel, $8.00 for the third, and $7.00 for 4th channel. If the tenant prior to you did not pay his or her bill, you may have to go down to the Manhattan Cable with your lease or other form of documentation to prove you legally live at your current residence.

INTERNET SERVICE PROVIDERS
National

America Online, 1-800-827-6364, has its plusses and minuses. If you want a user-friendly, cheerful and bland national internet service provider (ISP), this is the one for you. It's geared toward the typical American, and has lots of typical Americans chatting it up in a variety of chat rooms. This may or may not be your slice of pie. However, the 5 free hours they provide as part of the $9.95 Basic monthly fee get used up rather quickly, especially if you go onto the internet. Rates: There are two options for America Online members. The Basic plan is $9.95 per month, with the first 5 hrs free. Every hour after that is $2.95. The other option is called "20 for 20." You get 20 hours a month for $19.95, and then every hour after that is $2.95.

CompuServ, 1-800-848-8199 Another big national ISP, CompuServ tends to have a better rep for user support than AOL, and is also often used by businesses who want access to the web. Like AOL, there are two monthly package options. However, it's a little more expensive than America Online. Rates: The first option is $9.95/5 hrs ($2.95 per hour after 5 hours) The Super Value package is $24.95/month for 20 hours, and $1.95 per hour after that.

Compuserv's WOW, 1-800-848-8199, is a subdivision of CompuServ and is delightfully cheap for a national Internet Service. It's designed more for the home and family, which means that its graphics look very bright, tactile, and colorful, as if everything were made out of squishy rubber. It offers easy access to the internet, and can be easily sussed out by a six-year-old. But as it's relatively new, they're still working out the bugs, and it's slooooooow. $17.95 per month flat fee.

LOCAL

Interport, 989-1128. Interport has a sturdy rep for being no-frills and yes-functional. Almost German in its bland, pleasing efficiency, it's a no b.s. local gateway. Unlike AOL, the technical support is swift and painless, although it's only accessible during the week. $25/60 hours/month. (If you exceed that, it's either your first month online or you need to ungraft your fingertips from that keyboard and meet people. Off-line. Now.

Panix, 741-4400. This service lets you customize your path into the web. You can land directly at a particular site, and also graphic design your User Profile into a fine bit of eye candy. But it'll cost you . . . $35/month for unlimited access.

Spacelab.net, 966-8844. Offers Unix Shell access, a personal home page, e-mail and news. 28.8 K PPP is $16.95 per month, and 128K ISDN is $29.95 per month. You can also pay $229 for one year of unlimited 28.8 access. One week free trial. (http://www.spacelab.net, info@spacelab.net)

Tuna.net, 805-2470. Specifically for the Mac-users among us, and is accordingly characterized as warm, fuzzy, kind and gentle with their slogan: "TunaNet loves you more than anyone!" Their 28.8 dial-up service is available exclusively to Mac users. They also have great technical support, and are recommended by the New York Macintosh Users Group. Bonus: they provide house calls ($50 fee) for Manhattan subscribers. $20/month. (info@tuna.net, http://www.tuna.net)

Internet Channel, 243-5200. Offers free software, no set-up fee, 5 MB of storage for your home page, and no time limits for $25/month. They also feature a Homepage Creator program that "helps" you set up your own homepage. Pretty nifty. (http://www.inch.com, access@inch.com)

DRIVER'S LICENSE AND REGISTRATION

Department of Motor Vehicles, 645-5550, 141-155 Worth St.

Okay. Steel yourself for this brush with bureaucracy in blue eye shadow. It might help to think of the DMV as a tease—they get you all the way out there and then they say no. So make sure you have every bit of documentation you will need to get the goods. And call to make sure there haven't been any policy changes.

For registration, plates, and license, bring your body down to 141-155 Worth St. between 9:00 a.m. and 4:30 p.m. To get a car registration and plates for the first time, you'll be filling out form MV82. You need to bring:

- proof of ownership
- proof of New York State Insurance
- sales tax clearance.
- birth certificate
- proof of signature

New residents have thirty days to apply for their license and register their cars. You can pick up a license application, driver's manual, and auto registration form, or you can call the number above and have it sent (if you can get through). A valid out-of-state license exempts you from taking a road test, but you still have to pass the vision, road sign, and written test.

If your license has expired, or you are applying for the first time, you have to take the written test and then get your learners permit. You then have to take a three-hour course at a licensed driving school. After that, you can take your road test.

Currently, **to renew your license**, bring your current license, a proof of signature (such as a credit card), plus proof of your current address with a utility or credit card bill. You will pay a fee of $22.50. You will need to fill out an MV44 form there.

If you are getting a **car registration and plates** for the first time in New York, you'll need to fill out form MV82. You need to bring proof of ownership and proof of New York State insurance, and sales tax clearance. You will also need your birth certificate and proof of signature. Fees: $5/title, $5.50/plates, $15/surcharge. You'll also pay a fee depending upon the weight of your car.

INSIDER TIP: *If you're lucky enough to be a New York State resident already, and you need your license renewed, you can do so at LICENSE EXPRESS, 300 W. 34th St., where they promise to renew your driver's license in eight minutes. They're closed Friday, Saturday and Sunday, but open at 8:00 a.m. Monday through Thursday. To renew your license, you must bring your current license, proof of signature, and proof of your current address (a utility bill). This will run you $22.50.*

GARBAGE AND RECYCLING

Department of Sanitation, 219-8090. There are two acceptable kinds of containers for refuse: 20-32 gallon plastic containers or 13-55 gallon heavy-duty, opaque bags. Your landlord should provide these. Your landlord should also put the cans/bags at the curbside on the day the garbage is to be picked up; if you must do it, don't do it before 8 p.m. the night before it is picked up. Check the community pages of your Yellow Pages to find the day your garbage is picked up. No pickup on holidays or snow days.

Recycling: Check the community page of your Yellow Pages to find the day that your materials are picked up for recycling. Your landlord should provide a recycling bin for you to use, but you are responsible for separating your own recyclables. You should have separate bags—tightly secured—for plastic bottles, glass items, corrugated cardboard, paper items; each can go into the recycling bin. Your landlord is responsible for putting all the recyclable bags on the curbside the day on pickup. Milk containers are not recyclable.

Some buildings have indoor garbage chutes. Especially here, make sure that your garbage is tightly tied. Remember to separate your garbage from your recycling items; the above rules apply. Again, you must separate your recyclables—It's the law!

GET A JOB: EMPLOYMENT RESOURCES

If you're moving here without a job lined up, it's best to be super-prepared. First of all, get your resume in order. Make sure it's typo-free, interesting, one page only, laser-printed, and on a fine quality bond or laid paper. White and off-white are fine, but don't go crazy with the marble-ized, speckled, and neon paper unless you want to be thought of as overbearingly "wacky." Have several form cover letters prepared that you can customize to each job in the smallest amount of time.

Think about what you want to do, how much you want to get paid, and how you might need to prep your skills. It would be wise to be combing the *Village Voice* classifieds before you move, just to take the temperature. Also, contact your university alumni association to see if there are any active chapters in

OWNING A CAR IN THE CITY

All I have to say is, why? New York City lives to accommodate those without cars, as opposed to certain other west coast cities that shall remain nameless. For young people just starting out, it's an unnecessary headache. Parking rules are myriad and byzantine, parking spots are rare, and car insurance is more expensive here. You've got to be one clever fella to avoid the hated parking ticket, and the more hated towed-car status. However, more established people with a less stringent budget might appreciate getting around (and getting out of) the city with their own wheels. As long as they factor in the cost of this convenience (an annual average of $3,600 in garage fees, for starters), and are still cool with it . . .

But everything's not so cut and dry. Below are some ways that we skirt the issue.

How to have your cake and eat it too:
• Be rich. You won't be upset about parking garage rent, high car insurance, and other trifles.
• Keep your car cheaply parked out of "town" and subway, bus, or ferry to it for special occasions like weekend getaways, helping someone move, or going to the airport. People in New Jersey or the outer boroughs often rent their carports, garages, and driveway space to Manhattan car owners for a rock-bottom price. You can also keep it in West Harlem's WD Lot (304 West 135th St.) for a measly $100 per month.
• Rent. If the main reason you want your car is for weekend and longer getaways, you can rent a Ford Taurus for the weekend from Hertz for $165.62 (unlimited mileage). If you take ten weekend vacations and one long (9 day) vacation, it'll cost you $2,567, which is about $1,000 less than the cost of parking alone for one year.

INSURANCE
In New York State, the absolute minimum coverage you can have is a $20,000 liability coverage. However, many opt for the generally recommended $300,000 liability, along with collision and comprehensive (fire and theft) insurance. Liability coverage pays claims and covers the

legal defense expenses if you get in an accident. Collision insurance only pays for damage to your car caused by an accident. Comprehensive coverage covers paying for damages to your car due to fire, theft and other catastrophes. Collision and comprehensive often carry a deductible, which is, like with medical insurance, the amount you have to shell out before your insurance company will start paying.

If you live in Manhattan, have a car of median value (like a Taurus) and have a squeaky-clean record (but of course . . .), recommended coverage should run between $1200 and $1700 per year. Insurance companies love married, non-smoking drivers with boring cars that are loaded with safety devices like the Club, airbags, and a car alarm. However, if the car alarm goes off for an extended period of time, people are liable to get really mad and crowbar the dang thing. Nothing is more annoying to a New Yorker than one of those fancy, unrelenting car alarms with the varying alternation of bloodcurdling sirens, blips, yawps, and yodels.

HOW TO CHOOSE CAR INSURANCE

For an extensive array of data on the car insurance best suited for you, your budget, and your mean machine, get October 1995's Consumer Reports (the Auto Insurance issue).

If you were pleased with your car insurance pre-New York, see if it's available here too. Insurance companies are often known to give you a discount if you are a loyal customer, especially if they don't want to lose you.

NATIONAL INSURANCE COMPANIES

ALLSTATE INSURANCE COMPANIES, 21 locations in the metropolitan area, call 666-3000 for the location nearest you.

NATIONWIDE INSURANCE, 1596 Third Ave. (89th & 90th Sts.), 534-3320

LOCAL CAR INSURANCE COMPANIES

These companies are willing to quote you a price over the phone.

DART AUTO INSURANCE, several locations (718) 365-5656

GEICO INSURANCE, (718) 423-9000

1 STOP AUTO INSURANCE, 2592 Broadway (97th & 98th), 961-9425

PROGRESSIVE INSURANCE, 1-800-AUTO-PRO

Manhattan that have networking and job placement services.

If you're not sure what you want to do, it's best to take temporary assignments in different fields. Often, temps are offered the job full-time, once they see that this person is competent and works well with their company. And no matter how highly you think of yourself, it's still true that fast typers get higher hourly rates and also get their foot in the door of desirable companies. So start practicing!

If you're already established in your field, think of yourself as a valuable commodity. (If you have Computer Systems Management experience, you've got it made.) Headhunters make their living by finding you a great job at an optimum salary.

Head Hunters

Allegheny Personnel Associates, Inc., 6 E. 39th St., 532-1300

Computer Graphics Artists Creative Network Systems, 295 Madison, 986-9760

Don Waldron & Associates, 450 Seventh Ave., 239-9110

Executive Exchange, 450 7th Ave., 736-2350

Freelance Advancers, 441 Lexington Avenue, 661-0900

Head Hunters Executive Search, 352 7th Ave., 947-0300

Interspace Personnel, Inc., 50 E. 42nd St, 867-6661

The Bankers Register, 500 Fifth Ave., 840-0800

Kling Personnel Agency, 150 Broadway, 964-3640

Lynne Palmer Agency, Inc., The Agency for Publishing Professionals, 14 E. 60th St., 759-2942

Legal Support Personnel, 333 Seventh Ave., 695-3999

Macs to the Max, 611 Broadway, 674-0486

Paralegal Ivana Legal Services, 420 Lexington Ave., 286-9560

Sales Brownstone Sales and Marketing Group, Inc., 1133 Broadway, 727-7373

Thomas O'Brien Executive Recruitment, 832-6060

Womenspeak Inc, 111 E. 85th St., 722-3770

Best Classified Sections

New York Times (Sunday)—Snag this baby late Saturday night and type cover letters on Sunday. If you have a fax at home, fax the cover letters and resumes off that day. You can also fax from many drugstores, stationery stores, and office supply stores. Mail the rest on Monday morning. When employers place an ad in the *New York Times*, they can get several hundred responses, so it pays to be one of the first.

Village Voice—Get this paper Tuesday night at Astor Place so you can start faxing, mailing and calling right away.

Employment Agencies

Ad-van-tage Staffing Services, 1-800-299-9950

(Investment Banking Group, Legal Group, and Creative Group) This cheery, professional, youthful organization specializes in good matches. They support Citibank, Siemens, and many entertainment and publishing companies. A great way to get your foot in the door of many top companies.

Office:

Accounting Temps by Olsten, 1140 Avenue of the Americas, 730-8814

Aavis Resources, 485 Madison, 753-4272

Kelly Temporary, 1212 Avenue of the Americas, 704-2040

Legal:

Sporn Group, 56 Pine, 344-5050 (Lawyers)

Legal Support Personnel, 333 7th Ave., 695-3999 (Paralegal)

Legal Horizons, 317 Madison, 972-1300 (Legal Secretaries)

Domestic:

A Pavillion Agency, 15 E. 40th St, 889-6609
    (Child Care, Housekeepers)

Greenhouse Agency, 15 E. 40th St,
    889-7505 (Child Care, Housekeepers)

Best Domestic Services Agency,
    10 E. 39th St, 685-0351 (Domestic)

Graphic Design:

Creative Artists Systems, 295 Madison Ave., 986-9760

(Computer Graphic Artists)

Freelance Access, 286 Summer St., Boston MA 02210,
1-800-ART-TEMP. http://www.8000arttemp.com/freelance.
This agency also coordinates placements in Manhattan.

Computers:

Bob Ross Executive Search,
150 W 51st, 969-9030 (Computer
Technical Support)

Denver Associates,
171 Madison, 725-8300
(Data Processing)

Chefs:

Chefs International, 535 5th Ave., 867-1910

Medical:

Medi Temps, 18 W 45th St, 354-0129 (Medical personnel)
Home Helpers Nurses Registry, 165 W. 46th, 768-9758, (Nurses)

STORAGE FACILITIES

Yes, you've suddenly realized that you don't need all ten of those
boxes of letters and your Halloween costumes from first grade on. I'm
not going to say "I told you so," but I am going to tell you where to go.
Go to a storage facility. New York City is no place for baggage.

Manhattan Mini Storage, (212) STO-RAGE.
http://www.mini-storage.com
Call for the location nearest you—they're all over the city.

Chelsea Mini-Storage, 224 12th Ave./626 W. 28th St. 564-7735.
Offers one hundred different sizes, from a 2x3 cubby for $25 per
month to an 18x55 room for $1210 per month.

U-Haul Storage, 562 w. 23rd St. 620-4177. Two sizes are
available, both on two different levels divided by stairs.
For a 4x4 space on the more convenient lower level is $29.95
per month, or on the upper level, it is $23.95 per month.
For the 8x12 on the lower level, it is $154.95 per month,
or $134.95 per month on the upper level.

DAY CARE

In order to find the most current references for Manhattan Day Care Services, call the following organizations. They will be able to give you information, ratings, and referrals.

Child Care Inc., 929-4999

Day Care Council of New York, 398-0380

Trained counselors can match your child's needs and your budgeted amount with the appropriate program, picking from 4,500 licensed programs.

Chapter Five

NOW IT'S TIME TO FEATHER YOUR NEST. If you've brought the basics with you, then half the battle is won. However, it's nice to get items here, too, to reflect your new city self. Below are some great suggestions for ferreting out the perfect items for your new place.

FURNITURE

ABC Carpet & Home, 888 Broadway at E. 19th St., 473-3000. This is a must stop if you're going to be doing any nest-feathering. Besides all manner of quality rugs and carpeting, ABC has six floors of home merchandise, ranging from centuries-old antiques to little plastic thingies for your fridge.

Salvation Army, 69 Spring St., 925-1909. I snagged a boomerang-shaped coffee table with an inlaid ceramic tile chessboard nestled in its crook (perfect condition) here for $20. I also found a DKNY long black wool dress for $7.99. Plainly, a treasure trove.

Housing Works, 143 W. 17th St., 366-0820. This almost boutique-y Second-Hand Rose yields up beautiful bookshelves and the books and vases to place on them. All proceeds go towards helping homeless Manhattanites regain homes, jobs, and self-confidence.

Murphy Bed Center of New York, 110 W. 17th St., 645-7079. Beyond bedroom farces, Murphy beds are a worthy, space-preserving thing to have. (They're the kind that flip up into a cabinet or extant closet)

26th Street Flea Market (at Sixth Ave.). A motley crew of vendors ply everything from wire shoe sculptures to vintage cast iron bedframes, and bargains are plentiful.

IKEA 1000 Center St., Elizabeth, NJ 908-289-4488. Broadway Mall, Hicksville, L.I. 516-681-4532. Call 1-800-287-4532 for ways to get to IKEA via a special IKEA shuttle bus, which includes Swedish meatballs in its fare. Douglas Coupland deemed it

"Swedish semi-disposable furniture" in Generation X, but I've always wanted to have a sofa named Bjorggren, haven't you? Delivery available.

Christie's East, 219 E. 67th St., 606-0400. This auction house offshoot tends to have more inexpensive items than its higher-end mom. Drop in to "just look," and perhaps an item will strike your fancy, without giving your bank account a drubbing.

KITCHEN STUFF

Pottery Barn, call 595-5573 for the branch nearest you. Weighty ceramic plates, rustic table linens, and more.

Century 21 Department Store, 22 Cortlandt St., 227-9092 (Opposite World Trade Center, in the Financial District). This bargain paradise offers Le Creuset cookware, Krups coffeemakers, Corelle dish sets, whimsical coffeepots, etc.

Crate and Barrel, 660 Madison Ave., 308-0004. Relatively inexpensive housewares, from cooking implements to kitchen tables and fun glassware and dishes.

Ad Hoc Softwares, 410 W. Broadway, 941-6910. This is not a computer store—it's an approachably luxe Soho outpost filled with chi-chi items for your kitchen and bath.

Platypus, 126 Spring St., 219-3919. Good for high-end tablecloths, cooking ware, utensils and the like.

Fishs Eddy, 889 Broadway at 19th St.; 2176 Broadway, 873-8819; 551 Hudson St., 627-3956. The nostalgia queen in everyone will love this store crammed with dishes, silverware, and china from restaurants, hotel lounges and cruise ships gone out of business.

Pier One Imports, 71 Fifth Ave., 206-1911. Multi-culti inspired plates, glasses, and serving platters.

BATH STUFF

Portico Bed and Bath, 139 Spring St., 941-7722;

SETTING UP HOUSE

450 Columbus Ave. (81st and 82nd Sts.), 579-9500. Fetching ceramic soap holders, lush towels, and everything else to give your loo a touch of class.

Bargain Bazaar, 526 E. 14th St., 777-7980. If you aren't fussy, this is a radical-cheap secret more often frequented by Loisaida grandmas than, well, anyone else. Here you can find elaborate and inexepensive bathtub caddies, piles of towels and wash-cloths, plastic clothes hampers and trash cans, and Jesus clocks.

Boyd's of Madison Avenue, 655 Madison Ave. (between 60th and 61st), 838-6558. A very London place to pick up all your necessary ointments, potions, and other things that go in medicine cabinets.

Bed, Bath & Beyond, 620 Avenue of the Americas (Sixth Ave. at 19th St.), 255-3550. This truly huge store is packed with linens, bath indispensables, and a lot more. A perfect way to one-stop shop when faced with barren apartment anxiety.

See also **Century 21 Department Store** and **Ad Hoc Softwares,** previous page.

BEDROOM STUFF

Murphy Bed, 110 W. 17th St. (Sixth and Seventh Aves.), 2nd floor, 645-7079. The obvious choice for making the most of cramped quarters.

Macy's, 151 W. 34th St., 695-4400. This department store behemoth often runs sales on top-of-the-line bed linens. Look for their weekly circular in the New York Times. Recent find: a damask sheet set for $50.

ABC Carpet and Home, 888 Broadway (19th St.). ABC specializes in making you drool. Just don't get it on the merchandise, dearie. Dazzling items ranging from rococo to homespun.

See also **Century 21 Department Store, Portico Bed and Bath, Ad Hoc Softwares, Bed, Bath & Beyond,** and **Crate and Barrel** on previous page.

ARCHITECTURAL DETAIL STORES

Architectural Salvage Warehouse, 33 Berry St., Brooklyn. (718) 388-4527. The New York City Landmarks Preservation Commission rescues worthwhile fixtures, windows, doors, shutters and other interesting architectural items from city-owned buildings slated for demolition and sells them here. Prices start at $40.

Urban Archaeology, 285 Lafayette St., 431-6969. This huge space houses whole rooms filled with mantels, bookcases, pool tables, and other items, often over a century old.

Irreplaceable Artifacts, 14 Second Ave. (Houston St.), 777-2900. 12 floors of architectural ornaments, from gothic chandeliers to Arthurian round tables to mantels and stained glass.

FLEA MARKETS

Annex Antiques Fair and Flea Market, Sixth Ave. between 24th and 26th Sts., 243-5343. Saturday and Sunday, 9-5. Admission: $1

PS 44 Flea Market, Columbus Ave. between 76th and 77th Sts., 678-2817. Sunday, 10-6.

196 Bleecker Street, (outside the Little Red School House at Sixth Ave.), 564-1670. Saturday and Sunday, 9-5.

PS 41 Schoolyard, Greenwich Ave. between Sixth and Seventh Aves., 751-4932. Saturday, 11-7.

PS 183 Flea Market, 419 E. 66th St., 737-8888

Yorkville Flea Market, 351 E. 74th St., 535-5235. Saturday, 9-4 (no market June through August).

ART

Alphabets, 115 Avenue A, 47 Greenwich Ave., 475-7250. This store is governed by a sleek yet playful aesthetic. You can get a fancy cat food bowl or a lovely set of candles for your first dinner party.

Rescued Estates, 54 Second Ave., 674-4578. A mix of modern and antique sculpture, furniture, and tchotchkes.

Archetype Gallery, 115 Mercer St., 334-0100. An assortment of objets d'art sure to give your place a slick Soho feel.

Chimera, 77 Mercer St., 334-4730. This Soho find has enchanting shadow boxes, Isamu Naguchi lamps made of metal, mulberry wood, and bamboo, and candles.

Platypus, 126 Spring St., 219-3919. Chock-full of candelabra, decorative frames, pottery, and more.

NEW YORK DELIVERS!

Of course, we all expect the Chinese place or the pizza place down the block to deliver, but here, in true New York fashion, is a list of delivery services you might not expect:

URBAN ORGANIC, 230 7th St. (between Third and Fourth Aves.), (718) 499-4321, will deliver an assortment of certified organic fruits and vegetables to your doorstep, for a mere $28. You won't know what to do with the fresh herbs, strange fruit, and exotic veggies. It kind of feels like you have a vegan mom sending you care packages.

HÄAGEN-DAZS ICE CREAM, 5 Carmine St. (Sixth Ave.), 229-0140, and 33 Barrow St. at Seventh Ave. South, 727-2151, for the times "when you need it", Häagen-Daaz is there for you.

Cutting down on in-store mortification, CRAZY FANTASY, 333 Sixth Ave. (between 3rd and West 4th Sts.), 366-4444, will deliver pornos, as well as a gamut of adult toys, straight to your home.

PET TAXI, 222 E. 56th St., 755-6000, will deliver your pet to an appointment in style.

Hosting a raging house-warming party and too drunk to go out for a booze run? ASTOR PLACE WINES & LIQUORS, 12 Astor Place (Lafayette St.), 674-7400, has an extensive selection of wines and liquors and delivery is available throughout Manhattan. (Or Carnegie Hill Brewing Co., 1600 Third Ave. (at 90th St.), 369-0808 will deliver a keg of beer, and provide the tap too.

Can't figure out what to put over the mantle? MOUNTAIN ICE OF NEW YORK, 443 West 50th St. (between 9th and 10th Aves.), 397-1500, will chisel down a 300 pound of ice into the ice sculpture you've always dreamed of and deliver it straight to your home Have the polaroid camera ready, the masterpiece starts melting after five hours.

PEPPERMINT PARK, 1225 First Ave. (66th St.), 288-5054, will lessen the anxiety of throwing little Billy's fist birthday party in New York by delivering lunch, ice cream, cake, decorations and party hats.

DIAL-A-DINNER'S, 643-1222, tuxedoed waiters will pick up and deliver meals from restaurants which don't deliver (adding a 20% service charge to the bill).

NILOUFAR MOTAMED

STEREO EQUIPMENT AND COMPUTER EQUIPMENT

P.C. Richard and Son, 120 E. 14th St., 979-2600.

Nobody Beats the Wiz, 871 Avenue of the Americas (Sixth Ave.), 594-2300. This Greenwich Village store is a perfect replica of ones found in the suburbs—it's clean, well-lit, and has a large selection of stereo equipment and CDs.

J&R Music World, 31 Park Row, 238-9000. This downtown electronics mecca has a large selection of stereos, knowledgeable staff, and ok prices. Their sales on featured merchandise are often featured in the Post and the Daily News.

Vicmarr Stereo and TV, 88 Delancey St. (Orchard and Ludlow), 505-0380. This Lower East Side shop is known for its low prices and un-pushy salespeople.

East 33rd Street Typewriter and Electronics, 42 E. 33rd St., 686-0930. This midtown store offers good prices on computers, as well as fax machines and copiers.

Rockwell Computer & Software, 261 Madison Ave., 949-6935. This small Madison shop gets kudos for its non-mega-store compactness, its wide selection of notebook computers, competitive prices and excellent service.

APPLIANCES

Home Sales Dial-a-Discount, 513-1513. This is a really groovy way to get your appliances. Go into any major appliance store and note the exact make and model numbers of items you wish to purchase, along with their prices. Then, call the above number to see if they have the item in stock, and find out the price. This service is famous for offering a hefty discount. They sell air conditioners, major kitchen appliances, trash compactors, TVs and VCRs.

Black and Decker Outlet Store, 50 W. 23rd St., 929-6450. Whoever said you had to travel to go to an outlet store never stepped into this Flatiron discount heaven.

Century 21 Department Store, 22 Cortlandt St. (Opposite World Trade Center, in the Financial District), 227-9092. Offers all manner of vacuums, coffeepots, espresso makers, fans, and the like, at a nice price.

Tops Appliance City, Secaucus, New Jersey, (201) 902-6900. This isn't exactly located in Manhattan, but it's worth the haul. They sell everything from kitchen appliances to washing machines and stereo systems, and they deliver. Unlike many stores, you can strike a fair bargain, and the more you buy, the better the deal. They deliver to Manhattan and can take away your old nasty stove that hails back to the turn of the century. How cool is that?

See also **P.C. Richard and Son,** previous page.

PLANTS

If you're an early riser, the flower district in the west twenties is the place to go. **Union Square market** on 14th St. has plenty of greenery on Market days, Monday, Wednesday, Friday and Saturday. **The Flower District** (along Sixth Ave./Avenue of the Americas, between 27th and 30th Sts.) is a lovely little concentration of botanical shops, which have an extraordinary range of flora, from delicate Japanese bonsai to thick, lush vegetation. It's definitely a good place to pick out some housewarming presents for your new apartment.

ICE CREAM, YOU SCREAM

CHINATOWN ICE CREAM FACTORY, 65 Bayard St., 608-4170. After dinner at Canton or Golden Unicorn, head here for inventive flavors including green tea, mango, red bean and ginger.

CIAO BELLA AT FANELLI'S, 94 Prince St., 226-9412. When it warms up, this sidewalk stand is the most popular destination in Soho for its gelatos and sorbet flavors which include hazelnut, malted-milk-ball and blood-orange.

CUSTARD BEACH, 33 E. 8th St., 420-6039, if you can't make it to the boardwalk, this frozen custard will hit the spot.

DUANE PARK CAFE, 157 Duane St., 732-5555. If you're a fan of granita, the annual berryfest at this TriBeCa cafe will do you in. Don't miss the huckleberry beaujolais and sour cherry flavors, served with zabaglione and cookies.

OUT OF A FLOWER, at Grace's Market Place, 1237 Third Ave., 737-0600, For the grown up kids, ice creams with herbs and alcohol-try peach and champagne with mint or cranberry with port and tarragon.

LUTECE AT RICHART, 7 E. 55th St., 371-9369. Eberhard Muller's chocolate encased ice cream and sorbet creations such as lemon-verbena and passion fruit, in mini chinese-takeout containers

MR. CHIPS, 27 E. 92nd St., 861-4749. Join all the private school kids on the Upper East Side in indulging at this old-fashioned ice cream parlor.

PEPPERMINT PARK, 1225 First Ave., 288-5054. A perennial favorite for all kids big and small.

SAINT AMBROEUS, 1000 Madison Ave., 570-2211, if you can't make it out to East Hampton, a trip to the Upper East side will satiate the urge for this fabulous gelato.

SERENDIPITY 3, 225 E. 60th St., 838-3581. This is where to find New York's yummiest sundaes and the best frozen hot chocolate.

TWEENFONTEIN HERB FARM, at Union Square Greenmarket, 17th St. and Broadway. Stop by this stand after a day shopping or blading around town to sample flavors such as sage, lavender, and rosemary.

NILOUFAR MOTAMED

Chapter Six

GOING OUT:

ENTERTAINMENT FROM A TO Z

One thing you'll leave behind you when you move to Manhattan is the ability to say "There's nothing to do." This city is the center of the universe, and that's why every major band, sports team, play, musical, and celebrity touches down here for at least a little while. You'll never be at a loss for something to do; the hardest thing will be choosing between all the things that happen to be going on on the same night. It doesn't matter what you're into—it's happening somewhere in this city.

ART GALLERIES, HIP

Exit Art, 548 Broadway, 966-7445
Gen Art, 145 W. 28th St., 290-0312
Sperone Westwater, 142 Greene St., 431-3685
Dia Center for the Arts,
    155 Mercer St., 431-9233
    542 W. 22nd St., 989-5566
Mary Boone Gallery, 417 W. Broadway, 431-1818
Gagosian Gallery, 136 Wooster St., 228-2828
PaceWildenstein Gallery, 142 Greene St., 431-9224

BAKERIES

Although many specialty markets such as Dean & DeLuca, Grace's Marketplace and Balducci's, carry fresh bread begotten from specialty bakers such as Tom Cat Bakery and Companio, nothing quite compares to walking into a bread shop which is devoted solely to the creation of delicious bread, from start to finish. Whether its sourdough, semolina or foccaccia, here are some of the best:

Amy's Bread, 672 Ninth Ave., 977-3856. This Hell's Kitchen bakery's loaves are served at such upscale restaurants as Bouley. Try the raisin and fennel semolina bread or the savory twists with olives or cheese.

D & G, 45 Spring St., 226-6688. Go to this Little Italy institution early (before 11:00 am), if you expect to take home any of their famous brick oven creations. Try the round white loaf, with just the right balance of crust and chewy inside.

Ecce Panis, 1260 Madison Ave., 348-0040 and 1120 Third Ave., 535-2099. I melt at the mere thought of their airy, chewy, foccaccia rounds—either plain or baked with sun-dried tomato or caramelized onion. Its more than bread, its an experience.

Eli Zabar's Bread, EAT, 1064 Madison Ave., 772-0022. The "starter" of the bread movement in New York, Eli Zabar's prolific output almost puts him in a mass-produced/fast-food category. However, the quality of his onion sourdough baguettes or raisin pecan loaves, is consistently superb.

Vesuvio Bakery, 160 Prince St., 925-8248. Since it opened in 1920, this SoHo bakery has remained largely the same. If you're looking for glam, look elsewhere. If you want old-fashioned Italian white bread, the perfect accompaniment to just about anything, look no further.

Sullivan Street Bakery, 73 Sullivan St., 334-9435. At this minimalist SoHo outpost, their crusty loaves practically fly off the shelves. The savory pizza rossa-pizza topped with tomato sauce without cheese—is a perfect snack to eat on the bench right outside the store.

Orwasher's Bakery, 308 E. 78th St., 288-6569. This Yorkville bakery, opened in 1916, specializes in Old World recipes like rye and pumpernickel, sold by the pound.

WEEKLY LISTINGS SOURCES

TIME OUT NEW YORK: This magazine devotes itself entirely to chronicling the schedules of every venue and performance space in the city. If you can get beyond their fatuous ad campaign, it's a great tool. Good features, too. On newsstands.

OBSERVER: Dubbed "the school paper of the publishing world," this salmon-colored, dishy rag nonetheless has a delightfully snotty take on the week ahead's activities—the ones it cares about, that is. On newsstands.

NEW YORK (CUE): New York Magazine is the ultimate tool for enjoying, decoding, and handling New York City. Its features keep us abreast of all we need to know, while keeping NYC big cheeses on their toes. Cue is a snazzy, palatable weekly guide at the end of the book, with a "Kids" page that should be of special interest to parents. On newsstands.

NEW YORKER: A New York institution, which has of late been tweaking its refined readership's ears with allowances to the modern age. Listings in the front of the mag. On newsstands.

NEW YORK PRESS: This sneaky, relentlessly obnoxious (in a good way) freebie has been the tortoise to the Village Voice's hare. Although it doesn't have the feature story muscle that the Voice has, its columnists are more plentiful and engaging. Available at many dropoff points throughout the city, including drop boxes on street corners.

VILLAGE VOICE: This newly "giveaway" paper is a downtown institution, and it's in our prayers. Don't miss Michael Musto's column, La Dolce Musto, as well as the weekly Picks and monthly Voice Literary Supplement (read it to give those lulled, scholarly brain cells a swift kick). Available at many dropoff points throughout the city, including drop boxes on street corners.

THE NEW YORK POST: Their new Sunday entertainment section is worth a look for its edgy picks, pans and roundups.

CULTURAL AFFAIRS HOTLINE, 765-2787

BAGELS

New York is a bagel town, to be sure, but it's easy to end up with fluffy impostors, especially if you get yours at the corner deli. However, here are a list of bagel shops that still have some soul.

Columbia Hot Bagels, 2836 Broadway (near 110th St.), 222-3200. Provides the bagels sold at Zabar's and Murray's Sturgeon Shop. Chewy, dense, definitely old-school.

Ess-a-Bagel, 359 First Ave. (21st St.), 980-1010 and 831 Third Ave. (near 50th St.), 260-2252. These bagels are known for their astonishing girth. Not just notable for quantity, they have a stretchy, chewy character and are generously encrusted with your topping of choice.

Absolute Bagels, 2788 Broadway (near 107th St.), 932-2052. These score high on the flavor table, but are admittedly fluffier than the rest.

H&H Bagels, 2239 Broadway (80th St.), 595-8003. Famously tasty bagels abound at this non-glam (no seating, you can see the ovens and sweaty bagel elves) upper east side site. Consistently snags "Best of New York" laurels.

Dizzy Izzy's NY Bagels, 408 W. 14th St. (between Ninth and Tenth Aves.), 627-3777. This sprawling, no-frills bagels source in the Meat Packing District is the H&H of W. Villagers and Chelsea girls and boys alike.

Russ & Daughters, 179 E. Houston, 475-4880. If in this delightfully named bagelry and hors d'ouvre shop, we recommend the scallion tofu cream cheese. They also sell dried pineapple rings.

Other bagel shops of note:

Chelsea Hot Bagels, 300 W. 23rd St., 675-7171

Jo-Jo's Bagel Shop, 346 Ninth Ave., 736-1199

York Avenue Bagels and Appetizing, 1638 York Ave., 535-3838

Bagelicious, 3 Maiden Lane, 348-5858

BARS

Bars, with 70s Memorabilia

PollyEsther's, 77th and 2nd; W. 4th (between Barrow and Jones). Some people just aren't happy unless they're in polyester glad rags and platform shoes. Polly Esther's ensures that they'll always have a place to rage.

Bars with Pool Tables

Bleecker Bar, on Bleeker at Crosby. Dimly-lit downtown bar with one pool table in the back room.

Blue & Gold, 79 E. 7th St. (First & Second Aves.), 473-8918. This quiet, unadorned bar is inexpensive, unpretentious, and mellow. Perfect for pool.

Ace Bar, 531 E. 5th St. (B & C), 979-8476. Very young, post-grunge, hip scene with 2 pool tables.

Bars, Acoustic

Siné, 122 St. Mark's Place, 475-3991. Crowded, intimate venue that often spills onto the St. Marks sidewalk. Notable for its food, too.

Sun Mountain, 82 W. 3rd (at Thompson St.). Laid-back and relatively non-smoky.

New Music Cafe, 380 Canal St. (W. Broadway), 941-1019. Somewhat cavernous, with a questionable B&T crowd and boorish, giant bouncers.

Brownies, 169 Avenue A (between 10th and 11th Sts.), 420-8392. A perfect venue to spot up-and-coming, promising unsigned bands.

The Knitting Factory, 74 Leonard St. (between Church St. and Broadway), 209-3055. This three-floor Tribeca space is widely considered to be at the cutting edge when it comes to the arts, which naturally extends to music like John Zorn's as well as a multitude of experimental and alternative performances.

Ludlow Street Cafe, 165 Ludlow St. (between Houston and Stanton), 353-0536. On this hip block, little-known bands rock out to youthful patrons who also take advantage of the decent food.

Under Acme, 9 Great Jones St. (Lafayette St.), 420-1934. This dark, underground spot carries a regular array of fine bands and has a dinerish, kitschy decor.

Wetlands, 161 Hudson St. (Laight St.), 966-4225. For the greener ones among us, Wetlands is the closest NYC comes to harboring a total hippie refuge. Like, Tuesday is Dead Night? Snicker.

Mercury Lounge, 217 E. Houston St. (Essex St.), 260-4700. The strapping sound system, parade of hottie college music bands (in lieu of co-opted alternative), and hipster contingent makes the Mercury Lounge a fab venue.

CBGBs, 315 Bowery, 473-7743. CB's, to locals. That old punk dinosaur where one can bump into John McEnroe, Iggy Pop and Henry Rollins in one night. But put away your pen. New Yorkers are too cool to ever ask for autographs—or admit to doing so.

Bars, Blues

Chicago B.L.U.E.S., 73 Eighth Ave. (below 14th St.), 924-9755. Brings the Chicago blues music scene to Manhattan. Mixed crowd and comfortable, inspired atmosphere.

Terra Blues, 149 Bleecker St., 777-7776. This Greenwich Village spot is often the first name on everyone's list when it comes to cool, downtown blues.

Manny's Car Wash, 1558 Third Ave. (87th and 88th Sts.), 369-BLUES. National and local blues acts take the stage at this Upper East Side venue populated with post-collegiate fratties and yuppies in a state of love readiness. Also plays host to zydeco and jam sessions.

Bars, Corner

7B/Vazac's Horseshoe Bar, Corner of 7th St. and Avenue B. This is an old, basic, totally cool bar. You may have the privilege of sitting next to old codgers who were planted there decades before you were born. If you can work up the nerve, ask them to spin a yarn. Of course, they might just tell you to get lost.

Corner Bistro, 331 W. 4th St., 242-9502. This West Village haunt is guaranteed to contain plenty of well-groomed, over-educated slackers in search of diversion.

Old Town Bar, 45 E. 18th St. (Broadway and Park Ave. South), 529-6732. This Gramercy perennial gives you the feeling of being in a well-adjusted, comfy neighborhood bar. Note: the exterior of this very bar was featured in the opening credits of David Letterman's pre-NBC show)

Fanelli, 94 Prince St. (Mercer), 226-9412. This Soho oldster is definitively un-Soho—its red-checked tablecloths, staunch pub food and pressed-tin ceiling have everything to do with the best concept of a corner bar. You can also come here in the morning for a spot of tea.

Lakeside Lounge, 162 Avenue B, 529-8463. This corner bar borders on camp—it boasts a decidedly trailer trash feel and attracts low-profile rockers. But they come here to escape the b.s., so don't give them any.

Jim McMullen, 1341 Third Ave., (76th and 77th Sts.), 861-4700. An old-fashioned Irish bar on the Upper East Side, especially targeted by the hard-bitten after-work crowd.

Dublin House, 79th between Amsterdam and Broadway, aka the Harp Bar. Has your standard bar in the front room, and a room out the back with some booths in it. Cheap beer, but loud music at times.

Bars, Jazz

The Blue Note, 131 W. 3rd St., 475-8592. Feel the history. Attracts the biggest names in jazz. Quite expensive, from door charge to drinks, but the sound system and quality of genius in near incomparable. Dinner, too.

Iridium, 44 W. 63rd St. (Broadway & Columbus), 582-2121. If this surreal space makes you feel like you took a big bite of Alice in Wonderland's mushroom, the jazz will take you over the edge completely.

The Village Vanguard, 178 Seventh Ave. South (11th St.), 255-4037. This legendary, often packed house will make you feel like you're in a noirish "50s time zone. Call ahead for " quieter" nights.

Sweet Basil, 88 Seventh Ave. South (between Grove and Bleecker Sts.), 242-1785. Top names, fine stylings, and well-attended Sunday brunch.

Arthur's Tavern, 57 Grove St. (Seventh Ave. South), 675-6879. Here's the place to take in great jazz for free-just consider the overpriced drinks the price of your admission. Mixed crowd.

Bars, Global Music

S.O.B.'s (The Global Lounge), 204 Varick St. (at Houston), 243-4940. This West Village/West Soho space hosts everyone from Tito Puente to Brazilian sirens, and everything in between.

Latin Quarter, 2551 Broadway (96th St.), 864-7600. Get down with salsa.

Bars, Country

If you're a misplaced cowboy hoofing around in those eponymous boots, there are a few places where you might pretend you're back in the Lone Star State. However, NYC hasn't exactly thrilled to line dancing like other, well, more impressionable cities have.

Rodeo Bar & Grill, 375 Third Ave. (27th St.) 683-6500

Denim & Diamonds, 511 Lexington Ave., 371-1600

Bonus: **Joe's Bar** on 6th St. between A and B isn't a country bar per se, but its jukebox has enough country tunes to choke a hoss.

BEACHES

Coney Island (take the B, D, F, or N to Brooklyn Terminus). Still home to the Cyclone and a sepia-toned amusement park, it also has a lifeguard-protected beach filled with Brooklynites catching rays. Take the F or D trains to W. 8th St.

Brighton Beaches (D train), (718) 946-1350. Open Memorial Day through Labor Day, from 10 a.m. to 6 p.m. "Little Odessa by the Sea" features markets, cheap cafes and lifeguard-protected beach.

Jones Beach, Hempstead, Long Island, accessible by the Long Island Railroad, (718) 217-5477. Serious sand and super-waves draw surfers and locals alike.

Fire Island, a gorgeous stretch of beach that runs parallel to Long Island. Call LIRR train information (718) 217-5477 for information on their transportation package, which includes the ferry over there. Cherry Grove and the Pines are destinations for urban gays and lesbians happy to resurface there in bathing suits.

Long Beach. Take the LIRR Long Beach branch to its terminus. In just under an hour, you can be in the charming beach community which happens to be Billy Crystal's hometown. He's often spotted here getting bagels with his folks.

BOOKSTORES

Barnes & Noble Superstores, 2289 Broadway, 362-8835; 105 Fifth Ave., 807-0099; E. 54th (at Third Ave.), 750-8033. This last one has become the new hot spot for singles on the weekend, with the addition of the cafe and couches all over the store. These mega-stores offer a vast selection, rad discounts, popular reading series and house cafes where you can gear up on the caffeine and pastry while perusing a potential acquisition. Watch the sticky fingers!

Verso Books, 128 Eighth Ave. (16th St.), 620-3141. Thorough array of intellectual and hip tomes and cutting-edge fiction.

A Different Light, 151 W. 19th St., 989-4850. This gay and lesbian-themed bookstore has an extensive array of related books, and hosts readings for such luminaries as Dorothy Allison.

The Strand, 832 Broadway (12th St.), 473-1452. New York fixture Fran Lebowitz's haunt, and frequented by many other less quoted as well, due to the variety, new and used, of discounted books of every type and stripe.

Shakespeare and Co., 2259 Broadway (between 80 and 81st Sts.) and 716 Broadway (Washington Place), 529-1330. Regrettably, the uptown location—which has a great bargain basement, and sidewalk sale tables in the warm months—is scheduled to close in the Fall of '96, victim to the two Barnes & Noble megastores that have opened recently a few blocks to both north and south. The downtown location remains, though, featuring the usual suspects, and the more arcane. This is a good spot to get hooked up with heavy philosophy, as well as some poetry, film and art books.

Oscar Wilde Memorial Book Shop, 15 Christopher St., 255-8097. If Wilde's ghost isn't chilling in Paris' Cemetiere Pere Lachaise, he's almost certainly here.

Biblio's Bookstore & Cafe, 317 Church St. (between Lispenard and Walker Sts.). For well-honed, yet vibrant poetry readings and a fine selection of books.

Housing Works Used Books Cafe, 126 Crosby St., 334-3324. This newish bookstore/cafe is more reminiscent of a baronial library, with its balcony and liberal groupings of handsome furniture. The profits from these used books, furniture (often including a Naked Lunch-y typewriter or two), and sundry other offerings all go towards helping homeless Manhattanites regain homes, jobs, and self-confidence.

Corner Bookstore at 93rd Street, 1313 Madison Ave., 831-3554. Ray and Lenny Sherman have run this community-oriented book-store for close to two decades, and have preserved its architectural integrity by maintaining the terrazzo floors, tin ceiling, and extant woodwork. They carry books to interest each member of the family, with an eye toward belles lettres. Cute factoid: Children often come here after school when waiting for their parents to pick them up. The Shermans think that's just great.

New York Bound, 50 Rockefeller Plaza, 245-8503. This bookstore serves as one large reference center for all things Manhattanish, from architecture to art to guide books like this one.

Rizzoli, 31 W. 57th St. (Fifth and Sixth Aves.), 759-2424. Scope out their Soho and World Financial Center locations, too. Dark wood, sonorous music, and coffee table books galore. Don't forget to scope out the sale table.

Other Notables:

Three Lives & Co., 154 W. 10th St., 741-2069

Biography Book Shop, 400 Bleecker St., 807-8655

Coliseum Books, 1771 Broadway (at 57th St.), 757-8381

BREWPUBS

The Microbrew phenomenon has finally reached New York. Maybe we can attribute the sudden interest to medical studies which suggest that consumption of all alcohol—including beer—has marked health benefits. Or, maybe we just have to admit that New Yorkers have been slow to adopt the affinity the rest of the country, and in fact, the world, has for beer. Its never too late, so cheers!

AJ Gordon's Brewing Company, 212 W. 79th St., 579-9777. Serving caribbean-influenced food.

Bayamo, 704 Broadway, 475-5151. Cuban-Chinese restaurant-cum-brewery.

Carnegie Hill Brewing Company, 1600 Third Ave., 369-0808. Casual atmosphere and pub food draw a young crowd.

Chelsea Brewing Company, Pier 59, West St. at 18th St., 336-6440. Microbrewery attached to large restaurant, attached to Chelsea Piers complex.

Commonwealth Brewing Company, 10 Rockefeller Plaza, 333-2269. Steak and seafood restaurant serving British-style beers.

Hansens Times Square Brewery, 160 W. 42nd St., 398-1234. Didn't know Times Square had room to spare but this brewery, restaurant and pretzel bakery has made it home.

Heartland, 35 Union Square W., 645-3400. The Keg-crew enjoys the lagers at this American restaurant/brewery.

Nacho Mama's Brewery, 40-42 Thompson St., 925-8966. English-style ales and a Mexican-influenced menu.

Park Slope Brewing Company, 356 Sixth Ave., Brooklyn, (718) 788-1756. Neighborhood brewpub serving comfort food.

Typhoon Brewery, 22 E. 54th St., 754-9006. First NY brewery to serve Asian food.

Westside Brewing Company, 340 Amsterdam Ave., 721-2161. Pub atmosphere and food. Rowdy at night.

Yorkville Brewery and Tavern, 1359 First Ave., 517-2739. Young crowd packs in for brick-oven pizza and brew.

Zip City Brewing Company, 3 W. 18th St., 366-6333. The 1897 headquarters of the National Temperance Society, now serves brews galore.

CIGAR SHOPS

Nat Sherman, 500 Fifth Ave., 764-5000. This serious, deluxe smoke shop is more of an epicure's parlor, with fancy humidors and other puffing notions.

Davidoff of Geneva, Inc., 535 Madison Ave., 751-9060. Swanky, baby.

JR Tobacco, 11 E. 45th St., 983-4160; 219 Broadway, 233-6620. "Lowest Prices on Earth!" Um, not swank. Check this out.

Swank International Inc., 316 Fifth Ave., 594-9691

De La Concha Tobacconist, 1390 Avenue of the Americas (Sixth Ave.), 757-3167. Cigars, cigarettes, pipes, custom tobacco blending.

Barclay-Rex Pipe Shop, 70 E. 42nd St., 692-9680; 7 Maiden Lane, near Broadway. 962-3355. Established in 1910, they're Manhattan's most senior tobacconist.

CHURCHES AND SYNAGOGUES

Cathedral of St. John the Divine, 1047 Amsterdam Ave. (112th St.), 316-7540. The largest cathedral in the world, and truly stunning. Check listings in the paper or call about various events, from operatic singing and many activities during the holiday season.

CIGAR SMOKING YEAR 'ROUND

AHNELL, 117 Prince St. (between Thompson and Sullivan), 254-1260.

LE CIGAR, 151 E. 50th St. (between Lexington and Third Aves.), (212) 980-2877. Above Tatou: dancing, fine champagne, late supper, and cigars for an upscale, mannered audience. Memberships available.

CLUB MACANUDO, 26 E. 63rd St. (between Park and Madison), 752-8200. The latest in the evolution of the cigar phenomenon. For the true aficionado: cigar classes, tastings, and special events. New York magazine has named the club the best in New York, and it's hard to argue with the 500 available-for-lease humidors and the special smoke removal system. The club also offers business services (laptops, fax machines, etc.) and a relaxing, clubby atmosphere.

MONKEY BAR, 60 E. 54th St., 838-2600. Beyond the kitsch of drinks like the Sparkling Monkey and Purple Monkey, a selection of cigars for the old-money, jet-set crowd.

THIRD FLOOR CAFE, 315 5th Ave. (32nd St.), 481-3669. Settle in with a snifter of port and a Davidoff cigar.

FRANK'S RESTAURANT, 85 10 Ave. (5th St.), 243-1349. This meat-packing district institution has a smoking dining room (separated from the main dining room with a glass partition) always packed with carnivores with a penchant for cigars.

GRANVILLE, 40 E. 20th St. Complete with chandeliers, leather armchairs, and private humidors, this restaurant/Lounge exudes clubbiness.

THE GINGERMAN, 11 E. 36th St. This new tavern wants you to smoke—cigars, cigarettes and even pipes. The only caveat: legal substances only please.

O'NIEAL'S GRAND ST., 174 Grand St. (between Center and Mulberry), 941-9119. This former speakeasy's cigar selection is changed bi-monthly. The small dining room is smoker friendly.

CAFE AUBETTE, 119 E. 27th St. between Park and Lexington, 686-5500. Storefront cafe by day transforms a prohibition speak easy into a cigar bar and lounge by night.

Church of the Heavenly Rest, 2 E. 90th St. (Fifth Ave.), 289-3400.
A neighborhood family church. A private school occupies part of
the property. They often have concerts on the weekends.

St. Malacy's Church, 239 W. 49th St., 489-1340. Located in the
heart of the theater district, many actors attend mass here.

Grace Church, 802 Broadway (10th St.), 254-2000. A beautiful
gothic church for Episcopalians. There are even tours, which
are held Sundays at 12:15 p.m.

Dignity New York, 218 W. 11th St., 627-6488. Offers spiritual
support to lesbian, gay and bisexual Catholics. Also operates
an AIDS ministry.

Synagogues

Lincoln Square Synagogue, 200 Amsterdam Ave. (at 69th St.),
874-6100. Popular beginner's service.

B'Nai Jesharun, 270 W. 86th St., 787-7600. Held in a church, this
synagogue holds what has been described as "moving, unusual and
uplifting" services. It's not out of the ordinary for people to get up
and dance. Very warm and embracing atmosphere.

Temple Emanu-el, 1 E. 65th St., 744-1400. World's largest reform
temple. 76,000 pipes in the organ! There are over 2,000 members.
Lectures, organ recitals, tours and many other activities are offered.

Wall Street Synagogue, 7 Beekman St., 227-7543, 227-7800.
An orthodox temple down in the financial district. Lunch hour
services are held.

Congregation Beth Simchat Torah, 57 Bethune St., 929-9498.
A Reform synagogue for lesbians and gays. There's a special
Yom Kippur service at the Jacob Javits Center—the room
overlooks sunset on the Hudson river.

Central Synagogue, 652 Lexington Ave., 838-5122. New York's
oldest Jewish house of worship.

CLUBS
Clubs, country music

Denim & Diamonds, 511 Lexington Ave., 371-1600

Rodeo Bar, 375 Third Ave. (at 27th St.), 683-1600

Joe's Bar, 520 E. 6th St., 473-9093. This east village classic derives its country chops from its jukebox. Anyone who wanders in off the street and wants to pay for some tunes will be confronted with a jukebox filled with all those country singers, as well as crossover acts like Elvis and Patsy Cline. However, the patrons are just regular folk, with nary a ten-gallon hat among them.

Clubs, Dance

Disclaimer: club buzzes are so evanescent here that you might want to check out *Paper Magazine* for the latest word, but here are some tried-and-trues:

Webster Hall, 125 E. 11th St., 353-1600. Massive, with different kinds of music on each of the multiple dance floors. Even Bill Clinton has tapped a toe here.

Jackie 60, 315 Park Ave. South, 677-6060. A drag-queen heavy, dance-centric and 'tude throwing free-for-all.

Irving Plaza, 17 Irving Place, 777-6800. This club/music venue has different parties or concerts every night. Check local listings for the scoop.

Tunnel, 220 12th Ave., 695-7292. This club has managed to survive the 80s, barreling into the 90s with multi-levels, groove-heavy djs, and an unremittingly loyal following.

COFFEEHOUSES

Limbo, 47 Avenue A (3rd and 4th Sts.), 477-5271. This sherbety, retro joint encourages relaxation with a wide array of mags, from the erudite to the "guilty pleasure" categories. It also serves up yummy, fussy sandwiches, oversized pastries, and about 50 ways to get wired.

Espresso Madison, 33 E. 68th St., 988-7444. Deemed New York Magazine's best source for espresso, 1996.

News Bar, 150 E. 58th St. (Lexington and Third), 486-8862. 969 Third Ave. (57th & 58th Sts.), 319-0830; 2 W. 19th St. (Fifth Ave.), 255-3996; 107 University Place (12th and 13th Sts.), 260-4192; 366 W. Broadway (Broome St.), 343-0053. This is a media junkie's paradise. 450 periodicals line the walls, and three television sets relay CNN's latest message. Coffee and snacks are the perfect accompaniment to your information overload.

alt.coffee, 137 Avenue A. 529-2233. Technophobes, fear not. This
roomy, down to earth place resembles an off-campus housing living
room more than a weird cyber pod. Salvaged, seventies Louis
Quinze couches manage to be both lumpy and comfy, tables allow
for discourse ranging from the party last night to Roland Barthes,
and the baked grub is tasty. Sure, there are computers around, but
they're very personal.

Anna's, 131 Avenue A, 979-2662. This very welcome addition to
Avenue A (read: not another knee-jerkily "hip" bar) is an incredibly
sweet bakery and cafe. It's tiny, clean, and sells freshly baked bread
and other baked goods along with coffee and tea. Perfect site for a
leisurely reading of the Sunday Times.

Starbucks, call 477-7776 for nearest location. Although it has raised
the ire of the same folks who don't like Barnes & Noble superstores,
Williams Sonoma and Eddie Bauer in Soho, Starbucks is filled with
people who only sometimes look sheepish. In the summer months,
their Frappuccino (frozen, shake-like cappucccino) is the ultimate
in cryogenic summer caffeination, and has achieved a cult-like
status formerly akin only to Cherry 7-Up in 1987.

Caffe Reggio, 119 MacDougal St., 475-9557. Baroque furniture,
bruschetta, well-pulled espresso, and understated rococo atmo.

CONCERTS

An indispensable source for finding out when your favorite band is
coming to town is the listings section of local weekly newspapers and
mags like *NY Press, The Village Voice,* and *Time Out New York.*

Ticketmaster Hotline, 307-7171

The Beacon, 2124 Broadway (76th St.), 496-7070. Old-world theater, complete with red velvet curtains and swooping mezzanines.

Madison Square Garden, Seventh Ave. (between W. 31st and
33rd), 465-6741.

Irving Plaza, 17 Irving Place, 777-6800

Summerstage: Every summer, Central Park's Rumsey Playfield
(at 72nd St. and East Dr.) plays host to a FREE array of dance,
opera, alterna-rock, spoken word, and global music. Schedules
are distributed in most weekly newspapers at the beginning of
the season, or call 360-2777 if you miss it.

New York Philharmonic in Central Park, 875-5709

The Metropolitan Opera in Central Park, 362-6000

Charlie Parker Jazz Festival in Tompkins Square Park, takes place every summer in August, right across from Parker's former residence on Avenue B. Call 408-0226 for the exact date.

Classical

Half-price concerts, opera, and dance events, at Bryant Park, (40th to 42nd St., between Fifth and Sixth Aves.) Take advantage of the TKTS booth selling tickets. Call 382-2323 for hours on the day of the show.

Bargemusic, at the Fulton Ferry Landing, Brooklyn (just south of the Brooklyn Bridge). (718) 624-2083. $15 students, $20 seniors, $23

CYBER CAFES

Whether it's via information superhighways or alleyways, New Yorkers are into being on-line. We dig web sites and chat groups. We want a place to be social and to get our internet fix. And natch, we love to do so while munching on a bagel, sipping a cappuccino, and ogling other cute gearheads. Here are a few spots where you can be on-line but not anti-social.

@ CAFE, 12 ST. MARK'S PLACE, 979-5439. Fifteen terminals, decent food and a fully stocked bar make this cafe conducive to two types of interaction: interpersonal and internet.

ALT.COFFEE, 139 Avenue A, 529-2233. Five terminals connected via T1 and a great cup o' java.

CYBER CAFE, 273-A Lafayette St., 334-5140. The menu of light fare and pastries is the perfect complement to a hot and heavy surfin' session on one of the eight Pcs at this hip SoHo cafe.

INTERNET CAFE, 82 E. Third St., 614-0747. The first cyber cafe in New York is still ticking with four PCs and 56K ethernet access. Light lunch fare and training available.

VOID, 16 Mercer St., 941-6492. Dark groovy bar, lit mostly by candles, with only one terminal and oversized screen displaying Web sites or trancy, ambient videos.

NILOUFAR MOTAMED

others. Absorb the trilling of string instruments on board this 50-odd year old boat, which gives two shows a week, so reserve in advance.

The Juilliard School, 60 Lincoln Center Plaza (Broadway and 65th St.), 769-7406. Tickets for majority of concerts are free, $15 maximum. Juilliard sponsors about 550 concerts throughout the school year, and the price and quality can't be beat.

New York Philharmonic, at Avery Fisher Hall, Lincoln Center, Broadway and 64th St., 875-5030. Tickets $6-$60. The country's oldest such organization carries on in full force. Check out their July summer season, featuring lighter classics.

Carnegie Hall, 881 7th Ave. (57th St.), 247-7800. This tried-and-true venue offers dazzling acoustics in palatial environs.

<u>Other Options:</u>

Symphony Space, 2537 Broadway, 864-5400

Winter Garden of the World Financial Center, in Battery Park City, near the World Trade Center. 945-0505. Free concerts given by the New York Philharmonic, the Metropolitan opera, and the New York City Ballet. Call for dates and times.

DANCE COMPANIES

American Ballet Theater, Metropolitan Opera House, Lincoln Center, Broadway and 64th St., 362-6000. Everything from Twyla Tharp to Swan Lake.

The Joyce Theatre, 175 Eighth Ave., 242-0800. This Chelsea spot plays host to everything from the Eliot Feld Ballet to Native American ceremonial dance.

City Center, 131 W. 55th St. (Sixth and Seventh Aves.), 581-7907. This Moorish palace has regular performances by the companies of Merce Cunningham, Martha Graham, and Alvin Ailey American Dance Theater.

New York City Ballet, at The New York State Theater, Lincoln Center, Broadway and 64th St. 870-5570. The NYCB is widely regarded as the world's best company, and faithfully performs the many works of George Balanchine and Jerome Robbins.

<u>Others of Note:</u>

Danspace, St. Marks-in-the-Bowery Church, Second Ave. (E. 10th), 674-6377

Paul Taylor Dance Foundation, 552 Broadway, 431-5562

Merce Cunningham Dance Company, 55 Bethune St., 255-8240

DELIS, BEST JEWISH

2nd Avenue Deli, 156 Second Ave. (10th St.), 677-0606 (kosher)
Come for the matzoh ball soup. Stay for the noodle pudding.

Katz's Deli, 205 E. Houston St., 254-2246. (not kosher) Almost as
much as an institution as what Meg Ryan faked here famously in
When Harry Met Sally. "I'll have what she's having" ring a bell?

Russ & Daughters, 179 E. Houston, 475-4880. If in this delightfully named bagelry and hors d'ouvre shop, we recommend the
scallion tofu cream cheese. They also sell dried pineapple rings
by the pound.

Yonah Shimmel's Knishes, 137 E. Houston, 477-2858. Knishes
so genuine, they don't even resemble the ones sold in carts.

B & H Dairy, 127 Second Ave., 505-8056. Terribly cheap and delicious soup and challah bread, but skip the weird carrot cake.

Carnegie Delicatessen and Restaurant, 854 Seventh Ave. (at
55th St.), 757-2245. The best pastrami and corned beef in town
is served here, on gigantic sandwiches that give even ravenous
teenaged boys pause.

Stage Deli, 834 Seventh Ave. (53rd and 54th Sts.), 245-7850. What
is rumored to be New York's oldest continually run deli. 36 specialty sandwiches named after celebrities (who have actually
created them) are perfect for sharing, although you still may need
a doggy bag.

Kaplan's at the Delmonico, 59 E. 59th St. (Madison and Park Aves.),
755-5959. Another big sandwich source, this time in Midtown.

Fine & Schapiro, 138 W. 72nd St. (Broadway and Columbus
Ave.), 877-2874. This reliable kosher deli on the Upper W. Side
serves up standards with panache.

EDUCATION, CONTINUING

Cooper Union for the Advancement of Science and Art,
51 Astor Place, 353-4195

New York University, 50 W. 4th St., 998-1212

The New School for Social Research, 66 W. 12th St., 229-5690

CHEAP AND INVENTIVE NY DATES

In love and in need of a creative yet inexpensive N.Y. outing? Here are a few to try.

Take the F train to CONEY ISLAND for the day. Get whiplash on the Cyclone (good excuse to bury your face in your dates neck), mug it up in the photo booth, kiss at the top of the ferris wheel, and stroll on the boardwalk.

In the summer months, take advantage of the super-romantic BRYANT PARK OUTDOOR FILM SERIES, on 42nd St. between 5th and 6th Aves. every Monday at sundown. Check local listings for that week's movie, check the weather channel to make sure it won't rain, and get there close to 6 p.m. for a boffo position on the lawn. Make sure to bring a blanket some pillows, and a picnic basket or six-pack. Despite limited advertising, crowds are typically large.

Take the half-hour 50-CENT FERRY from Manhattan to Staten Island and back again, at night. The skyline's dreamy effect and that nautical vibe will give you both the warm fuzzies.

Catch the HAPPY HOUR (5:30-7:30 p.m.) free buffet at SFUZZI restaurant (58 West 65th St. between Columbus Ave. and Central Park West, 873-3700). Sfuzzi, to the uninitiated, is one fine Italian restaurant. That they give away pizza, pasta and stromboli is some kind of wonderful. You'll just have to spring for a few drinks, but dinner's on them.

Having a picnic at SHEEP'S MEADOW in the springtime in Central Park.

Gallery hopping in SOHO.

SUMMERSTAGE: Every summer, the Rumsey Playfield (72nd St. and East Dr.) plays host to a FREE array of dance, opera, alterna-rock, spoken word, and global music. Schedules are distributed in most weekly newspapers at the beginning of the season, or call 360-2777 if you miss it.

SHAKESPEARE IN THE PARK: Every summer, the Joseph Papp Shakespeare Festival takes place at the Delacorte Shakespeare Theatre (mid-park, at 79th St.) It's free! Call 861-7277 for details.

MODEL BOAT POND: Conservatory Water, 74th St. and Fifth Ave.

CENTRAL PARK ZOO/WILDLIFE CONSERVATION CENTER: (Fifth Ave. and 64th St.) 439-6500. Bring the little ones to this global collection of animals. Behind bars, unlike the ones on you see on the subway.

Columbia University, W. 116 & Broadway, 854-3774

The Learning Annex, 116 E. 85th St., 570-6500

New York Open Center, 83 Spring St., 219-2527

School of Visual Arts, 209 E. 23rd St., 1-800-319-4321 (x.34)

FISHING

The Harlem Meer, in Central Park at 106th St., (Meer is Dutch for "lake") was recently restored to glory. The pond is stocked with fish, and poles are available at the Charles A. Dana Discovery Center, which sits on the north shore.

If you are interested in chartering a boat for a fishing party, you'll probably end up on **Long Island,** as the only things coming out of the Hudson and East Rivers are whacked mafioso and toxic fish. Try the following:

Captain Lou's Fleet in Freeport, Long Island, specializing in bay fishing and cruises. (516) 766-5716

Marie III Charters, Freeport-Point Lookout. Half/Full day **Long Island fishing cruises,** specializing in trips off the beaten track. (516) 481-2841

FITNESS CLUBS

Rates change frequently! But expect to pay anywhere from $60 to $150 a month, plus an initiation fee. Always ask about specials and corporate discounts, as well as hours of operation if you like to work out particularly early or late.

Equinox, 19th and Broadway, 780-9300; Amsterdam between 76 and 77th Sts., 721-4200; Broadway between 91 and 92nd Sts., 799-1818. There's a $395 initiation fee—which cashes in for training, stretching, t-shirts, guest passes, fitness evaluation and so on. Then, you can either pay $105 monthly or $1050 all at once for one year.

Reebok Sports Club New York, 167 Columbus Ave. (at 67th St.), 362-6800. Ultra deluxe, ultra chic, with prices to match ($1000 initiation fee plus $140/month). Kevin Bacon and Kyra Sedgwick sightings abound. It has everything though, from a full size basketball court to a pool with underwater music. Plus the celebrities to match.

New York Sports Clubs. They have the most locations throughout

LEAVING MANHATTAN:
GREAT DAYTRIPS

Here are our picks for the must-do daytrips from the Big Apple.

PATSY'S PIZZA, 19 Fulton St., Brooklyn, (718) 858-4300. This is pizza. Under the Brooklyn Bridge, and Frank Sinatra's autographed photos everywhere.

PLANET THAILAND, 184 Bedford Ave., Brooklyn, (718) 599-5758. Best Thai in New York. And New York Press agrees.

LOEHMANN'S, 5740 Broadway at 236th St., Riverdale, (718) 543-6420. Take the Loehmann's bus from 62nd St. and Columbus for the ultimate discount shopping experience. Buses on Saturdays at 9, 12, and 3 p.m., and on Sundays at 10 and 1 p.m..

THE CLOISTERS, Fort Tryon Park, (212) 923-3700. A Metropolitan Museum of Art branch located around 190th St. This replica of a medieval monastery will transport back to more simple times. The gardens are splendid.

THE WESTCHESTER MALL, 125 Westchester Ave., White Plains, (914) 683-8600. Flanked by Neiman Marcus and Nordstrom's, with Saks and Bloomingdale's just a hop skip away, if you can't find it here...

THE SHORT HILLS MALL, Short Hills, New Jersey, (201) 376-7692. Luxury shopping center with over 200 retail shops and the benefit of New Jersey's low sales tax.

IKEA, Elizabeth, New Jersey, (908) 289-4488. For the ultimate in one-stop Skandinavian home shopping experience.

WOODBURY COMMONS, Route 32, Central Valley, NY, (914) 928-8082. Factory outlet schmorgasbord-Barneys, Calvin Klein, Donna Karan and Kenneth Cole etc.

BROOKLYN ACADEMY OF MUSIC, 30 Lafayette St., Brooklyn, (718) 636-4100. Home of the avant-garde, The Next Wave Festival always draws crowds away from the Manhattan venues.

NEW YORK BOTANICAL GARDEN, 100th St. and Southern Boulevard, the Bronx, (718) 817-8705. This 250-acre gem is renowned for its horticultural research center and provides the perfect arboreal respite from the city.

STEW LEONARD'S, 100 Wesport Ave., Norwalk, Connecticut, (203) 847-7213. Take the kids for an educational and yummy field trip to this produce wonderland.

NILOUFAR MOTAMED

Getting In & Out of New York City

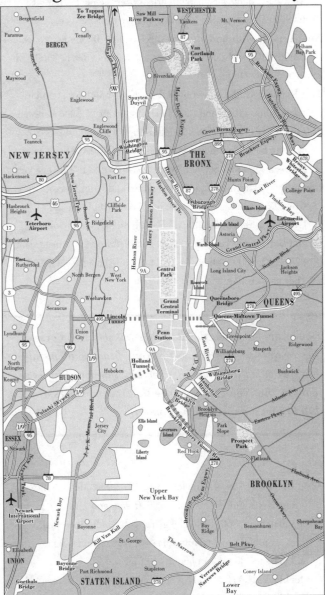

New York, with 16 in Manhattan alone. Some locations have squash and tennis. Call 1-800-796-NYSC for locations and info. They don't quote membership prices over the phone, but give them a call to see what kind of deal they can offer you.

New York Health and Racquet, 6 locations in Manhattan, call 1-800-HRC-BEST for info. One-time initiation fee of $500 and then $95/month thereafter.

The Vertical Club, owned by Bally's. Known to have great lap pools, plus squash and tennis facilities. 139 W. 32nd between 6th and 7th, 465-1750; 335 Madison at 43rd St., 983-5320; 350 W. 50th between 8th and 9th Aves., 265-9400; 330 E. 61st between First and Second Aves., 355-5100; $1199 for one year.

Crunch, 404 Lafayette St. (between Third and Astor Place), 614-0120; 152 Christopher St. between Washington and Greenwich Sts., 366-3725; 54 E. 13th St. between Broadway and University Place, 475-2018; 162 W. 83rd St. at Amsterdam, 875-1902; $899 for the year. Call to inquire about special deals! They happen a lot.

INSIDER TIP: *Most healthcare programs will reimburse you for at least half the cost of your fitness club membership, provided that you go a certain number of times a year (or that you can convince the staff members at the club to sign a paper saying you do).*

The Y's:

92nd Street Y, 1395 Lexington Ave., 427-6000. Membership Rates: Men's Full Membership: $960 Women's Full Membership: $860. Pool, two gyms, volleyball, basketball, track, aerobics, and exercise classes, yoga, steam, sauna, and massage, towel and laundry service.

Vanderbilt YMCA, 224 E. 47th St., 755-2410. Men & Women's Membership: $660. Two pools (one for lap, one for lessons), Nautilus, free weights, karate, yoga, StairMaster, Lifecycles, NordicTrack, aerobic and exercise classes, steam, sauna, and massage.

Westside YMCA, 5 W. 63rd St., 787-4400. Men & Women's
   Membership: $660. Silex, Nautilus, free weights, aerobics
   classes, pool, indoor track, handball, racquet ball, sauna,
   massage, Stair Master, and bikes.

YMCA, 610 Lexington Ave., 755-4500. Men & Women's
   Membership: $50, but you must pay extra for use of the
   facilities. Fitness room, pool, weight rooms, StairMaster,
   bikes, treadmills, indoor track, steam and sauna.

McBurney YMCA, 215 W. 23rd St., 741-9210. Men & Women's
   Membership: $663 per year, includes classes. StairMaster,
   treadmills, Universal equipment, indoor pool, indoor track,
   paddle ball courts, basketball, sauna, steam and massage.

INSIDER TIP: *Getting tickets for LIVE TV SHOWS is often as
difficult as holding out your hand and taking them from
the guys passing them out on the street—for pilots, test
screenings, and less popular shows. For the hotter tickets,
you often have to book weeks or months in advance by
sending in a letter.*

*For SATURDAY NIGHT LIVE, tickets for the whole season are
allocated in August, via a lottery held for postcards
received only in August at NBC, 30 Rockefeller Plaza,
New York NY 10020.*

For information on other shows call:
*DAVE (Letterman) 975-5853; MONTEL 989-8880; RICKI 889-
6767; ROLONDA 650-2077; SALLY 582-1722; GERALDO 265-8520;
CONAN 664-3055; MAURY 989-3622; RUSH 397-7367; REGIS AND
KATHIE LEE 465-3054. Some shows also have standby tickets
to fill the seats of no-shows; for Letterman, for example,
the line begins forming early in the morning for the 5 p.m.
taping, and there's no guarantee of getting in.*

City-Funded Recreational Centers

Asser Levy recreational Center, FDR Dr. at 23rd St., 447-2020.
   Membership: An unbelievable $25/year. Indoor/outdoor pools,

Universal and free weights, standard gym equipment. Pay by the aerobics class.

Carmine Street Pool, 3 Clarkson St., 397-3107

East 54th Street Recreational Center, 348 E. 54th St., 397-3154

FREE STUFF TO DO

Limbo Cafe, 47 Avenue A (3rd and 4th Sts.), 477-5271. Pick up the current readings schedule at Limbo, or call. Past readings have featured Jay McInerney, Stephanie Grant, and Elizabeth Wurtzel.

Kid Stuff

American Museum of Natural History, Central Park West at 79th St., 769-5100. For more Jurassic Park style fun, make sure to visit the two new dinosaur displays. On Fridays and Saturdays, the admission price includes an IMAX double-feature.

Central Park Children's Zoo and Carousel, 59th St. and Fifth Ave. Visit the neurotic polar bear and company and stop by the beautifully refurbished 1903 carousel.

Children's Garden Program at the Brooklyn Botanic Garden, 1000 Washington Ave., (718) 622-4433 ext. 216/276, lets your kids know where vegetables actually come from (not necessarily shrink-wrapped from the produce section).

Children's Museum of Manhattan, 212 W. 83rd St., 721-1234, Admission $5. This is the cream of the technological/interactive crop——your kids won't want to leave.

Forbes Magazine Galleries, 62 50th Ave. (12th St.), 620-2200. Extensive Faberge egg, toy boat and toy soldier collection.

Hayden Planetarium, 81st St. (Central Park West), 769-5100, Laser and sky shows always delight the tots. Both informative and fun. Special kids shows on Saturday mornings.

Intrepid Sea-Air-Space Museum, Intrepid Plaza, 245-2533. At the end of May, during Fleet Week, when 10,000 Navy and Coast Guard personnel are on shore leave, ships can be visited free and from 1 p.m.-4 p.m., there will be special exhibitions by the Marines.

Museum of Television and Radio, 25 W. 52nd St., 621-6600. Watch or listen to Uncle Milty, JFK, Lucy or Martin Luther King Jr. at your own private console.

Sony Wonder Technology Lab, 550 Madison Ave., 833-8100.
An interactive science and technology exhibition which lets kids edit music videos and design video games.

MOVIES

Movie hotline number:

777-FILM

Movie theater with the best art films:

Angelika, on 18 W. Houston and Mercer, 995-2000

The Film Forum, on Houston and Varick, 727-8110

Lincoln Plaza, on Broadway between 62nd and 63rd, 757-2280

Movie theater with the best screen to see an action flick:

Ziegfield, on 54th between 6th and 7th. Legendary.

Movie theaters to see classics on"

Film Forum, 209 W. Houston St., 727-8110

Bryant Park Film Festival, Sixth Ave. at 42nd St., 512-5700

Walter Reade Theater, Lincoln Center and W. 65th St., 875-5600.

American Museum of the Moving Image, 35th Ave. (36th St.), Astoria, Queens, (718) 784-4520. Take the R train to Steinway St.

American Museum of Natural History, Central Park West at 79th St., 769-5100

Anthology Film Archives, 32 Second Ave. (2nd St.), 505-5181

Casa La Femme, 150 Wooster St. (between Houston and Prince), 505-0005

Cinema Village, 22 E. 12th St. (between Fifth Ave. and University Place), 924-3363

A Different Light Bookstore, 151 W. 19th St. (between Sixth and Seventh Aves.), 989-4850

French Institute, 55 E. 59th St., 355-6160

Lighthouse Cinema, 116 Suffolk St. (between Rivington and Delancey), 979-7571

Museum of Modern Art, 11 W. 53rd St. (Fifth and Sixth Aves.), 708-9400

MUSEUMS

The Metropolitan Museum of Art, Fifth Ave. at 82nd St., 570-3753. This grand neoclassical behemoth has both an imposing permanent collection as well as exciting temporary exhibits. Don't miss the Egyptian collection.

The Frick Collection, 1 E. 70th St., 288-0700. Formerly Henry Clay Frick's domicile, this mansion is now merely home to a large, mostly European Renaissance art collection, featuring Fragonard. Note the period furnishings.

The Cooper-Hewitt Museum, 2 E. 91st St., 860-6868. The Smithsonian Institution's National Museum of Design, formerly Andrew Carnegie's home. This museum now preserves over 30,000 drawings and prints, mostly depicting architecture, ornament, and design.

The Jewish Museum, 1109 Fifth Ave. (92nd St.), 860-1888. Formerly the home of Felix M. Warburg, this museum is devoted to Judaica, and offers changing collections. There is a Sculpture Court, Jewish coins and medals, artifacts, paintings, drawings, and decorative arts.

The Solomon R. Guggenheim Museum, 1071 Fifth Ave., (89th St.), 360-3500. Frank Lloyd Wright's structure is home to over 4,000 pieces of art, from the Impressionist period to the present.

The Whitney Museum of American Art, 945 Madison Ave. (75th St.), 570-3600. Like the Guggenheim, this Marcel Breuer-designed building has a brave, new look to it. Patron and Ur-Trustafarian Gertrude Vanderbilt Whitney was responsible— her interest in things artsy and bohemian led to the funding of this institution. The Whitney's permanent collection is largely composed of 20th Century art.

American Museum of Natural History, W. 65th and Broadway, 769-5000. One of the largest and best museums anywhere for researching and displaying knowledge about the Earth and its life forms. For recorded information, call 769-5100.

Hayden Planetarium of the Museum of Natural History, 81st St. (Central Park West). Hi-tech sky shows are given daily, and get you in touch with your place in the universe. 769-5100.

The Museum of Modern Art, 11 W. 53rd St. (Fifth and Sixth Aves.), 708-9480. If you're tired of the Old Masters, this is the place for you.

MUSIC
Good Local Bands

The best way to get a grip on good local bands is to scan the more youthful weekly publications like *Time Out* and *New York Press.* They both spotlight local bands and have listings detailing the venue, date, and so forth. Additionally, popular band venues like Irving Plaza, Mercury Lounge, Continental, Brownies, and the Knitting Factory usually run an advertisement that lists their schedule of performers for a week or two in advance.

Artist Profiles

David Clement, singer/songwriter. It's a rare thing to be taken somewhere precious by someone standing alone with a guitar on a stage, to follow him or her: leaving inspired by dreamy images that are startling and lucid. David Clement, a 27 year old singer-songwriter, is to be closely watched, for he does just this. His voice is melodic silk, ringing with candid pain that manages to envelop and comfort. He doesn't sing boring love songs, or hide behind average pop. He is a minstrel filling a void and crossing barriers of old-style-gay-activist-folk into an open new field where anything can happen. David Clement performs frequently around downtown Manhattan.

Dorothy Scott, Irish songstress about town. Dorothy is the most humble, beautiful, Irish singer going on these days. I wasn't surprised to learn that both Sinead O'Connor and Carol King had both been so inspired by her that they joined her on stage. Her Celtic roots are sewn into her lyrical imagery and shocking vocal range. I've seen her turn three audiences into pensive and inquisitive mush within seconds.

Funk/Hip Hop/Soul

Groove Collective—This smart bunch grooves most in Giant Step, its spawning ground and home sweet home. Sweet sax and smoooove sensations all around.

Rock

The Authority—a heady blend of funk, rock and latin. Let lead singer Rene Lopez take you there.

Techno/Ambient
Mobius Strip—British invasion redux does Joy Division one better.

Alternative
Cake-Like—The State's very own Kerri Kenny sings lead vocals for this avant-pop, rough-edged, but ultimately gratifying femme trio. Catch them before they're too big for cozy venues like Mercury Lounge and the Cooler.

Country-Tinged
Star City—This winsome, boyish klatch spins tales and tunes, with a certain je ne sais cowboy.

OPERA COMPANIES
The Metropolitan Opera House at Lincoln Center, 362-6000
New York City Opera at New York State Theatre, 870-5570

OUTDOOR CONCERTS
Summerstage, 360-2777. Every summer, the Rumsey Playfield (72nd St. and East Dr.) plays host to a FREE array of dance, opera, alterna-rock, spoken word, and global music.

New York Philharmonic in Central Park, 875-5709

The Metropolitan Opera in Central Park, 362-6000

Charlie Parker Jazz Festival in Tompkins Square Park—takes place every summer in August, right across from Parker's former residence on Avenue B. Call 408-0226 for the exact date.

OUT-OF-TOWN GETAWAYS
Every summer, the **Long Island Rail Road** arranges day and weekend trips to historic and charming parts of Long Island. It's usually a train fare plus a tour or hotel stay. Call (718) 217-5477 for information or a schedule.

Fire Island, a gorgeous stretch of beach that runs parallel to Long Island. Call LIRR train information (718) 217-5477 for information on their transportation package, which includes the ferry over there.

Long Beach—Take the LIRR Long Beach branch to its terminus. In just under an hour, you can be in the charming beach community which happens to be Billy Crystal's hometown. He's often spotted here getting bagels with his folks.

The Hamptons—Expect to spend 3-4 hours stuck in traffic on your way out to a tiny resort community where summer rentals have been known to go for hundreds of thousands of dollars. But hey, you'll be buying your cole slaw next to Sting.

PARKS
Parks for Bike Riding

Central Park, 6.2 mile loop. Closed to traffic on weekday nights after 7:00 p.m. and all weekend, this is one of the most popular routes for bikers (as well as rollerbladers and runners). It winds its way completely around the park and contains some challenging hills. Danger depends upon the number of people out—it really can be mayhem on a sunny spring day.

New Jersey Palisades. For a more challenging ride, head up Riverside Dr. and over the George Washington Bridge and take a right turn into the New Jersey Palisades. Depending on how far you go, round trip is anywhere from 18-30 miles. It's kind of tricky finding your way from Riverside Dr. onto the GW Bridge, so it's best to ask before going.

Races:

Bike New York: The Great Five Boroughs Bike Tour. To register, call 932-0778 and ask for a registration brochure. Entry fees are $16 to $18. May 5.

This marathon of cycling attracts about 30,000 enthusiasts from all over the world every May. A 42-mile ride through the five boroughs begins at Battery Park and finishes at Fort Wadsworth Naval Station on Staten Island, where a gala celebration awaits.

Parks for Picnics

Tompkins Square Park, at 7th St. and Avenue A, on the lawn.
Central Park, Sheep's Meadow.

Parks for Running, Walking, and Rollerblading

The loop in **Central Park** provides the best road with the least amount of traffic, particularly when cars aren't allowed. **Carl Schurz Park** on the upper east side has a decent stretch of pavement alongside the East River, as does **Riverside Park** on the upper west side and **Battery Park** downtown. East River Park has a fine track overlooking the water, and the center often plays field to a heated soccer match.

Check out **The New York Road Runners Club** (9 E. 89th St., 860-4455). Call number for schedule of upcoming events This august running organization has partnered with Central Park to make running safer and less isolated. As the nasty number of park casualties climbs, your only option is to not run alone. The Road Runners Club will pair you up with runners at the same level as you. It also has a multitude of programs for all ages and skill levels.

PIZZA PLACES

It often seems like there's a pizza place on every corner here. And unlike in other cities, if the pizza stinks, the pizza place folds. We New Yorkers hold our pizza makers to a high standard, and they are most often happy to comply. So you can be reasonably sure that any place you go into (not counting a dubious chain) will leave you satisfied, especially if you're used to the weird stuff they call pizza everywhere else in the world. Below are some places especially worth checking out.

Two Boots, 37 Avenue A, 505-2276; 74 Bleecker St., 777-1033. This kid friendly, Cajun-inspired pizza place puts dang near everything on a pie.

John's Pizzeria, on Bleecker St. in the West Village, 243-1680 serves up steadily satisfying pies to the village contingent.

Village East Pizzeria, 180 Avenue C, 477-1926. Cheap, fast, and good.

Sofia Fabulous Pizza, 1022 Madison Ave. (79th St.), 734-2676

Garlic Bob's Pizza Bar, 1325 Third Ave. (76th St.), 772-2627

PLANETARIUMS

Hayden Planetarium, at the Museum of Natural History, 769-5920. Laser and sky shows always delight the tots. Both informative and fun. Special kids shows on Saturday mornings.

RADIO STATIONS

If it's rock and roll you're after, tune into 92.3 KRock, 102.7 WNEW, and 105.1 MIX 105. Alternative fans dig Z100FM, as well as 92.7 WDRE. If you're a news junkie, tune into 1010 WINS, AM.

RESTAURANTS
Restaurants, Diners

Whether you're in the mood for an omelette, mac and cheese or a pastrami sandwich, here are our choices for the best of the greasy spoons.

Aggie's, 146 W. Houston St., 673-8994. Upscale diner with a
   grouchy namesake.

The Bagel, 10 W. 4th St., 255-0106. West Village institution.

Buffa's, 54 Prince St., 226-0211. '70s luncheonette appeal.

Eisenberg's, 174 Fifth Ave., 675-5096. Best tuna fish
   sandwich around.

EJ's Luncheonette, 227 Amsterdam Ave., 873-3444;
   432 Sixth Ave., 473-5555. Blue plate specials and a soda jerk.

Googie's Luncheonette, 1491 Second Ave., 717-1122.
   Upper East Side booth site.

GREAT FOOD, BAD ATTITUDE

In New York putting up with unbelievable "attitude" is often the price one has to pay for a really yummy meal.

MELAMPO AKA "LITTLE SANDWICH SHOP OF HORRORS", 105 Sullivan St., 334-9530 Owner Giuseppe Guilandi has been known to throw people out of his sandwich shop for wanting to alter the ingredients in one of his culinary creations. Lovers of succulent Italian sandwiches should make this stop a must.

SOUP KITCHEN, 259 West 55th St. (between Broadway and 8th Ave.), 757-7730. Soup Man, a.k.a. Soup Nazi (for his strict insistence on proper soup-line procedure), has become a celebrity, thanks to a Seinfeld episode.

AGGIE MARKOWITZ AT AGGIE'S, 146 West Houston St., 673-8994. So many people waited on line for Sunday brunch at Aggie's that Aggie's Too was opened practically next door.

Gotham City Diner, 1562 Second Ave., 570-9334. Splendid
   french toast, beautiful waitresses.

Joe Jr.'s, 482 Sixth Ave., 924-5220; 167 Third Ave., 473-5150.
   Great chili and burgers.

Mayrose, 920 Broadway, 533-3663. Hip Flatiron district diner.

Moonstruck Restaurant East, 449 Third Ave., 449 Third Ave.,
   213-1100. Yummy Greek/American fare.

Odessa, 117 Avenue A, 473-8916. 24/7 Eastern European diner
   known for its $2 breakfast specials and Allen Ginsberg sightings.

Restaurants, Chinese

Bo Ky, 80 Bayard St., 406-2292. This noodle shop in Chinatown
   offers delicious soups in spare, communal surroundings.
   $, cash only.

Jimmy Sung's, 219 E. 44th St., 682-5678. Classic Hunan cuisine
   in a tasteful, elegant environment. $-$$

New York Noodle Town, 28½ Bowery, 349-0923. Skip the gilt
   and head for intensely flavorful fare in a no-frills environment. $

Peking Duck House, 22 Mott St., 227-1810. This restaurant lives
   up to its name by consistently reinventing the humble duck with
   their traditional and inventive recipes.

Tse Yang, 34 E. 51st St., 688-5447. Though on the expensive side,
   its impeccable service, breathtaking decor and delectable dishes
   are wildly lauded. $$$

Jing Fong, 20 Elizabeth St. (Bayard and Canal), 964-5256.
   Famous for its dim sum, and known for its hustle-bustle atmos-
   phere jammed with faithful devotees. $$

Restaurants, for Dates

Moving to New York can be a lonely experience. The best way to
accelerate the adjustment process is to interact with the natives or, to
go on dates. Getting to know someone new is, by definition, awkward.
To ease the first date jitters, it doesn't hurt to be bathed in flattering
soft lighting or enveloped by a soothing ambience, chock full of flowers. Trying to put your best foot forward in what feels like a heavy
metal concert is bound to spell disaster. Here are our picks for a guaranteed winner.

Alison on Dominick, 38 Dominick St., 727-1188

Au Troquet, 328 W. 12th St., 924-3413

Baraonda, 1439 Second Ave., 288-8555

Chez Michallet, 90 Bedford St., 242-8309

Flowers, 21 W. 17th St., 691-8888

Mary's, 42 Bedford St., 741-3387

ONieal's Grand Street, 174 Grand St., 941-9119

Provence, 38 MacDougal St., 477-4460

Sign of the Dove, 1110 Third Ave., 861-8080

The Grange Hall, 50 Commerce St., 924-5246

Restaurants, French

Cettes restaurantes c'est magnifique!

Bouley, 165 Duane St. (near Hudson), 608-3852. Reserve weeks in advance for seating at this consistently white-hot classic French restaurant in Tribeca, presided over by the revered maestro David Bouley. $$$

Chanterelle, 2 Harrison St. (Hudson St.), 966-6960. Husband and wife team Chef David and Karen Waltuck run this tastefully spare restaurant, but the mom-and-pop comparisons end there. Elegant, meticulous French cuisine is often said to be the downtown standard. $$$

L'Ecole, 462 Broadway (Grand St.), 219-3300. This bistro has something that sets it apart from others-its chefs are students at the French Culinary Institute. Let your taste buds benefit from their youthful exuberance. Closed Sundays. $$

Les Halles, 411 Park Ave. South (between 28th and 29th Sts.), 679-4111. This virtual Left Bank-on-Gramercy bistro is prized for its faithful renderings of such French stalwarts as onion soup, steak frites, and creme caramel. $$

Lutece, 249 E. 50th St., 752-2225. The name summons up an apogee of luxe French cuisine in Manhattan. Chef Eberhard Muller carries on eminence grise Andre Soltner's legacy, on a light note, with thrilling results. $$$

Jo Jo, 160 E. 64th St. (Lexington and Third Aves.), 223-5656. Vong's Jean-Georges Vongerichten does the French thing at this charming Upper East Side townhouse, and serves up smashingly light and transporting French cuisine. You won't break the bank by indulging in their $25 prix fixe lunch. $$$

La Lunchonette, 130 Tenth Ave., 675-0342. Known not only for its succulent bistro fare but for its fetching waitstaff as well.$$

Restaurants, Indian

Baluchi's, 193 Spring St. (between Thompson and Sullivan), 226-2828. Also, 1565 Second Ave., near 81st St., 288-4810. If you want your Indian food served Soho-style, with the requisite chichi trappings (and why not?), stop here and drink in the import-heavy surroundings along with your lassi. $$

Salaam Bombay, 317 Greenwich St., 226-9400. If you've tired of the Little India vibe, venture south to Tribeca, where this posh outpost of Indian cuisine awaits. Marble floors, a canopy above each table, a dance floor and a dizzying array of fine dishes (lots of veggie ones, too). $$

Dawat, 210 E. 58th St., 355-7555. The tandoori is cooked before your eyes at this upper east midtown outpost of Indian delights. $$

Panna, 330 E. 6th St., 475-9274. Right smack in the middle of 6th St.'s Little India, this oddballish-decorated gem serves up toothsome Indian standards at a terrifically low price. $

Mitali, 334 E. 6th St., 533-2508. On 6th St., Mitali is known as the Indian restaurant that Indian people go to. Need I say more? $$

Restaurants, Italian

Amici Miei, 475 W. Broadway, at Houston. 533-1933. Haute Soho Italian fare, downtown crowd, and wood-burning pizza oven make this restaurant appealing. $$

Diva, 341 W. Broadway (near Broome St.), 941-9024. Iron candelabra and blood-red walls set a gothic tone in this hip Soho eatery. A must: the lobster-stuffed black ravioli. $$

Asti, 13 E. 12th St., 741-9105. New York does have everything, including a 70-year-old Italian restaurant with opera-singing waiters. Menu features seafood fra diavalo, Black Angus steak, and Maine lobsters. $$-$$$

Ci Vediamo, 85 Avenue A (between 5th & 6th Sts.), 995-5300. This charming little underground eatery has a perfect mixture of attentive, unobtrusive service, uncomplicated, yet tasty fare, whimsical decor, and low prices. Plus, you get a free glass of port with your check. $

Il Bagatto, 192 E. 2nd St. (between A & B), 228-0977. Another smart East Village newcomer, combining atmosphere, economy, and imported diners from other neighborhoods.

Campagna, 24 E. 21st St., 460-0900. This trattoria is known for being a Media Corps magnet, and it's no surprise, as the fare is highly satisfying and the location (Midtown East) is central. Offerings include rabbit in polenta, gnocchi with wild mushrooms and truffle oil, and grilled tuna with beets. $$$

Restaurants, Japanese

Nobu, 105 Hudson St., 219-0500. The apex in Japanese cuisine, Tribeca's Nobu is elegant, pricey, and dispenses delectable sushi, sashimi, and other delicacies. $$$

Jo-An Japanese, 2707 Broadway (103rd and 104th Sts.), 678-2103. Classic, fresh Japanese fare in a comfy Upper West Side setting. $$

Fujiyama Mama, 467 Columbus Ave. (82nd and 83rd Sts.), 769-1144. This theme park of a Japanese restaurant is perfect for raucous parties and rambunctious chopsticks, although admittedly not very Zen. Draws a youthful crowd, uncowed by the blaring tunes and drawn by the hip vibe. $$

Takahachi, 85 Avenue A (5th and 6th Sts.), 505-6524. This super cheapie has offerings that truly shine, in a blond-wood East Village nook that would be serene if it weren't so packed with loyal regulars and newly initiated devotees. The tofu salad is a perfect beginning to whatever main course you choose. $-$$

Sushisay, 38 E. 51st St. (Madison and Park Aves.), 755-1780. This Zagats-laureled sushi autocrat is both calm and famously good. Do make a reservation days in advance, though. $$$

Restaurants, Unique

Melampo, 105 Sullivan St., 334 -9530. Melampo is famous for its fancy, haute sandwiches and attitude.

Serendipity 3, 225 E. 60th St. (2nd and 3rd Aves.), 838-3531. Just a stone's throw from Bloomingdales. The toy-store inspired motif and dreamy sundaes make this a treat for all ages.

Global 33, 93 Second Ave. (5th and 6th Sts.), 477-8427. The name
refers to the '50s airport lounge decor—low ceilings, bookoo
formica, prefab furniture and padded walls. The food (mediter-
ranean tapas) is quirky and yummy, and the crowd is sophisto.

Cowgirl Hall of Fame, 519 Hudson St. (10th St.), 633-1133. This
kitschy Tex-Mex restaurant is a popular spot for children's birth-
day parties, so a family dinner should be a breeze. Margaritas for
the big kids only.

Restaurants, Soul/Southern Food

5 & 10 No Exaggeration, 77 Greene St., 925-9024. This rustic
Soho restaurant-cum-collectibles shop lets you both partake of
succulent Southern cooking and take the chair home with you. $$

Jezebel, 630 Ninth Ave. (45th St.), 582-1045. Experience the
Theater District via this brothel-esqu Southern gem, where you'll
have to settle for chicken breasts and thighs, honey fried and
cozied up to yams. $$

Princess Pamela's, 78 E. 1st St. (Avenue A and First Ave.),
477-4460. Yet another East Village Soul food source, on the
divey side, and a place where you're liable to get your ass
kicked by Pamela herself. $$

Mekka, 14 Avenue A (Houston and 2nd Sts.), 475-8500.
Caribbean-Soul food fusion, with excellent results. A red toned,
pressed-tin interior is as heavy as the delightful wads of corn
bread and succulent jerk chicken.

Mama's Restaurant (on the corner of 3rd St. and Avenue B) is a
cheapie soul food spot, brimful of garlic mashed potatoes, sinful
macaroni and cheese, and fried chicken. Mmm. Rough-hewn
tables are packed in close, so don't plan on having a private conversation, although you might overhear one. And the walls are
plumb with framed paintings and photos of peoples' moms. Aww.

Cafe Beulah, 39 E. 19th St. (Broadway and Park Ave. South), 777-
9700. This Flatiron take on the Soul-food craze takes health and
wealth into account, the results being a slightly postmodern,
light, and pricier array of the usual church picnic staples. $$$

Sylvia's, 328 Lenox Ave. (126th and 127th Sts.), 996-0660. This archetypal Soul Kitchen must find it hard not to sneer at all the Johnny-Come-Latelys that have cropped up of late. An excellent reason to venture north of 96th St. $$

Restaurants, Spanish/Mexican

Rincon de Espana, 266 Thompson St., 475-9891. Cozy, intimate Spanish restaurant in the West Village. Paella and seafood are especially superb. $

Tio Pepe, 168 West 4th St., 242-9338. Festive, with both Mexican and Spanish offerings. Tapas, paella. Skylit garden room. $-$$

Bolo, 23 E. 22nd St., 228-2200. Neo-Spanish fare, surreal, over-the-top decor, and audaciously prepared dishes are the standard at this chic Flatiron eatery. $$$

Harry's Burritos, 241 Columbus Ave. (71st St.), 580-9494/230 Thompson St. (Bleecker and West 4th Sts.), 260-5588/91 E. 7th St. (Avenue A and First Ave.), 477-0773. Cheap, yummy, informal, crowded. $

El Parador Cafe, 325 E. 34th St., 679-6812. This congenial midtown spot's rep as one of the oldest Mexican restaurants in New York translates into a plenitude of premium tequilas, as well as tried-and-true dishes like mole poblano and carnitas. $$

Benny's Burritos, 93 Avenue A (6th St.), 254-2054/113 Greenwich Ave., at Jane St., 727-0584. Tremendously popular, youthful, fun, downtown Mexican food, and great margaritas. $

Zarela, 953 Second Ave. (near 50th St.), 644-6740. Combining a lively, margarita-propelled bar area with faithful regional cuisine. Try: chipotle-grilled salmon or tequila-braised chicken. $$-$$$

Restaurants, Thai

Thailand Restaurant, aka **Pongsri Thai,** 106 Bayard St. (Baxter and Mulberry Sts.), 349-3132. Don't let the crowds chase you away from this inexpensive and truly yummy source for heavenly downtown Thai. $-$$

Vong, 200 E. 54th St. (at Third Ave.), 486-9592. Haute Thai food with a French accent, in hushed environs, by maestro Jean-George Vongerichten. $$$

Sukhothai, 149 Second Ave. (9th and 10th Sts.), 460-5557

Sukhothai West, 411 West 42nd St. (Ninth and Tenth Aves.),
947-1930. Snazzy decor, delicious food at moderate prices.$$

Planet Thailand, 184 Bedford Ave., Brooklyn, (718) 599-5758.
Best, cheapest, and most out of the way Thai in New York. Their
Pad Thai will absolutely spoil you for everyone else's.

RUNNING EVENTS

The **New York City Marathon** attracts over 25,000 runners from
around the world. The Corporate Challenge- several race events held
in the spring in Central Park. New Year's Race at midnight in Central
Park. Sponsored by New York Road Runners Club.

New York Road Runners Club, 9 E. 89th St., 860-4455. Call
number for schedule of upcoming events

SAILING

<u>To Dock:</u> The **New York Sailing School Yacht Club,**
697 Bridge St., City Island, The Bronx. (718) 885-3074.

<u>Lessons:</u> **Land's End Sailing School,** (718) 885-2424. $395 for
27-hour sailing course.

SKATING, ICE RINKS

Lasker Rink, Central Park, near 110th St. and Lenox Ave., 996-1184

Wollman Rink, Central Park, Mid-Park at 63rd St., 517-4800

Chelsea Piers, 23rd & Hudson, 336-6666. The Sky Rink is open
year round. General skating begins at noon.

SKI RESORTS, Nearest

The nearest ski resort is **Great Gorge** in New Jersey
(201) 827-6000.

Ski Windham Shuttle trips M-W-F-Sun, Transportation
and Lift Ticket, call (718) 343-4444.

SKI TOURS

AAA Touring Company, 222 E. 24th St., 683-5810

Maximum Tours, 1-800-852-7979

Tours de Sport, 1-800-777-7650

KID STUFF, GREAT TOY STORES

A BEAR'S PLACE, 789 Lexington Ave., 826-6465. Educational toys such as Root Vue Farm —the ant farm turned on its head.

BOMBALULU'S, 101 West 10th St., 463-0897, and 332 Columbus Avenue, 501-8248.All manner of toys and gifts for the young and young at heart.

THE CHILDREN'S GENERAL STORE, 2473 Broadway, 580-2723. Innovative toys for kids of all ages.

DINOSAUR HILL, 302 9th St., 473-5850. Unique collection of puppets and marionettes.

FAO SCHWARTZ, 767 5th Ave. , 644-9400. If you don't mind the hordes of tourists, it is a toy-lover's paradise. You'll recognize it as the backdrop of the piano scene in the movie BIG.

JUST JAKE, 40 Hudson St., 267-1716. This two-year-old Tribeca store will settle your technology-crazed tykes down. Nothing here runs by electricity, and most toys and games require creativity.

MUD, SWEAT AND TEARS, 1566 Second Ave., 570-6868. Your kids and you can express your artistic side by painting ready-made pots. $5 1/2 hour painting session.

PENNY WHISTLE TOY, 1283 Madison Ave., 369-3868, and 448 Columbus, 873-9090. Educational toy emporium brought to us by television anchor Tom Brokaw's wife, Merideth.

PULLCART, 31 West 21st St., 727-7089. It can get pretty messy, but fun, as you and the kids throw your own pots.

UNCLE FUTZ, 408 Amsterdam Ave., 799-6723. If you can't get little Suzi out of your closet, head straight to Uncle Futz's.

NILOUFAR MOTAMED

SPORTS

For an exhaustive listing of sports activities and leagues offered in conjunction with **New York City Parks and Recreation,** call 360-8141. They'll be more than happy to send you the Green Pages, which details every excellent offering, from model boat ponds to boccie ball. Below are some to get you started.

Local pick up games and leagues—Cruise the parks for local pickup games. For team sports permits, call 408-0209

Racquetball

Chelsea Racquet & Fitness Club, 45 West 18th St., 807-8899

Softball

Central Park Softball League, 435 West 23rd St.,
956-6266

Women Athletes of New York, 800 Lexington Ave.,
759-4189

Soccer

Cosmopolitan Soccer League, 861-6606

Basketball

New York Urban Professionals League, 302 West 79th St.,
877-3614

SPORTS TEAMS, HOW TO GET TICKETS

Most Manhattan sports events occur at **Madison Square Garden,**
465-6741

The Yankees play at **Yankee Stadium,** 157th St. and Ruppert
Place, Bronx, (718) 293-4300.

The Mets play at **Shea Stadium,** Roosevelt Ave. and 126th St.,
Queens, (718) 507-6387.

The Giants and the Jets play at **Giants Stadium,** at Meadowlands
Sports Complex. East Rutherford, NJ. By car: Take the New
Jersey Turnpike to exit 16W. By bus: The Port Authority Bus
Terminal in Manhattan at Eighth Ave. and 41st St. offers bus
service to the Meadowlands Sports Complex. The Box Office, 1-
800-772-2222, located at Continental Airlines Arena, is open
Monday-Friday 9-6, Saturday 10-6, Sunday 12-5. Box Office:
(201) 935-3900 Group Sales: (201) 460-4370.

USTA National Tennis Center, Flushing Meadows-Corona Park,
Queens, (718) 592-8000

TENNIS COURTS

To play on tennis courts in applicable New York City parks (Central Park, East River Park, Inwood Hill Park, Fort Washington Park, Frederick Johnson Playground, Riverside Park, and an indoor bubble at Randall's Island), you need to get a tennis permit. This can be obtained by going to the **Arsenal in Central Park,** 360-8133 or calling them. **Central Park Tennis Center** at 93rd St. and West Dr. Call 360-8133 for info. You need a tennis permit to play, which can be obtained at the Arsenal in Central Park. Courts can be found at:

Central Park Tennis Center at 93rd St. and West Dr.

Riverside Park at 96th St.

East River Park, North of Delancey.

Private Tennis Clubs

Tennis Club, Grand Central Terminal, 15 Vanderbilt Ave., 687-3841. A private club, which believe it or not, does exist in Grand Central Station! Seasonal rates: 35 weeks Sept - May M-F $3,165. Sept - May Weekends $2,215. 52 weeks, M-F, $4,425. 17 weeks M-F $1265.

Trinity Tennis Club, 139 W. 91st St., 873-1650. Call after August 12 for information, or leave a message with the Building Services extension answering machine with your name and address, and you will receive their information by mail.

U.S. Tennis Association League, (914) 696-7000. This is a recreational league for adults only, and has different skill levels. Season is May to July. The membership fee is $20/person, plus $15/$25 per match that you play.

THEATER

The Atlantic Theater Company, 336 West 20th St., (Eighth & Ninth Aves.), 239-6200. This former Chelsea church gives a Mennonite flavor to the clean performances. Frequented by odd couple Woody and Soon-Yi.

The New York Public Theater, 425 Lafayette St., 260-2400. Often populist-tinged theater offerings, from *Blade to the Heat* to *Bring in Da' Noise, Bring in Da' Funk.*

Theater for the New City. 155 First Ave., 633-1292

INSIDER TIP: *TKTS, called "tickets" by New Yorkers, offers half-price theater, symphony, opera and dance tickets on the day of the performance at two booths, one at 47TH ST. AND BROADWAY, the other on the ground floor of 2 WORLD TRADE CENTER. The line is always longer on Broadway. Cash and traveler's checks only. No phone reservations. You never know what shows are going to be listed for that day, so be flexible. The most popular shows will never be available. Sales start at noon for matinees and 2 p.m. for evening performances. Some people get in line well before that, especially at the Broadway booth, while flexible, experienced theatergoers stop by in late afternoon, when the line is shorter, to see if any bargains are still available.*

WALKING TOURS

Adventures on a Shoestring, 265-2663. The name says it all—a journey through the streets of the city, including ethnic neighborhood tours, and completed with a restaurant visit. Consider them experts: they've been touring New York for thirty-three years.

Big Onion Walking Tours, 439-1090. Theme tours that last between two and two-and-a-half hours of alternative history. Past topics have included Immigrant New York and Historic Harlem.

The Cloisters, Fort Tryon Park, 923-3700. A Metropolitan Museum of Art branch located around 190th St. This replica of a medieval monastery will transport back to more simple times. The gardens are splendid.

Horticultural Society, 757-0915. Tour the Upper West Side's gardens (lotus gardens, rooftop gardens, and others). All tours $8.

Fulton Fish Market, South Street Seaport Museum, 669-9416. A ninety-minute tour starts 6 A.M., after which you can purchase the catches of the day; every first and third Thursday of the month starting May 1st.

Radical Walking Tours, 925-9060. Bruce Kayton gives eleven tours ranging from Wall St. to Harlem covering political topics and nontraditional histories of New York.

Sidewalks of New York, 517-0201. Narrated tours of New York's best known crime scenes, haunted bars and taverns in Greenwich Village and and Upper East Side "Tribute to Jackie" which walks you to the places associated with Jaqueline Kennedy Onassis,

Urban Park Rangers, 1-800-201-7275. The rangers give nature tours in all of the parks, including discussions of birdwatching, ecology, and history.

Wild Food Tours, (718) 291-6825, "Wildman" Steven Brill leads four-hour field walks where all manner of edible fruits, vegetables, roots and mushrooms are "unearthed'.

VOLUNTEERING

The Mayor's Voluntary Action Center, 61 Chambers St.,
788-7550

New York Cares, 116 E. 16th St., 228-5000

The Volunteer Referral Agency, 161 Madison Ave., 745-8249

The Federation of Protestant Welfare Agencies,
281 Park Ave. South, 777-4800

The United Jewish Appeal—Federation of Jewish Philanthropies,
130 E. 59th St., 753-2288

Catholic Charities of New York, 1011 First Ave., 371-1000

Chapter Seven
ESSENTIAL
NUMBERS &

Actors Institute 48 w. 21st St.,
924-8888
African-American Services
  Associated Black Charities,
  105 E. 22nd St., 777-6060
AIDS
  AIDS Coalition, New York,
  231 W. 29th St., 629-3075
  AIDS Education and Referral
  Service, 80 E. 11th St., 677-1777
  AIDS Hotline of GMHC, 129 W.
  20th St., 807-6655
Air Complaints (718) 699-9811
Al-Anon 200 Park Ave S., 254-7230
Alternate Street Parking Information
442-7080
Alternative High School and Program
Superintendent 206-0570
American Cancer Society 19 W. 56th
St., 586-8700
American Civil Liberties Union
944-9800
Arts Hotline 777-ARTS
Auto Pound, College Point
(718) 445-0100
Battered Women 24-Hour Hotline
1-800-621-4673
Big Brothers/Big Sisters of New York
City 223 E. 30th St., 686-2042
Blind services
  American Foundation for the
  Blind, 15 W 16th St., 620-2000
  Lighthouse, 11 E 59th St., 821-9200
Buses, City Information (718) 330-1234
Child Abuse and Neglect Reports
1-800-342-3720
Child Development
  Agency for, Information and
  Referral Service (718) 260-6000
Children's Aid Society 885 Columbus
Ave., 865-6337
City Clerk 669-2400
Citywide Information 788-4636
Consumer Affairs Department
487-4444
Courts
  Housing, 791-6000

  Landlord and Tenant, 791-6000
  Small Claims, 791-6000
Crack Hotline 374-5725
Crimes Victims Hotline 577-7777
Cultural Affairs Department 841-4100
Day Care and Head Start Information
(718) 367-5437
Deaf Services
  New York Society for the Deaf,
  817 Broadway, 777-3900
Dentists 1-800-243-4444
Department of Motor Vehicle 645-5550
Doctors 1-800-999-6266
Drug Abuse Prevention
  Council of Smaller Churches,
  69 W. 128th St., 876-7667
  Greenwich House Counseling
  Centers, 80 5th Ave., 691-2900
Fire Department (718) 694-2000;
  To Report a Fire, 911;
  Arson Hotline (718) 722-3600
Food and Hunger Hotline 533-6100
Foster Care Networks 43 W. 33rd St.,
643-0178
Hospitals
  NYU Medical Center, 550 First
  Ave., 263-7000
  Bellevue, 462 First Ave., 561-4141
  Beth Israel, 281 First Ave.,
  420-2000
  New York Foundling Hospital,
  590 Sixth Ave./Avenue of the
  Americas, 633-9300
  St. Vincent's Hospital and Medical
  Center of New York, 7th Ave. &
  11th St., 604-7000
  St. Vincent's Hospital and Medical
  Center of New York AIDS Center,
  412 Sixth Ave./Avenue of the
  Americas, 228-8000
  St. Vincent's, 153 W. 11th,
  790-1000
  Beth Israel, 281 First Ave.,
  420-2000
  Gouverneurs, 227 Madison St.,
  238-7000
  Beekman Downtown, 170 William,

312-5000

Mt. Sinai, 1 Gustav Levi Place, 241-6500

Lenox Hill, 100 E. 77th St., 439-2345 (has a great rep)

Metropolitan, 1901 First Ave., 230-6262

St. Luke's Hospital, 419 West 114th, 523-4000

Roosevelt Hospital, 428 West 59th St., 523-4000

Medical Arts Center, 57 West 57th St. 755-0200

NYU Medical Center, 550 First Ave., 263-7300

Roosevelt, 428 West 59th St. 523-4000

Housing Assistance

Metropolitan Council on Housing, 102-104 Fulton, 693-0550

Legal Aid Society, 2090 7th Ave., 663-3293

Legal Services for New York City, 350 Broadway, 431-7200

Federation of Protestant Welfare Agencies, 281 Park Ave., South, 777-4800

Human Rights Commission

Bias Hotline, 662-2427

Fair Housing, 306-7588

Public Information, 306-7530

Jewish Services

JACS Foundation, 426 W. 58th St., 397-4197

Jewish Association for Services for the Aged, 40 W. 68th St., 724-3200

Jewish Child Care Association of New York, 575 Lexington, 371-1313

Jewish Community Centers of North America, 532-4949

Jewish Education, Board of 426 E. 58th St., 245-8200

Lawyer's Referral Service 529-5950

Marriage License Bureau 669-2400

National Multiple Sclerosis Society 733 3rd Ave., 986-3240

92nd Street YM\YWHA 1395 Lexington Ave., 415-5630

Noise Complaints (718) 699-9811

Parking Violations Bureau Help-Line 477-4430

Parkinson Foundation, Inc. 122 E. 42nd St., 374-1741

Planned Parenthood 677-6474

Poison Control Hotline 764-7667

Police and Emergency 911

Pregnancy Healthline 230-1111

Rape Hotline 267-7273

Retarded Children's Services

Association for Help of Retarded Children, 200 Park Ave South, 780-2500

Senior Citizen's Services New York Foundation for Senior Citizens, 150 Nassau, 962-7559

Sex Crimes Report Line 267-7273

Street Lights Out, Reporting 442-7070

Subway, City Information (718) 330-1234

Suicide Prevention Hotline (718) 369-9608

Surplus Food Distribution Information (718) 291-1900

Taxi and Limousine Commission

General Information, 302-8294

Lost Property Information, 302-8294

Time of Day 540-8000

Tow or Boot (Auto) Information 788-7800

Unemployment Action Center 998-6568

United Nations Association Of USA Inc. 485 5th Ave., 697-3232

Veterinary Care

ASPCA's Bergh Memorial Hospital, 424 E. 92nd St. (First and York), 876-7700

East Village Veterinarian, 241 Eldridge St., off Houston. 674-8640. Homeopathic Medicine and Veterinary Care,

Pet Emergency Numbers

Animal Poison Control, 340-4494

24-Hour Emergency Animal Medical Center, 510 E. 62nd St., 838-8100

Pet Trekkers (House Calls!), 481-4111, (917) 706-4844 (pager)

Victim Services Agency 24-Hour Hotline, 577-7777

Violence Intervention Program 360-5090

Volunteer Referral Center 889-4805

Voter's Registration and Information 1-800-367-8683

Water Complaints (718) 699-9811

Weather 976-1122

Women's Services National Organization for Women, 807-0721

YMCA of Greater New York 630-9600

YWCA of City of New York 610 Lexington Ave., 755-4500

INDEX

Editor's Note: If you're looking for any of the following services—Schools, Police Stations, Post Offices, Hospitals, Libraries, Parking Information, Garages, Banks and ATMs, Cafes, Delis, Coffeeshops, and Diners, Community Resources, Convenience Stores, Synagogues, Churches, Pharmacies, Dry Cleaners, Laundromats, Gas Stations, Grocery Stores, Hardware Stores, Video Stores, Beer and Liquor stores—go to the neighborhood in which you're looking, and turn to the *Essential Resources* Pages.

Know someone who's moving to a major U.S. city?

BACKSTREET GUIDES' MOVING TO handbooks make the perfect gift!

Titles currently available:

Moving to Chicago

Moving to Los Angeles

Moving to New York City

Moving to Washington D.C.

And coming soon:

Moving to Atlanta

Moving to Boston

Moving to Dallas/Fort Worth

Moving to Houston

Moving to Philadelphia

Moving to San Francisco

Moving to Seattle

Make your move easy with Backstreet Guides—practical companions to new cities, from settling in to going out!